T0329572

A Vehicle for Change

Popular Representations of the Automobile in 20th-Century France

Studies in Modern and Contemporary France   10

Studies in Modern and Contemporary France

Series Editors

Assistant Professor Siham Bouamer, Sam Houston State University
Professor Denis M. Provencher, University of Arizona
Professor Martin O'Shaughnessy, Nottingham Trent University

The Studies in Modern and Contemporary France book series is a new collaboration between the Association for the Study of Modern and Contemporary France (ASMCF) and Liverpool University Press (LUP). Submissions are encouraged focusing on French politics, history, society, media and culture. The series will serve as an important focus for all those whose engagement with France is not restricted to the more classically literary, and can be seen as a long-form companion to the Association's journal, *Modern and Contemporary France,* and to *Contemporary French Civilization*, published by Liverpool University Press.

A Vehicle for Change

Popular Representations of the Automobile
in 20th-Century France

ÉAMON Ó COFAIGH

Liverpool University Press

First published 2022 by
Liverpool University Press
4 Cambridge Street
Liverpool
L69 7ZU

British Library Cataloguing-in-Publication data
A British Library CIP record is available

ISBN 978-1-80207-011-8 cased

Typeset by Carnegie Book Production, Lancaster
Printed and bound by CPI Group (UK) Ltd, Croydon CR0 4YY

Contents

Acknowledgements

I would like to thank the Moore Institute at the National University of Ireland, Galway for awarding me a grant in aid of publication. I am most grateful for this extremely useful financial support.

Most heartfelt thanks must go to my mentor and colleague Professor Philip Dine, without whose help this book would never have seen the light of day. I was very fortunate to have help from Dr Mary Cawley and Dr Marie Mahon from the Department of Geography who both contributed in no small way to this book. I would also like to thank Dr Noelle Higgins and Ruadhán Cooke for their keen eyes and astute suggestions.

I wish to thank the staff at Liverpool University Press, especially Chloe Johnson and Patrick Brereton and also Rachel Chamberlain at Carnegie Publishing, for the invaluable support, flexibility and advice.

Je tiens à remercier chaleureusement la famille de Paul Durand d'avoir si gentiment accepté que j'utilise le dessin de ce dernier pour la couverture de mon ouvrage.

Lastly, I would like to thank all my family, but in particular my wife Marie and my two children Sasha and Sam, for their patience and support. I want to dedicate this book to my parents who taught me always to be curious and to be me.

Note on Translations

All translations are the author's own unless otherwise stated. There are some words that remain in the original French, in italics. These are all explained, however the French version renders their meaning better than an English equivalent.

Introduction

Fetishizing the Automobile

In common with other manifestations of the commodity, as famously defined by Marx, the automobile appears 'At first sight, a very trivial thing and easily understood.'[1] Indeed, the motor car's capacity to transport someone from A to B is an obvious and inherent one. Thus, as a means of personal transportation, the automobile can seemingly be understood quite easily. One single intrinsic use-value cannot be applied to it, however, for while there is a whole range of activities for which the automobile cannot be used, it is also true to say that the number of roles of which it is capable is not fixed. Thus, its capacities vary according to the society in which it functions and the time frame within which it is being considered, as well as the demands placed on it by its owner. The use-value of a car is initially apparent; however, its corollary capacities are many and varied, depending on the setting within which it is placed.

Marx wrote of a world in which the radical – and technology-based – transformation of western societies since the Industrial Revolution had occurred, but the automobile had yet to be invented. Thus, in applying his theory of the commodity, and more specifically the fetishized commodity, to the car, we must be cognizant of the fact that it did not enter Marx's thought process when he wrote of the fetish and

1 Marx, Karl. 1990 [1867]. *Capital: A Critique of Political Economy*. London: Penguin, p. 81.

commodity fetishism. The automobile, at first sight, may seem to be trivial and straightforward; however, it has never embodied one single role or 'use-value.' A form of transportation, the motor car is consumed as much more than this. As John Urry has pointed out, 'Most car journeys were never made by public transport.'[2] Thus, the automobile was not invented initially as a means of transportation for the masses as it does not satisfy a specific pre-existing need or social role. The car became the embodiment of progress, a symbol of technology's role in improving society. As the latest in an ever-growing list of technological advances, the motor car was the vehicle, in every sense, by which society would be freed. People would find emancipation in the ability of the car to cast off the shackles of the city and provide its user with the freedom to conquer space and time in a hitherto unknown way.

De Brosses used the term 'fetishism' to refer to the adulation of inanimate objects as gods, as was done in 18th-century West Africa. It is ironic that the term originated in a practice that was ridiculed in the western world and that, in its attempts to 'civilize' these regions, France fetishized its newest symbol of modernity in parading the automobile through its colonies. Marx's access to the word was through de Brosses, and thus it was with religious connotations that Marx used the term, as highlighted by Bayley: 'This notion of the fetish worshipper's desire-driven delusion regarding natural objects, his blindness to the unprovidential randomness of physical events was an element in de Brosses's original theorisation of *fétichisme* as the pure condition of un-enlightenment.'[3] It is within this conceptual framework, as repurposed by Marx, that we will examine how the automobile has been fetishized in France. In examining the use of this object, we will also explore how its capacities are displaced and consumed to create an object of desire, specifically a desire to acquire and use the automobile in what became systems of automobility.[4] The practices which will be scrutinized have often led to the object acquiring a particular position in society. The evolution of the status of the automobile will

2   Urry, John. 2004. 'The "System" of Automobility.' *Theory, Culture & Society* 21 (4–5): 25–39 (p. 28).
3   Pietz, William. 1993. 'Fetishism and Materialism: The Limits of Theory in Marx,' in E. Apter and W. Pietz (eds), *Fetishism as Cultural Discourse*. Ithaca: Cornell University Press, p. 136.
4   Urry, 'The "System" of Automobility,' pp. 25–39.

be examined as it became valorized in such a way that it was perceived to enhance human capacities. By supplementing Marx's commodity fetishism with an exploration of use-value, Baudrillard examined the commodity as having a more active role in relation to humans, as we will argue in what follows regarding the motor car.

Taking the Second World War as a pivotal period in France's development, we will show how the automobile was consumed and fetishized before and after this conflict. This theoretical refinement and this social evolution together allow us to view French culture 'through the window' of the automobile as it embodied technology and progress in 20th-century France. After the Second World War automobile came to be fetishized as an everyday object. It became one of the standard household appliances, along with the fridge, the washing machine and the television, to such an extent that it now 'slept' in the house in a garage that was specially built for it. It was used to run errands and to commute to work. It thus came to be consumed for its use-value as a domestic vehicle. However, although it was consumed in this way, the car was not solely fulfilling its use-value. Marx refers to use-value as the ability of a product to fulfil the needs of its owner. But the automobile became ubiquitous across the classes in France and thus was fetishized in a new way. This constitution of the car as a need, an appliance without which a household cannot function, implies a fetishizing process or mechanism symbolic of a society then undergoing the economic expansion of the Trente Glorieuses.[5] As the car became inscribed in the domestic sphere, it began to represent a fetishized notion of progress that became attainable in this era of growth. Possession of a car was now considered a statement of a desire to engage with the nation's aim of advancing to a cleaner, more progressive, and more modern state.

---

5   Originally coined by Jean Fourastié in 1979, this term refers to the unprecedented economic and demographic growth which occurred from 1945 to 1975 following the end of the Second World War in France. See Fourastié, Jean. 1979. *Les Trente Glorieuses: ou la Révolution invisible de 1946 à 1975*. Paris: Fayard. Car ownership grew from 1 million cars in 1946 to 11.2 million in 1968 and 15.5 million in 1975 (p. 131). It is also important to note that some scholars, in particular Rémy Pawin, have questioned whether this period was as prosperous as has been claimed. See Pawin, Rémy. 2013. 'Retour sur les «Trente Glorieuses» et la périodisation du second XXe siècle.' *Revue d'histoire moderne contemporaine* 1: 155–75.

As automobiles became ubiquitous, French road infrastructure was unable to keep up, and automobility was inevitably compromised. The fetishized capacities of the car, especially its ability to liberate through freedom of movement at any time, were no longer being realized. Thus, while the car theoretically offered the means to escape, the reality was quite different. The car was consumed as an ideal of liberation rather than as liberation itself. Prominent cultural commentators, including Barthes[6] and Baudrillard,[7] discussed the impact of the car; Barthes, more specifically, that of the car in France. Both suggest that the car has been mythologized in a process through which it has been attributed a mystical aura. However, we shall see that as the automobile was democratized and domesticated, it began to lose this lustre and was consumed in a different manner. The car's accession to a place in the home led to it becoming a need in the Baudrillardian system of values of Trente Glorieuses France. The fetishized nature of the car can be seen to continue to exist, however, as Baudrillard argues that desiring an object because of its everyday use constitutes a form of fetishizing.[8] Barthes also suggests that a mythology of the car is no longer appropriate; the time has come for a mythology of driving.[9]

In what follows, these two Marxian thinkers, Roland Barthes and Jean Baudrillard, will together play an important part in the analysis of the automobile, which they each highlighted in their writings as an object of sustained moral and material investment in France. In their different ways, these distinguished intellectuals engaged incisively with the material culture of their homeland as the devastated country emerged from the Second World War and embarked on the process of economic reconstruction and social transformation that characterized the Trente Glorieuses. A paradox of this period of sustained growth and steadily increasing affluence was the high level of support retained by the French Communist Party (Parti communiste français or PCF),

---

6   Barthes, Roland. 2003 [1957]. *Mythologies*. Paris: Seuil; Barthes, Roland. 2002. *Œuvres complètes*. Paris: Seuil.
7   Baudrillard, Jean. 1968. *Le Système des objets: la consommation des signes*. Paris: Gallimard.
8   Baudrillard, Jean. 1972. *Pour une critique de l'économie politique du signe*. Paris: Gallimard, p. 151.
9   Barthes, *Œuvres complètes*, p. 1142.

in terms both of its membership and its popular vote, and specifically in spite of its exclusion from legislative and executive power throughout the Cold War. Without necessarily being members of the PCF, many on the left shared its Marx-derived social and cultural analysis, if not always the specific policies that the party derived from it. At the theoretical level, this broadly Marxist critique of the state-managed modernization and, for some observers, Americanization of France in the post-war period was combined productively with methodological innovations in the social sciences, including particularly structuralism, post-structuralism and, in due course, postmodernism. The widely varied intellectual interventions that resulted typically shared a Marx-inspired desire to reveal the workings of the capitalist system and its network of state supports, with a view to bringing about social and political change. This applied irrespective of whether the targeted apparatuses – to adopt the terminology suggested by leading Marxist theoretician Louis Althusser[10] – were understood as 'repressive' or 'ideological' and, by extension, whether or not they were primarily understood in terms of the country's economic base or its cultural superstructure.

Thus, influenced by the structural linguistics of Ferdinand de Saussure, Barthes would engage in the 1950s with semiology and the cultural meanings attached to systems of signs, as would Baudrillard in later decades. As Poster puts it, 'In *Mythologies*, Barthes illuminated the hidden, ideological significations of various communications systems,' as they revealed 'how simple, rational information became mythic supports of the social system.'[11] This process of sign-based mystification may be regarded as analogous to the fetishizing of commodities as theorized by Marx. Barthes's 'mythologies' were a series of critical essays on contemporary French society, covering subjects ranging from the gaudy images of food published in *Elle* magazine to the over-the-top antics of all-in wrestlers. His hyperbolic reflections on the Citroën DS may likewise be viewed as a contri-bution to this cultural critique. However, as Jonathan Culler has suggested, by the very fact of such a prominent intellectual engaging

10   Althusser, Louis. 1970. 'Idéologie et appareils idéologiques d'Etat.' *La Pensée* 151 (May–June), pp. 3–38.
11   Poster, Mark. 1979. 'Semiology and Critical Theory: From Marx to Baudrillard.' *Boundary* 2: 275–88 (p. 280).

with these subjects, Barthes was, in effect, adding to their mystique and encouraging their fetishization.[12] A decade later, drawing on the Marxist 'critique of everyday life' pioneered by sociologist Henri Lefebvre,[13] Baudrillard would develop his own critical semiology, as outlined in *Le Système des objets* (1968), *La Société de consommation* (1970) and *Pour une critique de l'économie politique du signe* (1972). Although their author was increasingly critical of prevailing Marxist economics, these early works together offered a toolkit for decoding the significance of objects within consumer society, particularly in an age of increasingly monopolistic capitalism. As Douglas Kellner explains: 'In his first three books, Baudrillard maintained that the classical Marxian critique of political economy needed to be supplemented by semiological theories of the sign which articulated the diverse meanings signified by signifiers into languages organized into systems of meaning.'[14] Crucially, Baudrillard's writing represents a 'deepening' of the analyses offered by both Marx and Barthes in that commodities are no longer viewed primarily as material objects but rather as signs which function within a system. Thus, they no longer need to function as signifiers of a use-value, having their principal existence rather in a system of signs. Significantly, both Barthes and Baudrillard engaged with the fetishized nature of the automobile. Of course, their respective analyses were themselves products of their historical moment and, more specifically, of the Marxian intellectual formation previously identified, with all that this implies in the way of inherent analytical limitations. Nevertheless, by drawing upon these two philosophers' sophisticated reworking of Marxist theory, we may better appreciate the evolution of the car's social meanings at this time. Indeed, their joint standing as eminent intellectual commentators means that their writings remain particularly apt for suitably nuanced application in our concluding analysis of automobile consumption in France in the period following the Second World War.

---

12   Culler, Jonathan. 2002. *Barthes: A Very Short Introduction*. Oxford: Oxford University Press, p. 28.
13   Lefebvre, Henri. 1947. *Critique de la vie quotidienne*. Paris: L'Arche.
14   Kellner, Douglas. 2020. 'Jean Baudrillard.' *Stanford Encyclopedia of Philosophy Archive* (winter edition), edited by Edward N. Zalta, https://plato.stanford.edu/archives/win2020/entries/baudrillard/.

Writing about the Car

While the automobile has established and retained a central role in human life, and especially mobility, since the early 20th century, it can be argued that it has not been adequately explored from a sociological or, indeed, from a representational point of view. The automobile, while initially a European product – invented in Germany and subsequently developed and improved in France – became an iconic product in the United States at an earlier date than in Europe. Perhaps as a result, the literature that focuses on the history of the American automobile is more extensive than that tracing the car's evolution in Europe. So, while numerous examinations of the automobile on American highways and its broader impact on American society have appeared, fewer such studies have been undertaken in the European context.

Although the iconic nature of the automobile has led to a voluminous general literature, it quickly becomes evident that much of this work focuses on an enumeration of cars, a sort of 'show and tell' of what exists, with perhaps a short biography of a designer or of the car itself to accompany it. Typically, these volumes are copiously illustrated, and as such are aimed at the general population to increase sales by satisfying the interests of an automobile-loving public eager to learn more about the latest models and their availability. Books written by car enthusiasts for car enthusiasts are the main staple. These works constitute the majority of the printed material relating to the automobile. However, academic engagement with the car and automobile travel is gradually increasing; the collection Automobilities is one notable example.[15] This 'relative neglect of the motor car as an object of scrutiny and analysis'[16] is reiterated by John Urry (2000), who finds this absence to be a 'particularly curious state of affairs, in part because automobile technologies have been profoundly involved throughout the 20th century in shaping and reshaping urban and non-urban spaces, ways of thinking and being, and modes of social interaction.'[17]

15   Featherstone, Mike, Nigel Thrift and John Urry, eds. 2005. *Automobilities*. London: Sage.
16   Inglis, David. 2004. 'Auto Couture: Thinking the Car in Post-War France.' *Theory, Culture & Society* 21 (4–5): 197–219 (p. 197).
17   Mimi Sheller and John Urry, qtd. in Inglis, 'Auto Couture,' p. 197.

In the early years, a number of periodicals devoted much space to the automobile in an attempt both to attract readers and also to promote the car itself. Initially named *L'Auto-Vélo* (1900–04), later renamed *L'Auto* (1904–44), the predecessor to *L'Équipe* was one such example. Other periodicals also emerged in this early period in an effort to embrace and promote the car. *Le Moteur* (1913–38) was a monthly magazine first issued just prior to the First World War and, after a suspension of printing during the hostilities, was resumed in 1924 under the name *Le Moteur et le Chauffeur Français*. With the subtitle *La grande revue de la vulgarisation automobile*, it was particularly concerned with making the public aware of the steady technological progress being made and how this could benefit the country. *La Vie Automobile* (1903–56) contained editorials that commented on the social need for the automobile and very often highlighted the evolving mechanical aspect of the car; it also contained regular articles on maintenance and repair. Other early newspapers included *La France Automobile* (1900–06), which, as technology advanced, became *La France Automobile et Aérienne* (1907–11), and then *La Journée Industrielle* (1918–39). These newspapers all featured abundant advertisements by the various car manufacturers. Their layouts and contents have not been analysed in any coordinated way in an attempt to gain insights into the public attitude towards the car or to obtain an understanding of the perceived needs and interests of the public. Chroniclers, interested in compiling a history of the car, have certainly used them, but to date these newspapers have not been examined as periodicals dedicated to the car's growth and democratization. Chapter 5 will explore some later general-market magazines during the period after the Second World War to trace the impact of the banalization of the car on the French population.

Extensive accounts have been written of the larger French automobile manufacturers. While, much like the more general histories, some of these works are simply chronicles of popular manufacturers, these volumes are important as they map out the evolution of the automobile. These often image-filled works provide an interesting tapestry of how each company's products and perceptions evolved over the years. The Michelin firm, notoriously slow to open up its archives, as attested to in Alain Jemain's *Michelin: un siècle de secrets* (1982), has arguably had least written about its enterprise, although Réné Miquel's *Dynastie Michelin* (1962) provides a comprehensive genealogy of the Clermont-based manufacturing company.[18] Miquel paints a negative picture of the family, nothing like the image portrayed through the jovial emblematic character of the Michelin man. A biography of the family-run company, Annie Moulin-Bourret's *Guerre et industrie* (1997), is a more comprehensive account of the development of the Michelin rubber factory. It traces the venture from modest beginnings through its acquisition of Citroën in 1933, exploring its efforts to innovate and to be at the forefront of both creativity and marketing.[19] This work also takes a more balanced and even favourable position with regard to the Michelin family. Much analytical work has been carried out on the marketing policies of the marque, as for example in Stephen Harp's *Marketing Michelin: Advertising and Cultural Identity in Twentieth-Century France* (2001), which examines the Michelin enterprise through its visibility in popular culture. His close reading of marketing material, the firm's 'lifestyle-oriented images,' and the development of Bibendum (the Michelin man) scrutinizes the impact of the company on the national consciousness.[20] The role of the Michelin company and also that of Citroën, specifically their effect on the growth of the automobile, will be explored in Chapter 3.

André Citroën is perhaps the man to whom most ink has been devoted. This is not surprising since his company was responsible for the creation of three of the most iconic cars in French automotive history.[21] Citroën, the man, has also attracted particular attention, as he was a very public figure during the 1920s and early 1930s. Regularly featured in newspapers, he embraced publicity and was constantly on the lookout for ways to enhance the Citroën brand. He organized publicity stunts, availed himself of innovative marketing ideas, and was open to acquiring the best practices from abroad, the United States in particular, for application in the manufacture of his vehicles. John Reynolds's biography, *André Citroën: The Henry Ford*

18 Jemain, Alain, and Bernard Hanon. 1982. *Michelin: un siècle de secrets*. Paris: Calmann-Lévy; Miquel, René. 1962. *Dynastie Michelin*. Paris: La Table Ronde.
19 Moulin-Bourret, Annie. 1997. *Guerre et industrie. Clermont-Ferrand: la victoire du pneu*. Clermont-Ferrand: Institut d'études du Massif Central.
20 Harp, Stephen L. 2001. *Marketing Michelin: Advertising and Cultural Identity in Twentieth-Century France*. Baltimore, MD: Johns Hopkins University Press.
21 The Citroën Traction Avant, Citroën 2CV and the Citroën DS.

of France (1996), is divided into three parts, 'The Engineer,' 'The Explorer,' and 'The Entrepreneur,' each dealing with significant periods in the life of a man who died at the age of 57.[22] Pierre Dumont dedicates his *Quai de Javel, quai André Citroën* (1973) 'to the memory of André Citroën, France's most important car manufacturer' ('A la mémoire d'André Citroën, le plus grand des constructeurs français') and includes photographs of the various cars to leave the Quai de Javel factory, some of which he examines in closer detail.[23] Numerous books have been devoted to the iconic cars to have emerged from the Citroën factories: the Traction Avant, DS and 2CV have each had several volumes dedicated to them.[24]

One notable exception to this relative lack of critical engagement with the automobile is Barthes's famous essay on the Citroën DS. In his celebrated collection of mythologies, he wrote about 'La nouvelle Citroën.' This treatise on the DS has become perhaps the most quoted text when referring to the groundbreaking car launched in 1955. In *Mythologies*, published in book form in 1957, Barthes compares the DS to a gothic cathedral, drawing on this new vehicle's otherworldly appearance.[25] He underlines how the shape of the DS belies its origins and utility.[26] This portrayal of the Citroën will be contrasted with another essay published in 1963, 'La Voiture, projection de l'égo' ('The Car, a Projection of the Ego'), in which Barthes singles out another Citroën, this time the 2CV, and highlights its place in the everyday life of French society.[27] These two essays, published just six years apart, albeit about two very different cars, are indicative of the evolution of perceptions of the automobile at the peak of the Trente Glorieuses. Jean Baudrillard also examined the automobile in his

22   Reynolds, John. 1996. *André Citroën: The Henry Ford of France*. New York: St. Martin's Press.

23   Dumont, Pierre. 1973. *Quai de Javel, quai André Citroën*. Paris: Éditions pratiques automobiles.

24   Wolgensinger, Jacques. 1995. *La 2 CV: nous nous sommes tant aimés*. Paris: Gallimard; Buffetaut, Yves. 1997. *La Citroën Traction de mon père*. Boulogne-Billancourt: ETAI; Serres, Olivier de. 2005. *Citroën DS: au panthéon de l'automobile*. Arcueil: Anthèse.

25   The religious undertone continues with the wordplay between DS and *déesse* (goddess).

26   Barthes, 2003 [1957], *Mythologies*, pp. 140–42.

27   Barthes, *Œuvres complètes*, pp. 1136–42. (This work was first published, as *La voiture, projection de l'égo*, in *Réalités*, October 1963.)

Le Système des objets (1968), where he describes accession to the use of the car as a rite of passage and the acquisition of the driving licence as an act of initiation for young people to prove their worthiness to be considered adults.[28] This engagement of leading social theorists with the automobile will be explored later in this study.

The earlier use of the automobile as a colonial tool in the 1920s is a theme to which a significant body of literature is devoted. The first automobile crossing of the Sahara desert in 1922 is chronicled in a work penned by the expedition leaders and prefaced by André Citroën.[29] A similar work was published after the so-called 'Croisière Noire' in 1926; however, it was the filmed account of this later expedition, in a 60-minute feature, which became the most significant work from this era.[30] Competing activity by Renault in North Africa in the 1920s has also been chronicled, the first such example being written by Gaston Gradis[31] and a subsequent journey recorded by the journalist and politician Henri de Kérillis.[32] These accounts form part of the colonial literature of the era. They place the automobile at the forefront of these expeditions. The automobile as the vehicle of modernity symbolizes *la mère patrie* on its *mission civilisatrice* as it maintains and promotes a France that is *une et indivisible*. Peter J. Bloom's *French Colonial Documentary: Mythologies of Humanitarianism* (2008) is largely devoted to the trans-Saharan films; Alison Murray also examines this period in the modernization of the colonies.[33] In an article about the Grand Rallye from Algeria to Dahomey in 1930 to celebrate the centenary of the French presence in North Africa, Philip Dine has also shown the impact of the automobile in demonstrating to the colonies the technical superiority which the *mère colonisatrice*

28   Baudrillard, *Le Système des objets*, p. 93.
29   Haardt, Georges-Marie, and Louis Audouin-Dubreuil. 1923. *La Première Traversée du Sahara en automobile: de Touggourt à Tombouctou par l'Atlantide*. Paris: Plon.
30   Sabatès, Fabien. 1980b. *La Croisière noire Citroën*. Paris: E. Baschet.
31   Gradis, Gaston. 1924. *À la recherche du grand-axe: contribution aux études transsahariennes*. Paris: Plon.
32   Kerillis, Henri de. 1925. *De l'Algérie au Dahomey en automobile: voyage effectué par la seconde mission Gradis*. Paris: Plon.
33   Bloom, Peter J. 2008. *French Colonial Documentary: Mythologies of Humanitarianism*. Minneapolis, MN: University of Minnesota Press; Murray, Alison. 2000. 'Le Tourisme Citroën au Sahara (1924–1925).' *Vingtième siècle. Revue d'histoire* 68: 95–107.

possessed.[34] The abundant capacity of cars to symbolize colonial modernity is highlighted here.

Motor racing in France dates back to the birth of the internal combustion engine and consequently has an abundant literature. As with general histories of the automobile, the rise of motor racing is often recounted in epic tones but, numerous volumes with plentiful images notwithstanding, the social significance of these races is rarely examined. *Le Sang bleu* (1978) by Serge Bellu is one such work, a chronicle of turn-of-the-century races compiled by a former racing driver.[35] *La Belle Époque à 30 à l'heure* (1984) by Claude Pasteur is another example.[36] Meticulously researched, these two accounts provide details of the races and, when these are considered within the societal context of the time, as suggested by periodicals, it is possible to identify the social role of the automobile and motor racing at the time. Early newspapers are particularly useful in providing a setting for these events. As the original motor trials and races were launched to boost press sales, this underlines the importance of consulting these periodicals. The significance of these early races in the growth of the automobile lies in their providing a platform upon which the French public could discover the capacities embodied in the car. This will be examined in Chapter 2.

The car's role in the democratization of tourism cannot be overstated. Initially, this linkage evolved slowly; however, with the establishment of paid holidays in 1936, followed by the economic boom of the Trente Glorieuses, a veritable tourism explosion took place which was, to a certain extent, linked with growing car ownership. In *La Roue et le stylo* (1999), Catherine Bertho-Lavenir traces the evolution of holidaymaking in France through the 20th century, emphasizing the growing democratization of the automobile.[37] This theme is also taken up by André Rauch in *Vacances en France de 1830 à nos jours* (1996), in which he refers to the direct effect the car had

34   Dine, Philip. 2010. 'Dresser la carte sportive de l'Algérie «française»: vitesse technologique et appropriation de l'espace.' In *L'empire des sports*, edited by Pierre Singaravélou and Julien Sorez. Paris: Belin, pp. 105–16.
35   Bellu, Serge. 1978. *Le Sang bleu: 70 ans d'histoire des voitures françaises de grands prix*. Paris: EPA.
36   Breyer, Victor. 1984. *La Belle époque à 30 à l'heure*. Paris: France-Empire.
37   Bertho-Lavenir, Catherine. 1999. *La Roue et le stylo: comment nous sommes devenus touristes*. Paris: Odile Jacob.

on the growth of holidaying on the French Riviera in the 1950s and 1960s.[38] Rioux and Sirinelli also make this point in *La France, d'un siècle à l'autre* (1999). They present the fuel crisis of 1973 as a watershed in the development of automobile holidays as this sudden shortage led people to question whether the ubiquitous use of the automobile – 'le tout-automobile,' as they put it – was sustainable.[39] The 1973 fuel crisis will form the cut-off point for the present volume as its economic impact forms a natural break from the economic expansion of the Trente Glorieuses.

After the Second World War, the growth of automobile use saw its influence extend to other forms of popular culture. The road movie, which had already been made popular in the United States, now came to France. *À bout de souffle* (1960) and *Un homme et une femme* (1966) became important films in the Nouvelle Vague, as the automobile began to play a more central role in modern life. In his song 'Nationale 7,' Charles Trenet evoked the summer holidays by referencing the road taken to get to the sun. The automobile also figures in the popular literature of the time; for instance, famous car lover Françoise Sagan's first novel *Bonjour tristesse* (1954), set on the Côte d'Azur, involves the death of a significant character in a car accident-cum-suicide.[40] The automobile and its destructive power were beginning to become part of popular discourse at this time. This process had been highlighted and intensified with the high-speed crash of James Dean in his Porsche Spyder in 1955. The incidence of death at high speeds quickly crossed the Atlantic. It began to figure in French cinema and in real life, with Sagan herself almost dying in an accident, and Albert Camus and Roger Nimier both meeting their end in a blazing car.[41] With larger numbers of cars on roads, the number of road deaths inevitably rose, and this began to be reflected in literature and the cinema. The novel *Les Choses de la vie* by Paul Guimard (1967) describes the final thoughts of a man as he lies dying at the side of the road, having crashed while driving at high speed. Less catastrophically, the ubiquitous nature of the car is explored and parodied in Jean-Luc Godard's *Week-end* (1967)

38   Rauch, André. 1996. *Vacances en France: de 1830 à nos jours*. Paris: Hachette.
39   Rioux, Jean-Pierre. 2002. *La France, d'un siècle à l'autre*. Paris: Hachette, p. 294.
40   Sagan, Françoise. 1954. *Bonjour tristesse*. Paris: Julliard.
41   Renou, Michel G. 1994. *Facel-Véga*. Paris: EPA, p. 43.

and Jacques Tati's *Playtime* (1967) and *Trafic* (1971), in the latter of which the car becomes the star.[42]

The car is featured in the work of many artists, Gerald Silk's *Automobile and Culture* (1984) and *L'art, la femme et l'automobile* (1989) being two examples of the scholarly analysis of this relationship between artist and automobile, as well as gender, in the latter.[43] In a notable example of this artistic interest, Henri Matisse (1869–1954), veering from his usual inspiration of life as seen through a window or in a mirror,[44] painted two landscapes encountered through the windscreen of a car.[45] Turn-of-the-century advertising quickly became an art form in its own right, and O'Galop, the cartoon artist who created Bibendum, became famous for the iconic posters he created depicting the Michelin man in various guises.[46] The cartoon has itself made ample use of the automobile; while fun is often poked at the car, it provided rich subject material for cartoonists, particularly during the growth of the car in the Trente Glorieuses. Two cartoonists in particular engaged with the car and modernity in the post-1945 era, as they lampooned the devotion to commodities that epitomized modernity yet also enslaved their owners. Chaval and Sempé both had their work regularly published in post-war periodicals; as commentators on modern France, their work is both socially informative and rich in cultural meanings.[47] All these interpretations of the car provide windows into the public image of the automobile, as these representations present a valuable insight into how the car was consumed.

42   Jean-Luc Godard, *Week-end* (France, 1967); Jacques Tati, *Playtime* (France, 1967); Jacques Tati, *Trafic* (France, 1971).
43   Silk, Gerald. 1984. *Automobile and Culture*. New York: Abrams; Néret, Gilles, and Hervé Poulain. 1989. *L'art, la femme et l'automobile*. Paris: EPA.
44   *Le Pare-brise: Sur la route de Villacoublay* (1916–17); *Route à Clamart* (1917).
45   Wollen, Peter. 2002. *Autopia: Cars and Culture*. London: Reaktion, p. 28; Danius, Sara. 2001. 'The Aesthetics of the Windshield: Proust and the Modernist Rhetoric of Speed.' *Modernism/modernity* 8 (1): 99–126. p. 118. Danius, Sara. 2002. *The Senses of Modernism: Technology, Perception, and Aesthetics*. New York: Cornell University Press, p. 136.
46   O'Galop was the pseudonym of Marius Roussillon. See Gonzalez, Pierre-Gabriel. 1995. *Bibendum: publicité et objets Michelin*. Paris: Le Collectionneur, p. 32.
47   Sempé is best-known for his illustrations of *Le Petit Nicolas*. See Corten-Gualtieri, Pascale. 2006. 'L'humour visuel de Sempé: une pratique de la sagesse populaire.' *Communication et langages* 149 (1): 29–44.

In its early days, the car was engaged with in different ways by the written media; it was even seen as being so dangerous that a campaign to ban the automobile was launched. Articles and letters received by newspapers were often negative in their views on the impact of the automobile on the lives of French citizens; indeed, many advocated a return to using horses. The pioneering architect Le Corbusier wrote extensively about the conversion of urban spaces to better manage the modernizing effect of the car. Le Corbusier accepted that modern life, which involved the automobile, inevitably implied living in a world where 'with traffic fury increasing, leaving your home meant that once you crossed the threshold, you became a possible prey to death, in the form of countless engines.'[48] Nevertheless, his *Urbanisme* (1924) proposes a city which, rather than rejecting the car, creates an urban utopia within which the automobile is central. The city is built around the ubiquity of the car, and the immense glass-and-metal structures illustrated in the book show a modernism that is not only utilitarian but also construed as a new object of beauty.

Cultural geographers in France and elsewhere have also engaged with the automobile in terms of its impact on urban and rural spaces. Henri Lefebvre and John Urry have both written about the car's conquest of space and how journeys have both been made shorter by the car's capacity to cover long distances and longer by the volume of automobiles on the road causing traffic jams.[49] Marc Augé has taken the idea of space further by suggesting that motorways and their corollaries are *non-lieux*, non-places, they are not lived in, not inhabited, but are simply crossed in order to get to where one wants to go.[50] The *non-lieu*, as a counterpoint to Pierre Nora's *lieu de mémoire*,[51] will be of importance especially in Chapter 4, where we will examine the significance of holidaymaking and the growth of the road network which inevitably led to the motorways and the *non-lieux* postulated by Augé.

---

48   'la fureur de la circulation grandissant, quitter votre maison signifiait qu'une fois le seuil franchi, vous deveniez une proie possible de la mort, sous forme d'innombrables moteurs.' Le Corbusier [Charles-Édouard Jeanneret-Gris]. 1994 [1924]. *Urbanisme*. Paris: Flammarion, p. 3.
49   Lefebvre, Henri. 2000 [1974]. *La Production de l'espace*. Paris: Anthropos; Urry, John. 2006. *Consuming Places*. London: Routledge.
50   Augé, Marc. 1992. *Non-lieux: introduction à une anthropologie de la surmodernité*. Paris: Seuil.
51   Nora, Pierre. 1997. *Les Lieux de mémoire*. Paris: Gallimard.

More recently, Matthieu Flonneau has written on the automobile, his writings mainly based on the use and perceptions of the car in Paris. His book *Les Cultures du volant* (2008) explores popular interaction with the car from its earliest days up to modern times.[52] In this comprehensive book Flonneau alludes to many instances where the car has had an impact on society. He makes use of resources ranging from popular songs to stamps as well as work by other writers who engage with the car. Ostensibly aimed at a French audience, there are a number of interesting links and representations mentioned, however many references and quotations are provided with little or no commentary. Flonneau's 2016 publication *L'automobile au temps des Trente Glorieuses* is aimed at a much broader, albeit francophone, audience. This image-laden work is less critical and more accessible as it endeavours to introduce what Flonneau terms 'automobilism' to a less consciously academic public.

Established in the early 2000s, two academic associations, the Association Passé-Présent-Mobilité (P2M) and its international counterpart, the International Association for the History of Transport, Traffic & Mobility (T²M), are dedicated to the exploration of transport and mobility. Gijs Mom and Mathieu Flonneau were early members and have both published extensively on the automobile. Mom, the founding president of T²M, has published widely on the development of the automobile throughout Europe and his 2014 publication *Atlantic automobilism: emergence and persistence of the car, 1895–1940* is considered the definitive history of early car development on both sides of the Atlantic.[53] This sprawling account explores novels, poems and films in several countries and gives a close analysis of parallels between these western nations. Mom uses the First World War as a dividing line between the 'emergence' and the 'persistence' of the car, the two periods of automobile expansion explored.

The edited volume *Automobile et littérature* (2005) analyses appearances of the car in English- and French-language literature.[54] However, it

52   Flonneau, Mathieu. 2008. *Les cultures du volant: essai sur les mondes de l'automobilisme, XXe–XXIe siècles*. Paris: Autrement.
53   Mom, Gijs. 2014. *Atlantic Automobilism: Emergence and Persistence of the Car, 1895–1940*. New York: Berghahn.
54   Monneyron, Frédéric. 2005. *Automobile et littérature*. Perpignan: Presses universitaires de Perpignan.

focuses mainly on American literature, with the notable exception of the exploration of *La 628-E8* by Octave Mirbeau (1907), whose title refers to Mirbeau's licence plate. The road movie genre is one which we almost immediately associate with American cars and Route 66. In his wide-ranging book *The French Road Movie: Space, Mobility, Identity* (2012), Neil Archer analyses a wide range of French films starting with references to the Nouvelle Vague before carrying out some excellent analysis of later 20th- and early 21st-century French and Québécois cinema.[55]

There has been a significant amount written about the perception and consumption of the car in French society and culture, particularly in recent years. This book will build upon the existing literature as it explores how the car has been perceived through popular represen-tations and how these representations have evolved as a result of the growing ubiquity of the car. This examination will take place in the context of the Marxian fetish, with the analysis reinforced by later critiques in the area. The first chapter is devoted to this theoretical discussion, exploring the reasons for this critical approach, as well as its limits.

55   Archer, Neil. 2012. *The French Road Movie: Space, Mobility, Identity*. New York: Berghahn.

Chapter 1

Theorizing the Car as a
Fetishized Commodity

Fetishizing the Modern

As modernization began to take hold in the late 19th century, symbols of this transformation were ostentatiously displayed as iconic landmarks of progress. Urban networks 'along with their "urban dowry" – water towers, dams, pumping stations, power plants, gas stations etc.' came to be constructed in the city as 'iconic embodiments of and shrines to a technologically scripted image and practice of progress.'[1] These urban networks reflected the commodification of technology. The automobile symbolized modernity and was displayed as the embodiment of a new emancipatory movement. It thus became both symbol and vehicle of a technologically enhanced world.

An early aspect of modernity was a quest to improve city and society through the newfound wonders of technology. Technology would improve living standards, and the car was a tool by which this improvement could be obtained. Kaika and Swyngedouw posit that 'As long as there was "progress," there was no fear of going "backward," no question or doubt about the positive trajectory of fulfilment of history's destiny, if not mission.'[2] The industrialization of nations, the expansion of free trade and the mass movement of goods from the mid-19th century augmented the need for improved connections in the world. Rail and steam travel preceded the motor car as 'Being

---

1   Kaika, Maria, and Erik Swyngedouw. 2002. 'Fetishizing the Modern City: The Phantasmagoria of Urban Technological Networks.' *International Journal of Urban and Regional Research* 24 (1): 120–38 (p. 121).
2   Kaika and Swyngedouw, 'Fetishizing the Modern City,' p. 125.

connected became an icon and expression of progress.'[3] The capacity of the car to conquer space by facilitating this connection was an expression of this modernity. The car's ability to tame nature, and to render the countryside trivial, placed it at the forefront of progress. As the automobile established itself further and became more familiar, it started to become aestheticized, as did other talismanic objects. The Eiffel Tower, which initially served as both a symbol of and shrine to modernity, is the ultimate example of this aestheticizing of the modern. Originally intended as a temporary construction, after its completion in 1889 the decision to tear it down was reversed. This symbol of technology has remained on the Parisian skyline as a reminder of how a new aesthetic appreciation could be afforded to technology.

Susan Buck-Morss suggests that the eminent German cultural theorist Walter Benjamin would define the fetish as an object of delight and desire in itself.[4] It is thus the representational value of the commodity that is emphasized, rather than that which is concealed:

> Everything desirable from sex to social status could be transformed into commodities as fetishes-on-display that held the crowd enthralled even when personal possession was far beyond reach. Indeed, an unattainably high price tag only enhanced a commodity's symbolic value.[5]

As a fetish, the automobile not only facilitated physical freedom for its owners, it also embodied the promise of a new world. In consequence, the desire to acquire a motor car constituted much more than the desire for its use-value; it was the desire to partake in progress, to participate in the emancipation offered by technology. The display of the motor car kept the dream of betterment alive, while the city and the streets were the shop window in which this commodity was put on display. Steps were taken to infuse this good further with an ideology of advancement. The car was actively promoted through the use of sporting events, through advertising, and later as a vehicle of propaganda in colonial expeditions in Africa.

---

3   Kaika and Swyngedouw, 'Fetishizing the Modern City,' p. 125.
4   Benjamin, Walter. 1999. *The Arcades Project*. Cambridge, MA: Harvard University Press; Buck-Morss, Susan. 1989. *The Dialectics of Seeing: Walter Benjamin and the Arcades Project*. Cambridge, MA: MIT Press, p. 82.
5   Benjamin, qtd. in Buck-Morss, *The Dialectics of Seeing*, p. 82.

The fetishized nature of the automobile was to evolve and change particularly after the watershed of the Second World War. Initially fetishized as an object of desire, specifically as an emancipator, the motor car gradually came to be fetishized for its mundanity, as a household object, the 'mechanical bride' of the Trente Glorieuses, as McLuhan referred to it.[6] Technology as a necessity was embodied in the refrigerator, the television and eventually the car. The emphasis moved to the importance of cleanliness inherent in the modernizing project: 'High modernity emerged from the 1930s onwards, with its obsession with clarity of form, purity, functionalism and cleanliness, translating the myth of the machine from the distant future into everyday experience.'[7] Over time, the functionality and efficiency of the machine supplanted the imaginary of desire previously afforded to it. This availability gradually became a reality and the 'urban technological cathedrals whose aesthetics belied the social realities'[8] were less desired. The automobile was regarded as a necessity in the modern household.

The Car as a Fetishized Commodity

In his study *Sex, Drink and Fast Cars* (1986), Stephen Bayley argues that the car is 'the ultimate talisman' of the 19th and early 20th centuries.[9] Through the appropriation of the car, by naming and anthropomorphizing it, people created gods from these machines.[10] Car expositions still provide sites where new versions of cars can be viewed, desired and consumed as anthropomorphic images. The process of the followers of the car all coming to one place in order to worship it has been compared to that of attending church or, indeed, a cathedral:

> The colors, the lights, the music, the awe of the worshippers, the presence of temple priestesses (fashion models), the thronging crowds – all these would represent in any other culture a clearly liturgical service … The cult of the sacred car has its adepts and its initiati. No gnostic more eagerly awaited a revelation from an

---

6   McLuhan, Herbert Marshall. 1967. *The Mechanical Bride*. London: Routledge.
7   Kaika and Swyngedouw, 'Fetishizing the Modern City,' p. 132.
8   Kaika and Swyngedouw, 'Fetishizing the Modern City,' p. 135.
9   Bayley, Stephen. 1986. *Sex, Drink and Fast Cars*. New York: Pantheon, p. 45.
10   It's worth mentioning the wordplay between DS/*déesse* (goddess) here.

oracle than does an automobile worshipper await the first rumors about the new models.[11]

The image of the cathedral in relation to technology is a motif that has been widely used. The early fetishizing of urban networks and the services they provided led to the creation of 'cathedrals of power' such as the early electricity generating stations built ostentatiously in the public eye: 'With upwardly-thrusting, gravity-defying lines and elaborate buttressing against wind pressures, a cathedral structure may seem to conquer elemental force just as surely as Concorde.'[12] Barthes compares the Citroën DS to the great gothic cathedrals and, in an early article on the car, Proust likens it to the cathedral of Reims as he makes his way to Paris.[13] The car may conveniently be regarded as a cathedral of progress. It is imbued in its physical character with the wish image of a better world, much as a traditional cathedral would be. In implying a link between the two, the quasi-religious worship of the automobile is portrayed in terms of a desire. As the cathedral symbolizes the wish for something better, so too can the automobile, which embodies the possibility of social progress through a commodity.

The desire to acquire this good does not always depend on the consumer's buying power; the early car was desired even though it could not be afforded by the majority of people. The desired nature of the motor car served to distance it from its original production value further: 'The price the consumer is prepared to pay for a commodity depends heavily on the ability of the market to render opaque the socioenvironmental relations embodied in the production process of commodities and to celebrate their uniqueness and phantom-like character.'[14] Thus the car's fetishistic character turned it into an object of desire in itself. As a symbol of modernity, the automobile not only physically emancipated its owner, it also carried the promise of a better society for its less privileged admirers. This image was nurtured

11   Dettelbach, Cynthia Golomb. 1976. *In the Driver's Seat: The Automobile in American Literature and Popular Culture.* Westport, CT: Greenwood, p. 99.
12   An Anglo-French construction, Concorde was a supersonic passenger airliner which operated from 1976 to 2003. Pacey, Arnold. 1983. *The Culture of Technology.* Cambridge, MA: MIT Press, p. 91.
13   Proust, Marcel. 1907. 'Impressions de route en automobile,' *Le Figaro*, 19 November, p. 1.
14   Kaika and Swyngedouw, 'Fetishizing the Modern City,' p. 123.

through the illusion of a happier life facilitated by the arrival of technology, most notably the car.

Although Marx's concept of the commodity fetish predates the car, technology more generally fits his definition of the fetish as 'a bewildering thing full of metaphysical subtleties and theological capers.'[15] The automobile became the outstanding embodiment of an imagined progress and a vehicle in the fullest sense for the quasi-religious belief that a better world was taking shape. Marx's theory of the commodity fetish is apt for exploring the consumption of the motor car, especially during early modernity. At a methodological level, a focus on commodity fetishism allows for the examination of economics, politics and culture. The automobile became a techno-logical fetish, admired, coveted, marvelled at; it enacted an ideology of progress in turn-of-the-century France. The fetishizing of the car went hand in hand with its commodification. The commodity assumes a new identity, alienated from that of its production and often alienated from its use-value. It is this commodification that creates the alienation between the use-value and the exchange-value of a manufactured object, as we shall explore in the specific case of the automobile.

Marx's Theory of the Commodity Fetish

Marx's landmark critique of capitalist economics, *Capital* (1867), includes a section entitled 'The Fetishism of Commodities and the Secret Thereof' in which he theorizes on the properties appropriated by the commodity as distinct from the utilitarian values of any given item.[16] The fetishism of commodities leads to objects becoming alienated from their origins and assuming values that are unrelated to the role envisaged for them. It is this change in value that interests Marx. An analogy employed by Marx is that of wood being altered to be made into a table; it is still wood but has acquired a utilitarian value in its new form as a table, and while this is clear:

> so soon as it steps forth as a commodity, it is changed into something transcendent. It not only stands with its feet on the

15   Marx, *Capital*, p. 24.
16   Marx, *Capital*, p. 25.

ground, but, in relation to all other commodities, it stands on its head, and evolves out of its wooden brain grotesque ideas, far more wonderful than 'table-turning' ever was.[17]

Through becoming a commodity, a 'mystical character' is conferred upon the table which, Marx claims, does not originate from its use-value: 'Whence, then, arises the enigmatical character of the product of labour, so soon as it assumes the form of commodities?'[18] Marx's answer lies in his concept of the fetish.

Perhaps the first example of engagement with the fetish is that of Charles de Brosses, in a work written in 1760.[19] The De Brossian image of the fetish draining humanity from the idolater is taken up by Marx in his treatment of the commodity fetish. De Brosses claims that this process of fetishizing leads to a situation 'in which the idol is more alive than the idolater.'[20] Pietz points out that Marx had engaged with 19th-century anthropology and had in particular studied 'primitive' religion, stating that: 'As early as 1842 he had read Charles de Brosses's classic *Du culte des dieux fétiches*, and he continued to take voluminous notes on ethnology and history of religion throughout his life.'[21] Marx posited that societies concealed the 'real' basis of existence in religious illusions. In *Capital*, he states that in order to understand 'the fantastic relation between things ... we must take flight into the misty realms of religion.'[22] Thus, borrowing heavily from the anthropological literature, Marx's concept of the commodity fetish criticizes capitalism for deluding its followers. The appropriation of the word 'fetish' for a commodified good links the properties this good acquires with those associated with primitive relations, and this process is seen as merely superstitious in modern society. Thus, Marx's commodity fetish forms a two-pronged critique of modern capitalist society and the religion underpinning it. In linking the origin of the fetishized character of a good to religion, Marx highlights how a product of

17   Marx, *Capital*, p. 25.
18   Marx, *Capital*, p. 25.
19   Brosses, Charles de. 1988 [1760]. *Du culte des dieux fétiches*. Paris: Fayard.
20   Cited in Mitchell, W.J. Thomas. 1986. *Iconology: Image, Text, Ideology*. Chicago, IL: University of Chicago Press, p. 190.
21   Pietz, William. 1985. 'The Problem of the Fetish, I.' *RES: Anthropology and Aesthetics* (9): 5–17 (p. 7).
22   Marx, *Capital*, p. 164.

human imagination can obscure its 'real' essence and, by extension, the world.

The Marxist concept of the commodity fetish is derived from the analysis of the relationship between the use-value and the exchange-value of a product. The use-value of an object in Marx's thesis is objective and thus 'real.' It satisfies human needs and performs no other function. Exchange-value, however, is much less clear. Exchange-value is the value placed upon a good as it goes through the process of exchange in capitalist society. In order to accrue a higher value, a product is perceived as a commodity and is thus alienated from its use-value, the processes through which it was produced being concealed. The 'real' value of a product should be calculated as a function of the social labour involved in its production; however, as a product is commodified, it takes on further properties. The fetishizing of a commodity is the attribution of qualities to an inanimate object, which fosters a misconception of the true value and true uses of the product. Thus, for Marx, while an object may appear simple at first sight, it is 'a very queer thing, abounding in metaphysical subtleties and theological niceties.'[23]

The Marxist theory of the fetish is, in essence, a critique of capitalist society. The real value of a good should, according to Marx, originate in the social labour involved in its creation. Thus, the exchange-value of a good is a misrepresentation of the true origins of value in capitalism. The central idea of the fetish is that an object is embraced by people and is venerated in a form of idolatry. The term 'fetish' was coined in the 15th century by the Portuguese in describing the religious practices of West Africa.[24] Marx, in the 19th century, extended this concept to the world of capitalism and more specifically to the category of the commodity. The fetishizing of technology accords it a certain godlike character, indeed the idea that technology has a life of its own recalls the animism prevalent in 'primitive' West African fetishism.

According to Tylor, an object is considered a fetish when a spirit is believed to be embodied in it. The object conceived is 'talked with, worshipped, prayed to, sacrificed to, petted or ill-treated with reference to its past or future behavior to its votaries.'[25] Thus, the fetishized

---

23   Marx, *Capital*, p. 165.
24   Pietz, 'The Problem of the Fetish,' p. 7.
25   Tylor, Edward B. 1970. *Religion in Primitive Culture*. Gloucester, MA: P. Smith, p. 231.

object becomes a god, venerated for invisible powers it embodies and capable of affecting the lives of those who worship it. Fetishism, according to William Mitchell, provided a rationale for 19th-century missionaries to convert North Africans to enlightened capitalism. This *mission civilisatrice* is a theme that was to form the backbone of the imperial campaign. The view of Africa was thus changing 'from an unknown, blank space, a source of slave labor, to a place of darkness to be illuminated, a frontier for imperialist expansion and wage-slavery.'[26] That much of this 'civilizing' process was accomplished through the use and misuse of totemic objects provides us with a valuable entry point into technology's function as a fetish in colonial Africa. Lewis Mumford refers to the machine as western culture's totem animal, half god and half slave.[27] This image is precisely that which was characteristic of French activity in Africa after the First World War and will be explored in Chapter 3, in which the *mission civilisatrice* in North Africa is examined.

Marx writes in *Economic and philosophical manuscripts of 1844* that the supporters of the capitalist regime are 'fetish-worshippers.'[28] Their veneration of private property has replaced real human relations, and objects thus appear to wield a power over subjects. Marx uses the term 'fetish' to criticize capitalist culture and, more broadly, social organization. 'Private property' and, later in this same work, 'metal money' are the only fetishes actually named. As previously mentioned, Marx's most famous work, *Capital*, also delves into the world of the commodity fetish. It follows the ideas already posited, namely, that the concept of private property is replaced by that of the commodity form. The 'real' value of a commodity is determined by the amount of labour required for its production and is unrelated to its material form. The exchange-value, however, is dependent on the relationship of the good with other objects. However, this perceived value is illusory since the relationship between objects leads to what is termed a 'fantastic' relationship. These 'fantastic' goods thus hide their real value in the capitalist market.

26   Mitchell, *Iconology*, p. 205.
27   Mumford, Lewis. 1952. *Art and Technics*. New York: Columbia University Press, p. 16.
28   Marx, Karl, and Friedrich Engels. 1988. *Economic and Philosophic Manuscripts of 1844*. Amherst, NY: Prometheus.

The acquisition of exchange-value, through the obscuring of the social values that underlie production, enables an Althusserian reification of the commodity, as the appropriation of imagery creates a good which functions over and above its use-value. This reification underlines its desirability and makes the customer prepared to pay a price unrelated to either its production costs or its use-value. Indeed, the price itself of a commodity plays a role in the creation of the value accorded to it. Hence, a good is fetishized through commodification. Marx refers to this process as abstraction: 'commodities become fetishes when quantification of qualitative relations allows for abstraction to take over.'[29] With this abstraction, 'commodities supply their own ideology in the market.'[30]

Fetishizing is the appropriation of desire, of reverence, of worship for an inanimate object. This may be done in a religious, economic or erotic context. Fetishism is the imbuing of objects with properties, and thus their consecration as commodities. This transformation is a social process. Therefore, identifying these social relations affords us an understanding of the true nature of the object; moreover, it allows us an access point through which we can examine the social and cultural movements at play in and through this object. An examination of the fetishizing of the automobile in France will shine a light on significant changes in society during the last century.

Fetishizing a Need: The Baudrillardian Fetish

In his treatment of the commodity fetish, Marx engaged in a form of cultural critique. He explored the displacement of real human relations and criticized their substitution with objects. Marx's work was intended for the liberation of human nature as it highlighted the oppression of man through the valorization of objects; the effects of living in capitalist society were thus responsible for repressing social life. The Marxian fetish belied the true nature of goods, and it was this misrepresentation that created a class distinction in society. However, Marx does not examine how these objects impacted on individual humans. In his *Système des objets*, Baudrillard examines this relationship

29   Marx, *Capital*, p. 35.
30   Eagleton, Terry. 1991. *Ideology: An Introduction*. London: Verso.

in terms of 'sign-values' and even goes so far as to suggest that objects have a causal effect on social beings.

The use-value, which Marx claims to be simple as it responds to a human need, has been identified by Marxist commentators such as Leiss, Sahlins and especially Baudrillard as an area in which Marx's critique is flawed. These writers posit that in separating use-value from exchange-value, and by placing all symbolic importance on exchange-value, Marx is omitting an important element in his treatment of the commodity. For instance, Leiss states that 'the idea of the symbolic constitution of utility is indispensable for a critique of consumer behaviour.'[31] Sahlins likewise argues this point, saying that use-values are also subsumed in the symbolic: 'In so far as "utility" is the concept of "need" appropriate to a certain cultural order, it must include a representation of the object, of the differential relation between persons.'[32] Thus regarded, Marx's materialist conception of society ignores the symbolic value of socially created needs. Baudrillard similarly questions Marx's differentiation of the use-value and exchange-value of an object. Baudrillard suggests that Marx's claim that use-value does not lead to the fetishizing of an object is mistaken. Much like Sahlins, Baudrillard points to the use-value of an object, and argues that it too is imbued with symbolic values:

> This is where Marxist idealism plays out, it is here that we must be more logical than Marx himself, in his own sense, more radical: use-value, utility itself, just like the abstract equivalence of commodities, is a fetishized social relation – an abstraction, one of the system of needs, which takes false evidence from a concrete destination, from a specific finality of goods and products – just like the abstraction of social work which founds the logic of equivalence (exchange-value) is hidden under the illusion of the 'infused' value of commodities.[33]

---

31   Leiss, William. 1976. *The Limits to Satisfaction: An Essay on the Problem of Needs and Commodities.* Toronto: University of Toronto Press, p. xix.

32   Sahlins, Marshall David. 1976. *Culture and Practical Reason.* Chicago, IL: University of Chicago Press, p. 150.

33   'C'est ici que joue l'idéalisme marxiste, c'est ici qu'il faut être plus logique que Marx lui-même, dans son propre sens, plus radical: la valeur d'usage, l'utilité elle-même, tout comme l'équivalence abstraite des marchandises, est un rapport social fétichisé, – une abstraction, celle du système des besoins, qui prend l'évidence fausse d'une destination concrète, d'une finalité propre des biens et des produits – tout comme l'abstraction du travail social qui fonde la

Thus, use-value for Baudrillard is not independent of symbolic constructions as needs are constructed as 'the equivalent of abstract social work' and 'on them the system of use-value is based.'[34] In short, 'use-value' is itself a mystified relationship. While exchange-value is a constituent of the fetishizing of an object, its use-values can equally be mystified. Marx stated that there is nothing mysterious about use and that a commodity is only mystified in exchange. Baudrillard posits that utility is not an absolute term and that needs can be socially created just as exchange-values are. In what follows, we shall explore these differing views with specific reference to the automobile.

The commodity fetish in Marx's writings involves the relationship between humans and objects. In his critique, Marx saw the attribution of properties to objects as a constitutive feature of the commodified world of capitalism. The concept of the fetish consists in the conferring of agency upon objects, which in reality is not possible as agency is limited to human beings. A century after Marx, Baudrillard draws on the theory of the commodity fetish in his exploration of objects. He explores the object's gaining of value 'through the social exchange of sign values, showing how objects are fetishized in ostentation.'[35] As explored by Marx and then reconfigured by Baudrillard, the theory of the fetish will form the framework for the present work. The fetish has not influenced exchange-value; in addition, and crucially, cultural representation of the object, as Baudrillard makes clear, has placed the automobile at the centre of semiotic fetishizing. As an ostentatious symbol, consumed for its sign value, the Baudrillardian fetish of the car overlooks the use-value of the commodity. It is not only through ostentation that the motor car is fetishized; additionally, the valorization of its capacities as a means of transport, as a mechanism for emancipation must also be examined in an exploration of its fetishized nature.

logique de l'équivalence (valeur d'échange) se cache sous l'illusion de la valeur "infuse" des marchandises.' Baudrillard, *Pour une critique de l'économie politique du signe*, p. 155; Baudrillard, Jean. 1981. *For a Critique of the Political Economy of the Sign*. Translated by Charles Levin. St. Louis, MO: Telos Press, p. 131.
34 'l'équivalent du travail social abstrait,' 'sur eux se fonde le système de la valeur d'usage.' Baudrillard, *Pour une critique de l'économie politique du signe*, p. 155; *For a Critique of the Political Economy of the Sign*, p. 131.
35 Dant, Tim. 1996. 'Fetishism and the Social Value of Objects.' *The Sociological Review* 44 (3): 495–516 (p. 496).

Viewed as a misconception and thus not real, the Marxian fetish did not offer a theoretical basis for examining the ability of one commodity to be more fetishized than another. Baudrillard, however, establishes such a hierarchy and moreover suggests that the automobile carried more ostentatious prestige than many other commodities in Trente Glorieuses France. We will use the concept of the fetish not to criticize but rather as a tool with which to explore the political, economic and cultural context of a rapidly modernizing country. Baudrillard's expansion of the fetishism theory is relevant here as the car will be examined as a sign of social value; it becomes part of a system of Bordelian distinction in which the object is seen to embody the owner's social status.[36] The fetish is no longer denied as not 'really' existing; rather, Baudrillard sees it as 'a means of mediating social value through material culture.'[37] The car consequently fits into his theory of the attribution of properties to commodified goods.

Baudrillard based much of his work on the nature of the object on the Marxian analysis of the fetish. However, in focusing on the relationship between the social subject and the object, he significantly developed Marx's theory, particularly regarding the object's impact on the subject. Whereas Marx strove to assert the primacy of the human subject, Baudrillard's work is a development of the subject/object relationship. In his critique of Marx, Baudrillard suggests that use-value is just as fetishized as exchange-value. This is because the object functions in a system of signs and values. Baudrillard argues: 'It is nothing but the different types of relations and significations that converge, contradict themselves, and twist around it.'[38] The object is not consumed as a direct response to a human need; instead, it exists as a sign in a system of relations with other objects. Thus, consumption is not a human need but the social exchange of signs and values. Objects for Baudrillard function in a system which operates on two planes, functionality and ostentation. It is the extent to which a good achieves ostentation that transforms it into a fetish.

36   Bourdieu, Pierre. 1979. *La Distinction: critique sociale du jugement*. Paris: Minuit.
37   Cited by Dant, 'Fetishism and the Social Value of Objects,' p. 498.
38   'Il n'est rien que les différents types de relations et de significations qui viennent converger, se contredire, se nouer sur lui.' Baudrillard, *Pour une critique de l'économie politique du signe*, p. 60; *For a Critique of the Political Economy of the Sign*, p. 63.

Baudrillard uses the television as an example to explain this point. Even if broken, in a society where a television can hardly be afforded, the television becomes a 'pure fetish' for its ostentation value. The television functions as a machine that mediates information which is consumed; it is also consumed in itself, its possession signifying membership of a community as 'a guarantee of social legitimacy.'[39] According to Baudrillard, the television has a sign value well in excess of its functional capacity. Each object 'only makes sense in the difference with other objects, according to a code of hierarchical meanings.'[40] It is this 'système des objets' which involves sign values and their social exchange that Baudrillard calls 'consommativité.' This is a system of needs which is imposed on consumers, including the need for choice. Needs are not created in a void, but rather are established in the consumer through the 'stratégie de désir,'[41] which ensures that, through the exchange of signs, the use-value of objects is distinguished. In *Séduction*, Baudrillard further develops his theory of the fetish as he explores how objects seduce the subject. This blurs the distinction established by Marx between subject and object. The determining effect of the social sphere is questioned: 'The reaction to this new state of affairs has not been a resigned abandonment of old values, but rather a mad overdetermination, an exacerbation of these values of reference, function, purpose, causality.'[42] For Baudrillard, the fetish symbolizes the power of the object to determine the subject and thus to reverse causality.

In his system of objects, Baudrillard examines objects according to their system of meanings in conjunction with their use-value. This involves examining the quotidian consumption of objects, that is, how they are experienced as a result of their capacities. Baudrillard rejects

---

39   'un gage de légitimité sociale.' Baudrillard, *Pour une critique de l'économie politique du signe*, p. 60; *For a Critique of the Political Economy of the Sign*, p. 54.
40   'ne prend de sens que dans la différence avec d'autres objets, selon un code de significations hiérarchisées.' Baudrillard, *Pour une critique de l'économie politique du signe*, p. 61; *For a Critique of the Political Economy of the Sign*, p. 55.
41   Baudrillard, *Pour une critique de l'économie politique du signe*, p. 61; *For a Critique of the Political Economy of the Sign*, p. 55.
42   'La réaction à ce nouvel état de choses n'a pas été un abandon résigné des anciennes valeurs, mais plutôt une surdétermination folle, une exacerbation de ces valeurs de référence, de fonction, de finalité, de causalité.' Baudrillard, Jean. 1986 [1983]. *Stratégies fatales*. Paris: Librairie générale française, p. 15.

Marx's analysis of the object as incomplete as it does not accord any semiotic worth to the use-value of an object. However, he follows Marx's theory as he examines the images concealed in the design of vehicles, much as Barthes did in his analysis of the DS. In his famous discussion of tail fins on American cars, Baudrillard exposes the ways in which design contrives to nurture an image of speed, which in reality leads to the opposite:

> [Tail fins] have other meanings, too: scarcely had it emancipated itself from the forms of earlier kinds of vehicles than the automobile-object began connoting nothing more than the result so achieved — that is to say, nothing more than itself as a victorious function. We thus witnessed a veritable triumphalism on the part of the object: the car's fins became the sign of victory over space — and they were *purely* a sign, because they bore no direct relationship to that victory (indeed, if anything they ran counter to it, tending as they did to make vehicles both heavier and more cumbersome).[43]

As these tail fins symbolize speed, yet their weight and bulk means that they actually slow the car down, the sign value of the automobile has partially replaced its use-value. The tail fins were derived from the fighter planes of the Second World War. Baudrillard and the general public believed that they originated from shark fins and birds' wings, a belief that echoes Futurism's animism of the automobile, in which machines were afforded the characteristics of different animals as they interacted with nature.[44]

Baudrillard also insisted on the everyday capabilities of the car, claiming that it had the capacity to be used as an abode. Thus, the

43   '[Les ailes de voiture] ont d'autres significations encore: à peine dégagé des formes des véhicules antérieurs et structuré selon sa fonction propre, très vite l'objet automobile ne fait que connoter le résultat acquis, se connoter lui-même comme fonction victorieuse. On assiste alors à un véritable triomphalisme de l'objet: l'aile de voiture devient le signe de la victoire sur l'espace, — signe pur parce que sans rapport avec cette victoire (la compromettant plutôt, puisqu'elle alourdit la voiture et en accroît l'encombrement). Baudrillard, *Le Système des objets*, p. 83; Baudrillard, Jean. 1996. *The System of Objects*. Translated by James Benedict. London: Verso, p. 59.

44   Campbell, Timothy. 2009. 'Vital Matters: Sovereignty, Milieu, and the Animal in Futurism's Founding Manifesto.' *Annali d'Italianistica* 27: 157–73 (p. 161).

automobile embodies a home away from home, one that can serve as a refuge, a place of privacy and intimacy, outside the house. As we shall see, Tati's 1971 film *Trafic* explores this as the vehicle that is to be brought to an exhibition incorporates all the functionalities of a house but is built on the mobile platform of a car in order to facilitate holidaymaking. Baudrillard, in his famous dialectic of the automobile as both projectile and dwelling place, shows that whether or not the motor car is perceived as a symbol of speed in its appropriation as a quotidian object, it is alienated from its 'real' use-value: 'But basically, like all functional mechanical objects, [the car] is experienced – and by everyone, men, women and children – as a phallus, as an object of manipulation, care, and fascination. The car is a projection both phallic and narcissistic, a force transfixed by its own image.'[45] This image of the phallus further underlines the distancing of the car in popular perception from its origin as, according to Baudrillard, it is experienced not as a 'simple' means of transport but rather as a much more complex phenomenon as it becomes ever more invested with meaning.

Baudrillard accepts that abstraction occurs in the exchange of an object. However, use-value and the perception of a need, which are indisputable for Marx, in Baudrillardian theory figure in a system of needs which is just as fetishized as the exchange object. Thus, that which may appear to be a need has become fetishized, crucially, and is also historically determined, as what may be perceived as needs are continually changed and updated as pertaining to a specific social order, and this order is based on the fetishizing of certain signs. In post-1945 France, the home was the site for the transmogrification of these signs, as fridges, televisions and cars came to be perceived as needs in a culture that was beginning to define itself according to a new standard of cleanliness and progress.[46] Baudrillardian theory posits that the commodity fetish not only occurs as a result of social abstraction in which the value of an object is defined by its capacity for exchange

---

45   'La voiture est d'abord, – et par tous, hommes, femmes, enfants –, vécue comme phallus, objet de manipulation, de soins, de fascination. Projection phallique et narcissique à la fois, puissance médusée par sa propre image.' Baudrillard, *Le Système des objets*. pp. 98–99; *The System of Objects*, p. 69.
46   Ross, Kristin. 1998. *Fast Cars, Clean Bodies: Decolonization and the Reordering of French Culture*. Cambridge, MA: MIT Press, p. 5.

but also through the abstraction of the need system in society. While the car gradually ceased to be considered a mythological or excessively desired object, becoming a symbol of mundanity as it started to acquire a domestic function, it nevertheless remained within a system where it was fetishized. Evolving from an object of desire to become a part of the home that was fetishized as a need, the automobile continued to function in a system of signs. Whether as goddess or as maid, the automobile remained a fetishized commodity, whose role became greater as its image became more mundane and commonplace.

Marx's seminal work *Capital* is a critique of a rapidly industrializing world. His concept of the commodity fetish challenged the perception of industrial goods as he posited that in the context of a market, in order for greater profit to be obtained, the process of exchanging any given product leads it to be alienated from its origin. The religious or anthropological metaphor as used by Marx focuses attention on the fetishizing of an object. This trope is a means of understanding commodity fetishism, which can be applied, according to Marx, to any product consumed within a capitalist framework. There are many different forms of fetishizing of commodities. It is a phenomenon that typically adapts to its cultural surroundings, making this concept a particularly useful one for the purposes of this study. While we might not necessarily accept all the arguments made by later Marxian critics regarding the fetishizing of the car, they nonetheless provide a fruitful commentary on their specific time and society. We will apply Marx's theory of the commodity fetish – revised and refined in the light of the reflections of Baudrillard and others – to the automobile. More specifically, this concept will be used as an entry point into French society's consumption of the car. The car as fetishized vehicle of modernity is consequently apt as the primary focus for this analysis.

Chapter 2

Motor Sport in France

Commodifying the Car

Central to the initial growth of the automobile was motor sport, which was born in France in the 1890s, on the model of the bicycle races that had successfully linked up the nation's major towns. Turn-of-the-century city-to-city races provided stern tests for these early vehicles, becoming advertising platforms upon which manufacturers displayed their models to an initially reluctant public. Pioneering manufacturers, such as Renault and Peugeot, quickly realized that it was necessary to participate in these events to ensure the commercial viability of their vehicles.[1] The new sport was inevitably costly, and it was thus France's upper classes who were the first to test and promote the automobile. However, motor sport gradually served to democratize the car as a broader public began to take an interest in it. Gordon Bennett served as an important catalyst in the emergence of the sport when he inaugurated the first international races. Le Mans, just 200 km to the west of Paris, also played an active role in the early development of motoring.

Motor racing appealed to large numbers of people as it served to build the social perception of the car while at the same time testing its capacities. In asking the car to reach destinations that were further and further away in shorter and shorter times, the car's surplus capacity, its ability to exceed its original use-value, was the means through which it began to be fetishized. Speed became the principal criterion by which a motor car was judged. The linking of French towns in a new way, via automobile, also promoted the transformative aspect of the horseless carriage, as it proved capable of carrying passengers at greater speeds than

---

1   Michelin, Peugeot and Bollée are examples of three *familles artisanales* who adapted their businesses to automobile production.

hitherto imagined to places which were previously out of reach. Speed and modernity as embodied by these hugely popular races brought the image of the motor car in motion to turn-of-the-century France.

This chapter will discuss the genesis of motor racing in France, showing how sport helped the automobile establish a foothold in society. The impact of an American, Gordon Bennett, in placing the sport on the international stage will also be examined. Additionally, a case study of Le Mans, birthplace of the Grand Prix and synonymous with French motor sport, having now hosted its iconic 24-hour race for over 80 years, will shed light on this growth in popularity. In its infancy, motor sport was an important testing ground for the newly invented motorized vehicles, and early races gave manufacturers the opportunity to trial and promote their cars on public roads. This provided the opportunity for a *marque* to stand out by showing the world its potential. Finally, two more modern examples of engagement with motor sport will be examined. Firstly, Claude Lelouch's *Un homme et une femme* (1966),[2] in which motor racing plays a central role, and secondly a short film entitled *Le Sport et les hommes* (1959), a documentary written by the cultural critic Roland Barthes and which does not appear in his *Œuvres complètes*.[3] These two films will be used to explore the manner in which motor sport continues to be fetishized in the latter half of the 20th century.

Early Automobile Racing

Although Gottlieb Daimler invented the internal combustion engine in Germany in the 1880s, the automobile developed more rapidly in France for a number of reasons. Firstly, the more established road network allowed the transition from horse-drawn vehicles to the automobile to be made without undue difficulty. Napoléon Bonaparte's creation at the turn of the 19th century of a star-shaped road network with Paris as the hub allowed easy access to and from the capital.[4]

2   Lelouch, Claude, dir. 1966. *Un homme et une femme*. France, Les Films 13.
3   Aquin, Hubert, dir. 2012 [1961]. *Le Sport et les hommes*. Montreal, Office national du film du Canada.
4   Pinkney, David H. 1958. *Napoleon III and the Rebuilding of Paris*. Princeton, NJ: Princeton University Press, pp. 125–27.

Paris was itself capable of accommodating the motor car, having been rebuilt in the mid-19th century by Baron Haussmann on the orders of Napoléon III. Fashionable houses were built on elegant boulevards with open intersections which had been designed to deter the building of barricades by rebels, but which now allowed for the coexistence of both horseless and horse-drawn carriages.[5]

A second major factor was the foresight of French entrepreneurs, anxious to make up ground lost as a result of France's belated and partial industrial revolution. The traditional *famille artisanale* only began to industrialize in the latter half of the 19th century. These small businesses typically engaged in trades such as metal- and woodworking. Thus, they had both the necessary flexibility and the existing infrastructure to turn their workshops into automobile manufacturing plants. These family-run businesses rapidly established themselves as the core of what came to be known as the Second Industrial Revolution.[6] Thus, by the turn of the 20th century, France had over 600 car manufacturers compared with fewer than 100 in the rest of Western Europe and the United States combined.[7]

The upper classes accepted the motor car with open arms for the most part. It became the latest in a series of inventions to grab their attention, in much the same way as the steam engine and the bicycle had previously. Many figures in society embraced it for varying reasons. Baron de Zuylen, who was to become the first director of the Automobile Club de France (ACF), was a major advocate of the car, not only because he believed in its potential but also, intriguingly, because of his love for horses. He specifically saw the automobile as a means of lessening the workload placed upon Parisian horses.[8] More generally, the link between aristocracy and horseracing at the time was strong, as exemplified by the Jockey-club de Paris, a gathering of the elite of 19th-century society. Members of this exclusive club formed two-thirds of the founding committee of the Automobile Club de France in 1895.

5   For more information on the redesign of Paris as well as the use of barricades in conflict, see Lefebvre, Henri. 1965. *La proclamation de la Commune, 26 mars 1871.* Paris: Gallimard, pp. 92–94.

6   Levin, Miriam R. 2010. *Urban Modernity: Cultural Innovation in the Second Industrial Revolution.* Cambridge, MA: MIT Press, pp. 13–75.

7   Laux, James Michael. 1976. *In First Gear: The French Automobile Industry to 1914.* Montreal: McGill-Queen's University Press, p. 40.

8   Laux, *In First Gear*, p. 31.

The Comte de Dion, Baron de Zuylen and Paul Meyan, a journalist with *Le Figaro* and editor of the newsletter *La France Automobile*, met in September 1895 to create the world's first automobile club. De Dion was nominated club president, a role he immediately ceded to de Zuylen as he saw his position as a major manufacturer as a conflict of interest with the broader promotion of the car. Although the creation of the Association Internationale des Automobile Clubs Reconnus (AIACR) in 1904 may be seen as the logical development of a world governing body for automobile clubs, this predecessor to the FIA (Fédération Internationale de l'Automobile), which came into being in 1947, was essentially the body by means of which the ACF organized its international races. Its headquarters are located next door to that of the ACF at 8 Place de la Concorde, and until 1963 the body had the same series of presidents as the ACF. Indeed, the link between motor sport and the aristocracy endured through much of the 20th century; to this day, only four out of the 11 presidents of what is now known as the FIA have not had noble titles.[9]

The growing importance of automobile racing was also to have an impact on the highly politicized arena of journalism. The Comte Albert de Dion and Pierre Giffard found themselves on opposite sides of one of the biggest political scandals in French history: the Dreyfus Affair, which involved the wrongful conviction (and later exoneration) of a Jewish officer in the French army on charges of treason. Giffard founded *Le Vélo* in 1892 and pursued an active role in promoting both bicycle and automobile sport; as a result, his paper was widely used for the advertising of these vehicles by manufacturers.[10] One such figure was the Comte de Dion, a vocal anti-Dreyfusard. De Dion became involved in a highly publicized spat with French president Émile Loubet at the Auteuil races, for which he was jailed for 15 days. Having been heavily criticized by Giffard in the newspaper he sponsored extensively, de Dion removed his advertising from *Le Vélo* and created a new newspaper. He and a number of other industrialists, including the Michelin brothers, launched *L'Auto-Vélo* in 1900,

9   Laux, *In First Gear*, p. 205. The last four presidents have not been linked to the nobility, a further indication of the strong association between motor racing and the upper classes in its earlier years.
10   Dauncey, Hugh. 2008. 'Entre presse et spectacle sportif, l'itinéraire pionnier de Pierre Giffard (1853–1922).' *Le Temps des médias* 2: 35–46 (p. 36).

with Henri Desgrange as editor-in-chief. It became *L'Auto* in January 1903, when Giffard successfully sued the paper for infringement on his own paper's name. It was *L'Auto* that was responsible, in 1903, for the creation and organization of what was to become the largest sporting event in France: cycling's Tour de France.

At this time, the popular press was also experiencing substantial development, reflecting growing levels of literacy in society, and each newspaper was striving to create ideas that would attract members of the reading public and encourage them to buy its issues. A firm link developed between journalism and the expansion of sport, seen by journalists as a means of acquiring and maintaining a high readership. The coverage of a sporting event that lasted over a number of days or even weeks was used as a tool to promote the purchase of newspapers on a regular basis. In a precursor of the Tour de France, Pierre Giffard, the then editor-in-chief of *Le Petit Journal*, the newspaper with the largest circulation in the 1890s, had organized a bicycle race from Bordeaux to Paris in 1891. This was followed later the same year by Paris–Brest–Paris. These bicycle races allowed Giffard to create a daily column relating to build-up to the race and the preparations involved in it, encouraging readers to buy his paper each day, for the duration of the race, in order to learn about the progress each competitor was making.[11] It was only a matter of time before this technique of newspaper marketing was adapted and used as a model to promote a motoring event.

The first attempt to test the efficiency of automobiles in public was organized as early as 1887, when the newspaper *Le Vélocipède illustré* announced the holding of a 'reliability' trial.[12] The event involved a short journey, from Paris to Versailles. Only one competitor showed up, however, and the event had to be abandoned. The following year, the same trial was organized, and this time two automobiles turned up; the trial was completed, but little importance was given to it since the two cars involved were both by the same manufacturer, namely the Comte de Dion. An automobile was allowed to take part in the Paris–Brest–Paris bicycle race of 1891. This race also marked the first competitive appearance of pneumatic tyres. The *frères* Michelin convinced the renowned cyclist Charles Terront to use their invention

11   Dauncey, Hugh, and Geoff Hare. 2003. *The Tour de France, 1903–2003: A Century of Sporting Structures, Meanings, and Values*. London: Frank Cass, p. 60.
12   Studeny, Christophe. 1995. *L'invention de la vitesse*. Paris: Gallimard, p. 305.

on his bicycle. While he had to stop to repair numerous punctures, the pneumatics' ability to cope with the rough terrain helped Terront to a famous victory.[13] He actually finished the course some 17 minutes before any of the cars, which is perhaps indicative of why the first automobile race was not to take place for a number of years. Having sponsored the Paris–Brest–Paris bicycle race, Pierre Giffard decided to apply his model to a motoring trial. Having seen the automobile first-hand in 1891, Giffard organized and publicized a competition for *voitures sans chevaux* to be held on the public roads between Paris and Rouen in 1894.[14] It was not a race but rather a reliability trial intended to assess the potential of the motor car. Cars were expected to 'be safe, easy to handle for travellers and not cost too much on the road.'[15] Unlike previous attempts, this event mustered a high level of interest, not least due to its constant front-page promotion by Giffard in *Le Petit Journal*. It gradually began to attract the attention of the public, and what has been qualified as a 'significant' crowd turned out at the Porte-Maillot for the departure on 11 June 1894.[16] Of the 102 entrants, 21 actually appeared on the start line, and 17 made it to the finish. It was not the automobile that finished first that was awarded first prize, however. The Comte de Dion crossed the line first, on a steam engine of his own invention; his vehicle, as it required a stoker, was deemed to be impractical, and first prize was jointly awarded to the second- and third-placed *marques*, both of which were petrol-powered. De Dion covered the distance of 127 km in a time of six hours and 48 minutes, giving him an average speed of just over 18 km/h, but it must be taken into account that all competitors stopped for lunch during the event.

Thus, the early attempts to promote the automobile were trials, testing grounds that publicized the ability or use-value of the car. With the support of the newspapers of the time, the commodification of the car had begun. While speed was not the goal of these trials, asking the early car to link two cities was a first step in valorizing its surplus capacity. These trials highlighted, first, the function of the car

13   Souvestre, Pierre. 1907. *Histoire de l'automobile*. Paris: H. Dunod, p. 227.
14   Studeny, *L'invention de la vitesse*, p. 306.
15   'être sans danger, aisément maniable pour les voyageurs et ne pas coûter trop cher sur la route.' Bellu, Serge. 1984. *100 ans d'automobile française*. Neuilly-sur-Seine: L'Automobile magazine.
16   Varey, Mike. 2003. *1000 Historic Automobile Sites*. Oakland, CA: Elderberry, p. 332.

by enhancing the ability of its user to travel. Second, they enhanced its capacity through ostentation, as it is evident that the early automobile users formed part of an elite social group. The decision to take the time to stop for lunch during the trial highlights the place of both the automobile and its user within a codified performance of privilege. The car's ability to reach greater speeds soon meant that a fetishizing of speed itself and an associated aesthetics of speed came to the forefront as trials were replaced by races that covered longer distances.

Giffard was immediately approached to organize an automobile race in 1895 but declined as he was unwilling to take responsibility for an event on open roads with vehicles capable of reaching what were perceived at the time to be dangerously high speeds. De Dion and Baron de Zuylen duly organized the Paris–Bordeaux–Paris race themselves. The choice of route may have been modelled on the first city-to-city bicycle race, which was successfully run from Bordeaux to Paris in 1891. This route was also chosen in order to show those still sceptical about the automobile that it could not only cover a great distance with a minimum of mechanical problems but also, by linking two of France's largest cities, to confirm the car's utilitarian role. Bordeaux was also a notably sporting city at this time, so doubly suitable for the race. De Dion showed, in the rules, that he was aware of what was at stake:

> It is important to remind competitors about the main rules that must be observed, just as much for their own safety as to ensure the success of this important demonstration of the progress made in automobile construction, which the organizing committee aimed to highlight in organizing this race.
>
> As a result, all strict rules notwithstanding, the organizing committee asks all competitors to remain cognizant of the fact that this 1,200 km test in which they are participating may prove to be decisive in the current and future use of everyday automobile locomotion.[17]

---

17   'Il se borne uniquement à rappeler aux concurrents les principales règles qu'ils doivent observer, tant dans leur intérêt propre que pour la réussite de l'importante manifestation des progrès réalisés dans la construction des automobiles et que le Comité a eu principalement en vue de faire ressortir dans l'organisation de cette course.
   En conséquence, à l'exclusion de toutes règles strictes, le Comité invite les concurrents à ne jamais perdre de vue que l'épreuve de 1,200 kilomètres,

While car trials were a thing of the past, as a desire for speed was beginning to take over, the use-value of the car remained a concern. Hence, although Émile Levassor finished the race first in a Panhard, with a time of 48 hours and 48 minutes (24.5 km/h), he was not awarded the first prize due to the fact that his automobile only had two seats and was thus not considered a viable option.[18] Nevertheless, the ostentation of speed is what was remembered, as Levassor's achievement is commemorated by a statue situated at the start/finish line at the place Porte-Maillot, Paris. Commissioned by the Automobile Club de France in 1898, a year after Levassor's death, the monument was originally to be sculpted by Jules Dalou. However, upon his death in 1902, one of his students, Camille Lefèvre, completed the Greco-Roman-style triumphal arch in 1907. The arch, which depicts Levassor in his car being watched by onlookers, remains there to this day.[19] Its epic nature evokes a fetishized impression of the car; this was to be a recurrent theme in the early 20th century.

The success of this race led the newborn ACF to hold city-to-city races on an annual basis. Race organizers chose routes that always incorporated Paris as the starting point but gradually moved destinations further away. Thus, if Paris–Bordeaux–Paris covered a total distance of almost 1,200 km, the following year's race distance was extended to more than 1,700 km for the Paris–Marseille–Paris race. In 1898, the race may have been shorter but had a much more significant destination as it was from Paris to Amsterdam. National borders were crossed and the automobile was proved capable of linking countries. Races linking Paris with Berlin, Vienna and Madrid followed, interspersed with some national competitions, including the Tour de France Automobile in 1899, organized by Paul Meyan and *Le Matin*, a full four years before the cycling version.[20] Indeed, the largest sporting event to take place in 1903 was not, as most would assume, the inaugural Tour de France bicycle race, but the Paris–Madrid road

à laquelle ils prennent part, pourra être décisive au point de vue de l'usage pratique, présent et à venir, de la locomotion automobile.' Paris–Bordeaux race rules. *Le Vélo*, 1 June 1895.

18   Volti, Rudi. 2004. *Cars and Culture: The Life Story of a Technology*. Westport, CT: Greenwood, p. 13.

19   Laux, *In First Gear*, p. 23.

20   Cadène, Jean. 2005. *L'automobile: de sa naissance à son futur*. Perpignan: Cap Béar, p. 59.

Figure 1 Sculpture at Porte Maillot, Paris commemorating the
1895 Paris–Bordeaux–Paris motor race.
© Éamon Ó Cofaigh (August 2014).

race organized by the ACF. It left Versailles on 24 May 1903 in front of a reputed 200,000 spectators.[21] A further 2 million people lined the roads from Paris to Bordeaux and, according to newspaper reports, another 200,000 people came out in Bordeaux to see the arrival at the end of the first major stage of this race.[22] However, a spate of fatal accidents brought about the cancellation of the Bordeaux–Madrid stage of the race. Among the victims was Marcel Renault, brother of Louis, co-founder of the company that still dominates both motor sport and French automobile production today.

As the automobile was becoming more celebrated, it was also beginning to find detractors in both the journalistic and literary fields; among others, Léon Bloy stated in *Le Journal* (26 May 1903) that 'all ambitious automobilists *are premeditated killers*.'[23] Motor racing had taken a firm hold, however, on the imagination of the public, and the promotional potential of up to 3 million people attending a single race could not be ignored. After 34 races held on open roads between 1896 and 1903,[24] the ill-fated Paris–Madrid race signalled the banning of city-to-city races, as it was deemed impossible adequately to marshal motor races on open roads.[25] The predecessor to circuit racing came into being as a result; this was the closure of roads to public use in order to form a circuit, the compromise required by the authorities to allow races to take place.

Motor racing increasingly commanded a large viewing public and this growth allowed manufacturers to display further the abilities of their vehicles. As discussed above, speed was the predominant surplus capacity to be fetishized in motor racing; however, at the turn of the century, motor racing also became an arena within which a highly publicized struggle between energy sources was fought out. Speed and distance constituted the yardsticks for a set of one-on-one races, organized to decide which power source was the 'best.' In testing these two objectives, the events underlined the fetishized nature of

21   Dauncey and Hare, *The Tour de France, 1903–2003*, p. 60.
22   Dauncey and Hare, *The Tour de France, 1903–2003*, p. 60.
23   Léon Bloy, qtd. in Laux, *In First Gear*, p. 40.
24   de Penfentenyo, Jehan-Charles. 2016. *2, 3, 4 roues, le grand prix de Picardie de 1913*. Paris: Michel de Maule, p. 28.
25   Rousseau, Jacques. 1985. *La commémoration de la course Paris–Madrid: 24 mai 1903*. Bordeaux: Automobile-Club du Sud-Ouest, p. 4.

the perception of the car. The public nature of this power struggle strengthened the growing link between the desire for, and the ostentatious display of, two surplus capacities of the car.

While certain race organizers were intent on conquering the roads of France and Europe, and at a later stage the world, others were still not convinced of the feasibility of the internal combustion engine. Thus, the late 1890s saw a competition between three forms of vehicle: internal combustion, steam and electric power. Each system had its own qualities and weaknesses. Electric cars were quiet and reliable; however, their batteries never lasted for more than 40 or 50 kilometres and were difficult to recharge outside the city. Electric cars were essentially seen as city cars. Steam-powered automobiles worked along the same lines as locomotive engines, albeit in a much smaller form. These cars required a *chauffeur*, literally 'a heater,' to feed the engine with fuel in order to provide the necessary steam to propel the car. Steam cars therefore required two people to operate them at any one time and were generally quite large and cumbersome. They were also slow to start, as 20 minutes was generally needed for an automobile to build up a head of steam. Internal combustion engines were noisy, smelly, and largely unreliable; however, they could cover large distances, and for those who converted from steam, their *chauffeur* was now actually driving the car.

La France Automobile, which was essentially the journal of the ACF, initiated a series of short speed tests in the late 1890s that captured public attention for a different reason from the city-to-city endurance tests; their purpose was not long-distance driving but speed alone. A straight stretch of road at the Parc Agricole d'Achères near Paris was the venue chosen for these sprints, and it was here in 1898 that Gaston de Chasseloup-Laubat set the world's first land speed record when he achieved 63 km/h driving a Jeantaud, an electric vehicle.[26] In 1899, Camille Jenatzy would become the first person to break the 100 km/h barrier driving another electric car named La Jamais Contente (Never Satisfied).[27] This proved to be the electric car's peak, the beginning of its downfall, as it was becoming more and more apparent that there was at that time no scope for improvement in the power or longevity

26   Chanaron, Jean-Jacques. 1983. *L'industrie automobile*. Paris: La Découverte, p. 8.
27   Souvestre, *Histoire de l'automobile*, p. 381.

of electric batteries. Steam and, especially, internal combustion remained the more viable options. The Le Mans-based *famille* Bollée persisted with steam power until the late 1890s before converting to petrol, as did the Comte de Dion. Léon Serpollet, the last of the great steam-powered vehicle producers, made one late flourish in securing the land speed record in April 1902 driving his Œuf de Pâques along the Promenade des Anglais in Nice reaching a speed of 120 km/h.[28] This was usurped within a matter of months when prominent American industrialist William K. Vanderbilt II reached 122 km/h in a French Mors, the first internal combustion-powered automobile to hold the land speed record. Serpollet continued to work on steam power until his death in 1907, which signalled the gradual demise of steam-powered transportation in France. Across the Atlantic, the success of the Stanley Steamer and the Doble steam car meant that steam power retained a commercial market in the United States until the late 1920s. However, the advent of electric ignition for internal combustion, which simplified starting a car and offered greater affordability, allowed Henry Ford and his celebrated Model T to take control of the automotive market.[29]

This turn-of-the-century struggle for power demonstrated the two main criteria that were coming to the fore in the public desire for a car. The ability to cross space and the ability to do so at speed were the use-values that increasingly became fetishized as the automotive world moved into an era of standardized motor racing. As the automobile gained acceptance, it was no longer the practicality of the vehicle that was of interest, but its ability to surpass that which had gone before. Gordon Bennett identified the technical ability of a car to cross more space at increasing speeds as an area in which he could enhance his name in the early 1900s. The Gordon Bennett races, precursors to the first Grand Prix, brought a further international dimension to these early competitions.

28   Chanaron, *L'industrie automobile*, p. 8.
29   The advent of the assembly line helped Ford produce cheaper cars that sold in much larger numbers than the workshop-built models in France.

Gordon Bennett: Modern Motor Sport Arrives

Although by 1898, the automobile had successfully crossed borders by reaching Amsterdam and other capitals, it still faced resistance in other countries. Seeing this, a wealthy American journalist named James Gordon Bennett Jr. decided to sponsor an international race inviting competitors from different countries to compete for the Gordon Bennett Trophy.[30] Bennett (1841–1918) was born in New York. He was the son of an Irish-American mother and a Scottish-American father who owned the famous *New York Herald*, the leading American newspaper of the day. When Bennett took the reins from his father in 1866, he was 25 and keen to spread the family firm abroad. Gordon Bennett had a keen sense of the newsworthy, and he introduced daily weather forecasts to Europe as well as wireless telegraphy for sending news dispatches. He had earlier been responsible for Henry Morton Stanley's 1869 search for explorer David Livingstone, which resulted in one of the most celebrated journalistic scoops of all time and the universally quoted greeting: 'Dr. Livingstone, I presume!'[31] Another scoop he managed to obtain was the reporting of the Custer massacre at Little Bighorn in 1876. Bennett was also an avid sailor, having won the first transatlantic yacht race in 1866. As a sports fan and, much like Pierre Giffard, seeing sports promotion as a means of improving newspaper readership, he inaugurated competitions in yachting, football and boxing. He publicized his *Herald* with a series of spectacular stunts, such as sponsoring Arctic and African expeditions, predecessors to the Citroën 'Raids' of the 1920s and '30s, which used exploration to promote sales.

Bennett moved to Paris in 1877, where he established the *Paris Herald* ten years later; he was, therefore, in France at the birth of the motor car and was ideally placed to observe its progress. Consequently, when he announced the inauguration of his Coupe Internationale, he was aware of the automobile's potential and hoped his helping hand would make it into a truly international vehicle. These first international races followed a set of rules devised by Bennett but enforced by the ACF. Each annual race was open to a maximum of three entries per nation, and the country

---

30   Bennett was later to sponsor an annual ballooning competition (1906–38).
31   Besquent, Patrice. 1985. *La coupe Gordon-Bennett 1905*. Clermont-Ferrand: La Montagne, p. 5.

Figure 2 The Gordon Bennett Cup.
© Motoring Picture Library/Alamy Stock Photo.

of the winner would hold the next year's race.[32] The cars of each nation
were to be painted a national colour irrespective of their manufacturer.
French cars were painted blue, Americans red, Belgians yellow, Italians
black and Germans white. As there was no British entry in the inaugural
race and since the three traditional colours from the British flag were
taken by other countries, the Napier driven by Selwyn Edge in 1901,
and which won in 1902, was green – reputedly the origin of British
Racing Green.[33] The Coupe Internationale added another layer to the
affective investment in the surplus capacity of cars. By distinguishing
competitors according to nationality and by demarcating cars visually,
Gordon Bennett was valorizing the aesthetic quality of the cars as they
were now recognizable through national colours. The trophy awarded
to the winner of the race also implied a fetishizing of sorts. The Coupe

32   Besquent, *La coupe Gordon-Bennett 1905*, p. 7.
33   Frank McNally, 'An Irishman's Diary,' *The Irish Times*, 9 September 2010.

Gordon Bennett – a sculpture of a winged female figure standing on top of a turn-of-the-century motor car upon which a boy, reminiscent of images from Greek mythology, sits holding aloft an Olympic-type torch – utilizes classical imagery to fetishize motor racing. The use of these two characters on the trophy is indicative of a growing association between symbols of modernity and those of Greek mythology.

While initially quite farcical affairs, with only France filling its quota of three cars, it was not until the French were defeated that manufacturers and the public opened their eyes to the potential of the competition. In its third year, a British car, once again a Napier, won the Paris–Vienna race, albeit in somewhat fortunate circumstances as the three leading cars, all of which were French, each broke down in quick succession. Nevertheless, this foreign victory brought an end to the perception of French invincibility not only among the French but also other nations. A dramatic rise in the number of entries in the qualifying competition the following year is indicative of the importance attached to this result. In 1903 the competition saw the largest number of entries to date, twice the number of the previous year, and with full quotas of competitors for the first time from France, Germany, Britain and the USA. As a British driver had won the previous race, it was now Britain's responsibility to host, which proved problematic. Britain had always been hostile to the automobile. The Red Flag Law set a speed limit of 12 miles per hour on all British roads and stipulated that all motor cars must be preceded by a man on foot waving a red flag.[34] Although this law had been repealed by 1903, speed limits were still maintained. Thus, it was decided that the race should be hosted in Ireland, where a relaxation of speed laws was permitted on rural roads, but not in towns.

The racing track consisted of two parts forming a figure of eight centred on the town of Athy, Co. Kildare.[35] At seven points where the track passed through towns, there were non-racing zones where the cars followed a bicycle through the streets. This was the first example of an international motor race taking place outside France; it was also the first time motor sports attracted global attention. Camille Jenatzy, who had previously driven La Jamais Contente during speed trials,

34   Laux, *In First Gear*, p. 72.
35   'After the Race' is a short story by James Joyce set against the backdrop of this race. Joyce, James. 1926. *Dubliners*. New York: Modern Library.

won the race driving a Mercedes, taking the Gordon Bennett Trophy to Germany along with the privilege of hosting the following year's competition. The final two Gordon Bennett races in 1904 and 1905 took place in a highly charged political atmosphere. The Franco-Prussian War of 1870 was still fresh in collective memory, and this was no more evident than in Alsace, which France had ceded to what was to become Germany in the aftermath of France's high-profile military defeat. Léon Théry's 1904 victory on German soil and subsequent triumphant return to France through Alsace, where he and his supporters were ordered to hide their *tricolores*, demonstrated the potential of the motor car to become a symbol of national pride.[36] The ostentatious welcoming of Théry by the President of France on the Champs-Élysées further augmented the political impact of the event.[37] These races took place against the backdrop of a series of events that would ultimately bring about the First World War. Germany's policy of *Weltpolitik* and the subsequent signing of the Entente Cordiale in 1904 between the United Kingdom and France heightened international tensions, and the automobile – as a symbol of progress, modernity and technicity – became a powerful player in the build-up to the First World War. The final Gordon Bennett race was organized by the Michelin brothers; it took place in the Auvergne and was the centre of media attention worldwide.[38] Léon Théry's triumph for the second year in a row was front-page news simultaneously in France, Britain and the US, among other countries; it even relegated the Russo-Japanese War to page 2.[39]

While the Gordon Bennett Cup races (1900–05) had been a success in terms of the internationalization of motor sport, these competitions had left France increasingly frustrated. While other nations had to struggle to assemble a team, France had to hold separate qualifiers to choose its representatives. Thus, with only three French cars out of 29 qualifying for the 1904 race, manufacturers like Clément-Bayard, Darracq, De Dietrich, Gobron-Brillié, Hotchkiss, Panhard,

36   Champeaux, Antoine. 2006. *Michelin et l'aviation, 1896–1945: patriotisme industriel et innovation*. Panazol: Lavauzelle, p. 27.
37   Breyer, *La belle époque à 30 à l'heure*, p. 71.
38   Bonnet, Olivier, and Philippe Gazagnes. 2002. *Sur les traces de Michelin, à Clermont*. Clermont-Ferrand: Le Miroir, p. 209.
39   Besquent, *La coupe Gordon-Bennett 1905*, p. 5.

Figure 3 Advertising poster by H. Bellery-Desfontaines: Richard-Brasier automobiles, which won the Gordon Bennett Cup in 1904. © Photo 12/Alamy Stock Photo.

Serpollet and Turcat-Méry found themselves without an opportunity to prove themselves on the international stage. When the Gordon Bennett Cup was inaugurated in 1899, the motor industry was still struggling to make its products viable. However, by 1905, the US had overtaken France as the world's largest automobile producer.[40] To an even greater extent, motor racing was becoming the arena in which manufacturers marketed their products. Seeing this gradual erosion of its power, the ACF decided to boycott the 1906 Gordon Bennett competition. It inaugurated a race in which all manufacturers could have a chance to compete without limiting entries. In turn, Bennett withdrew sponsorship from his motor race and created the Coupe Aéronautique Gordon Bennett for balloons in 1906, an event that exists to this day.[41] He followed this, in 1909, by sponsoring the Gordon Bennett aeroplane race in Reims, which continued until

40   Laux, *In First Gear*, p. 210.
41   Dauncey, Hugh, and Geoff Hare. 2014. 'Cosmopolitanism United by Electricity and Sport: James Gordon Bennett Jnr and the Paris *Herald* as Sites of Internationalism and Cultural Mediation in Belle Époque France.' *French Cultural Studies* 25 (1): 38–53 (p. 42).

the First World War. It is particularly apt that the street named in Bennett's honour in Paris is located beside the Stade Roland-Garros, which itself commemorates a renowned First World War pilot and the first person to fly across the Mediterranean, although the stadium is, of course, primarily associated with tennis.

Le Mans: Continuities and Changes

Whenever the town of Le Mans is mentioned, it is the 24-hour car race that springs to mind for the majority of people. While it is true that the Le Mans 24 Heures is universally recognized, the role of this town in the evolution of motor sport goes back much further than the first 24-hour race in 1923. As host of the world's first Grand Prix in 1906, Le Mans holds a singular place in motor sport history, but the automobile link stretches back even further in the history of the town and its surrounding area, which can justifiably claim to be the hub of motor sport in France. The growth of motor sport in Le Mans will be examined with a view to tracing how the evolving sport developed and how a fetishizing of the surplus capacity of the cars was adjusted to allow for a gradual banalization of the car. This will be seen not only in the creation of the 24 Heures but also in post-1945 engagement with the area and the race.

The department of La Sarthe was the home of the *famille* Bollée. Initially bell makers, this *famille artisanale* took up car construction when steam locomotion was being developed. Amédée-Ernest Bollée invented L'Obéissante, a 12-seat estate car that was advertised as the 'first road locomotive' in 1873.[42] This vehicle made national news in 1875 as Bollée drove it the 200 km that separate Le Mans and Paris. In 1878, La Mancelle, meaning a female native of Le Mans,[43] became the first automotive vehicle to be presented at the Exposition Universelle de Paris.[44] Such was the lack of familiarity with this new mode of transport that, being steam-powered, it was classified at the Exposition

---

42   Bonté, Michel, François Hurel, Jean-Luc Ribémon, and François Bruère. 2006. *Le Mans: un siècle de passion.* Le Mans: Automobile club de l'Ouest, p. 21.
43   The gendered names given to these vehicles are clearly indicative of the patriarchal society in which they were produced.
44   Cadène, *L'automobile*, p. 37.

in the railroad section. The family's Nouvelle took part, as previously mentioned, in the first ever automobile race, the 1895 Paris–Bordeaux. Many different vehicles built by *les Bollée* won various small races over this period, including Paris–Dieppe (1897) and Paris–Trouville (1898), while in 1898, Léon Bollée took part in the highly publicized world land speed record attempts, averaging 60 km/h. The Bollée family was a prime example of the success that could be achieved with the automobile. Their achievements inspired an ethic of innovation in the region of La Sarthe, which encouraged an entire community to mobilize in order to attract what was to become the largest race of the time to their *département*.[45]

In late 1905, the ACF announced that a new Grand Prix[46] would be held the following year, allowing three entries from each automobile manufacturer. The newspaper *L'Auto* announced 'La Course au circuit' (the race for a circuit) on 1 December 1905.[47] Among the 17 proposals was one from Georges Durand on behalf of the Circuit du Mans, received on 15 December, just 14 days after the original advertisement. Before the end of 1905, Durand had acquired the financial backing of the Conseil Général of the Sarthe and had convinced the board members of the ACF to visit the proposed circuit, a triangular formation joining the towns of Le Mans, Saint-Calais and La Ferté-Bernard.[48] After examining the proposal and visiting the projected site between 14 and 16 January, the ACF declared on 17 January 1906 that La Sarthe would host the inaugural Grand Prix de l'ACF in 1906. The Automobile Club de la Sarthe was created on 24 January 1906 and immediately made the Baron de Zuylen (the then president of the ACF) and Amédée Bollée honorary presidents.[49] Durand himself was elected general secretary, having turned down the opportunity to become president. An energetic

---

45   See Plessix, René. 1992. 'Au berceau des sports mécaniques: Le Mans.' In *Jeux et Sports dans l'histoire. Tome II: pratiques sportives.* Aubervilliers: Éditions du CTHS, pp. 205–28 (pp. 207–09).

46   The term 'Grand Prix' was a borrowing from horseracing, which had inaugurated a 'Grand Prix de Dieppe' in 1870. However, the origins of the term may actually stem from the world of art: a 'Grand Prix de Rome' was offered as early as 1803. This term was also applied to races previously hosted by the ACF. The Paris–Bordeaux–Paris race was thus retrospectively named 'Le premier Grand Prix de l'ACF.' de Penfentenyo, *2, 3, 4 roues*, p. 31.

47   Bonté, Hurel, Ribémon and Bruère, *Le Mans*, p. 29.

48   Cadène, *L'automobile*, p. 111.

49   Plessix, 'Au berceau des sports mécaniques,' p. 223.

fundraising campaign ensued, the 103.16 km circuit was prepared and on 26–27 June the race took place. Every car had to complete the circuit six times on each of the two days. Twenty-three French cars took part in this race, which despite significant attendance, made a loss for the ACS, since most of the spectators decided to watch the race from areas where it was free rather than paying for entry into the main stand.[50] This setback notwithstanding, the weekend as a whole was deemed a success by the ACF, and Le Mans went down in history as having hosted the first automobile Grand Prix.

In an effort to promote the Grand Prix series, the ACF moved the 1907 and 1908 editions of the race to other circuits, and Le Mans found itself in need of a way of remaining at the cutting edge of innovation.[51] The next big step in technology was also embraced with the creation of the Aéro-Club du Mans in 1908. Ballooning was becoming more and more popular and in August 1908 Léon Bollée, son of Amédée, took the logical next step in aviation promotion by welcoming Wilbur Wright to Le Mans.[52] The main straight of the Le Mans Grand Prix circuit, La Ligne Droite des Hunaudières (known as the 'Mulsanne Straight' in English), was used for a series of flight exhibitions over a number of days. Wright left after a week of stunning the large numbers of spectators, amongst whom was Louis Blériot, who would alter be the first man to fly across the English Channel.[53] The use of part of the Le Mans circuit to showcase this newest form of technology is, perhaps, an indication of the strong role of motor sport in generating public interest in modernity; but it could also be seen as an evolution in that popular interest. As we shall see, motor sport lost some of its popularity at a time when aviation was gaining in attractiveness. This was reflected in the inauguration at Le Mans of the Coupe Michelin Internationale, the first edition of which was hosted in December 1908 and was won by Wilbur Wright.[54] It is possible that a previously automobile-centred fetishizing of speed was transferred to aviation during this transitional period.

---

50   Bonté, Hurel, Ribémon and Bruère, *Le Mans*, p. 55.
51   Delaperrelle, Jean-Pierre. 1986. *L'invention de l'automobile. Bollée: de la vapeur au turbo*. Le Mans: Cénomane, p. 106.
52   Bonté, Hurel, Ribémon and Bruère, *Le Mans*, p. 71.
53   Studeny, *L'invention de la vitesse*, p. 343.
54   de Penfentenyo, *2, 3, 4 roues*, p. 34.

In the event, a period characterized by a relative lack of interest in motor sport followed these first Grands Prix, during which France lost the national events two years in a row to German competition. In consequence, French manufacturers took the radical decision to pull out of competitive international motor racing. Subsequently, the ACF decided to discontinue its Grand Prix just three years after its inauguration.[55] This first 'depression' in French motor racing would appear to be linked to a disenchantment among manufacturers following the realization that other countries were capable of providing stiff opposition. Rather than lose to what they saw as inferior rivals, these manufacturers decided to withdraw from competition altogether. Economic interests may also have been a factor, as the financial investment in high-speed cars was significant, while Grand Prix cars were becoming increasingly different from road cars. Smaller national races were still popular, and Le Mans continued to host events through this period of transition. As general secretary of the ACS, Durand decided in 1911 to host the first Grand Prix de France in Le Mans on a circuit of just over 54 km.[56] This new Grand Prix, which was seen as a distinct entity from the Grand Prix de l'ACF, turned out to be such a success that the Grand Prix de l'ACF was revived and run in Amiens the following year, while the Grand Prix de France remained in Le Mans. That two Grands Prix were held in France within one calendar year was indicative of the swing in popularity once again in favour of motor racing, which was to continue until the outbreak of the First World War.[57]

Georges Durand and the Circuit du Mans had one more role to play before the birth of their most famous offspring, the 24 Heures du Mans. Durand took the decision to attempt to bring French motor racing out of its post-1918 doldrums by launching the Coupe des Voiturettes in 1920.[58] This was the first motor race to take place in the wake of the Great War. While the country was still reeling from the effects of this conflict, Durand saw an opportunity for the ACS to come to the fore once again in the world of motor racing. This initiative provided the impetus for hosting the first post-war Grand Prix de l'ACF, run in Le

55   Cadène, *L'automobile*, p. 112.
56   Plessix, 'Au berceau des sports mécaniques,' p. 222.
57   Cadène, *L'automobile*, p. 112.
58   Plessix, 'Au berceau des sports mécaniques,' p. 224.

Mans the following year. Le Mans and Durand thus were instrumental in the growth of the automobile and motor racing in France. Durand not only oversaw the inauguration of the first automobile Grand Prix, he also ensured the maintenance of Le Mans as a site for motor racing as he attempted to relaunch public interest in the sport both before and directly after the First World War. The drop-off in interest in motor racing at the time was to become a source of concern for car manufacturers. Many withdrew from motor racing as they saw that it no longer fulfilled the role for which it had originally been conceived. In its earliest form, motor racing served to make the public aware of the capacity of the car. Through the overdetermination of its use-value, it created a fetishized image of the automobile that increased its exchange-value and thus increased its affective attraction. As city-to-city races evolved into Grands Prix, the type of car used in races developed to become a one-seater, large-engined vehicle. These racing cars were developed with the single goal of winning races and thus satisfied the requirement to demonstrate surplus capacity regarding speed, but no longer satisfied the more basic use-values of a car, namely transporting a small group of people. In the next section, we will discuss a motor sport modification of the fetishizing of use-value, as the 24 Heures du Mans can be seen as an overdetermination of the values of the everyday car, carried out in tandem with the consumption of those contrasting values via the ongoing Grand Prix races.

Les 24 Heures du Mans

As Grand Prix racing became more specialized, Georges Durand saw an opportunity to return to the roots of motor racing and to promote its original ideals. While Grand Prix racing continued to fetishize the surplus capacity involved in obtaining ever higher speeds, the construction of purpose-built racing cars meant that the public felt alienated from them and, therefore, its ability to identify with these vehicles was diminished. Thus, the first stage in a transformation of how motor racing was perceived and fetishized became apparent. The creation of the 24 Heures du Mans consequently stemmed from an urge to make motor racing both more practical and more relevant to the public.[59] As we have seen, the Le Mans event came

---

59   Plessix, 'Au berceau des sports mécaniques,' p. 225.

after more than 20 years of groundwork, and it was to become the world's most famous annual race. The 24 Heures du Mans was the brainchild of Georges Durand, who, becoming worried about the relevance of motor sport in its current form, held a meeting during the Salon de l'Automobile of 1922 with Charles Faroux, of the newspapers *L'Auto* and *La Vie Automobile*, and with Émile Coquille of Rudge-Whitworth, the well-known British wheelmakers.[60] It was decided that motor racing needed to be simplified and made more accessible. It was by now apparent that cars were reasonably reliable and could reach high speeds. The problem was that race cars were moving further and further from vehicles on the roads, and the resulting technical advances were no longer of direct benefit to the everyday driver. Coquille believed that car lights and starters were particularly behind the times and that, in the interests of building a safer car, a high-profile night race was needed.[61] Durand suggested a 24-hour race instead as this would not only put the lights to the test but would also test man and machine to the limit. It was agreed that the resulting race of 'tourist cars' would take place during the second half of June, when days are at their longest, and that the race would be run from four o'clock in the afternoon until the same time the following day. Thus, while this new race continued to fetishize the surplus capacity of the automobile, the fact that it targeted normal cars is indicative of how motor racing was beginning to promote the automobile for its more everyday features.

The 'Le Mans start' was an initiative introduced to test the cars' starters; this involved the drivers lining up on one side of the road and, once the French flag was dropped at four o'clock sharp, they would run across the road, jump into their respective vehicle, start it up and drive off. The advent of racing harnesses did nothing to stop this practice, and it took the actions of a prominent racing driver to show the lunacy of competing at getting ready to race. In 1969, instead of running across to his car, Jacky Ickx, the eventual winner, made a point of walking slowly across the track and belting up carefully before driving off.[62] The following year would see the race start with the drivers already strapped into their cars. The Le Mans start did,

60 Bonté, Hurel, Ribémon and Bruère, *Le Mans*, p. 136.
61 Plessix, 'Au berceau des sports mécaniques,' p. 224.
62 Montgomery, Bob, 'Past Imperfect,' *The Irish Times*, 11 June 2008.

however, ensure that Durand and Coquille accomplished the two goals they had set for themselves, namely testing the starters and lights of the cars:

> It is indisputable that, in the beginning, a race like that of Le Mans, contested over 24 hours, night and day, and in any weather, played a primordial role in the development of the automobile industry. Thanks to Le Mans, constant improvements have been made to tyres, brakes, lighting and road surfaces. In short, the 24 Heures perfectly justified their existence as long as they remained faithful to their title of 'endurance prize.'[63]

The 24 Heures continued to be used as a testing ground for new technologies, and aerodynamics improved immensely in the early years due to the long straights on the circuit. Disc brakes were first used at Le Mans in 1953.[64] Alternative fuel sources have also been tested here, from ethanol, used on a class-winning Porsche in 1980, to a diesel-powered Audi that won three successive races from 2006 to 2008. Audi managed to achieve with diesel a similar speed to that obtained typically from a petrol car. This, allied with the fuel economy of diesel, meant that the Audi pitted fewer times than other cars, giving it the necessary margin to win.[65] The 2012 and 2013 versions of the race were also won by Audi TDI engines, but these were significantly different from their predecessors in that they were the first cars to win this race using a hybrid electric engine.

Le Mans is also the site of the single most devastating accident in motor sport, which had severe repercussions not only in France, but throughout the world. In 1955, just seven hours into the race, French driver Pierre Levegh, driving a Mercedes, was forced to swerve wildly

63   'Pourtant, à l'origine, il est incontestable qu'une course comme celle du Mans, disputée pendant vingt-quatre heures, de nuit et de jour, et par n'importe quel temps a joué un rôle primordial dans le développement de l'industrie automobile. Grâce au Mans, des améliorations constantes ont été apportées aux pneumatiques, aux freins, à l'éclairage et au revêtement des routes. En somme, les 24 Heures ont parfaitement justifié leur existence tant qu'elles sont restées fidèles à leur titre de "prix d'endurance".' 'Plus de monstres au Mans,' 27 July 1956, *L'Express*, p. 8.
64   Montgomery, Bob, 'Past Imperfect,' *The Irish Times*, 8 June 2005.
65   Broscoe, Neil, 'Le Mans 24hrs Race Is the Glastonbury of Motorsport,' *The Irish Times*, 17 June 2009.

by another car, lost control and flew into a packed stand.[66] He died instantly, along with 82 spectators. The decision to continue the race was taken in order to allow emergency services to get access to the circuit, as stopping the race would have flooded the roads with over 200,000 people in attendance. Later in the race, Mercedes withdrew its two other participating cars and retired entirely from competitive racing until 1987. When the curtain fell on this event, it would be followed by the cancellation of a number of races throughout the world, including the Grand Prix de France for that year. It also brought about a complete ban on circuit racing in Switzerland, which stands to this day.[67] The following year an article entitled 'Plus de monstres au Mans' ('No more monsters at Le Mans') appeared in *L'Express*, which questioned the continuing relevance of the 24 Heures, stating that 'the desire for speed has prevailed', suggesting that the race had moved away from its original objective as a race designed to test different components of a car and had regressed to a fetishizing of speed:

> The question of whether car racing is useful – or is just a mind-blowing spectacle – has never been clearly resolved. The big French manufacturers, in any case, seem to unanimously deny the usefulness of the competition, since they do not make the slightest effort to take part in it.
>
> Originally, the 24 Heures du Mans was a testing ground for production cars. This is what made it so popular. Even in 1951 and 1953, when Jaguar tripled its sales figures after winning at Le Mans, it was because, for many people, this race was still a practical test, intended to showcase normal cars.
>
> In fact, this hadn't been true for a long time. From precisely when organizers agreed to enter what are called 'prototypes' at Le Mans. This word should designate a model, a first copy. In fact, it designates a monster.[68]

---

66 Ambroise-Rendu, Anne-Claude. 2007. 'Dangers et tourments du sport.' *Le Temps des médias* 9 (2): 267–72 (p. 272).
67 Setright, Leonard. 2003. *Drive on! A Social History of the Motor Car.* London: Granta, p. 99.
68 'Le problème de savoir si les courses d'automobiles servent à quelque chose – ou ne sont qu'un spectacle hallucinant – n'a jamais été résolu clairement. Les grands constructeurs français, en tout cas, semblent unanimement nier l'utilité de la compétition, puisqu'ils ne font pas le moindre effort pour y prendre part.
   A l'origine, les 24 Heures du Mans étaient un banc d'essai des voitures de

It would seem that, by the 1950s, the 24 Heures was no longer fulfilling the role for which it had been conceived. However, the enduring popularity of the race meant that the ability of the car to exceed its use-capacity continued to be fetishized even though a closer link to everyday cars served to reduce the alienation experienced by spectators.

The Le Mans 24 Heures has a mythical quality. It is difficult to define why it has acceded to this status, but its significant history certainly contributes. The race's enduring and ever-growing popularity also has much to do with the fact that it is one of the few races left in the world that uses public roads as part of the circuit. Much like the Tour de France, the 24 Heures evokes strong feelings in spectators as it strives to maintain relevance to the ordinary person, while locals from each town cheer on competitors from the area taking part on their roads in this prestigious event. Equally, there is a sense of pride evident in seeing the biggest *marques* in the world participating alongside French cars on a local road. In Le Mans, the Bugatti Circuit (named in honour of Ettore Bugatti, a famous French car manufacturer of Italian extraction) joins up with public roads, for one weekend of the year, to form the 13 km track which is covered on average 250 times over the 24 hours. The fascination of seeing these cars race on public roads that have been closed to traffic just for this special weekend in June is exceptional. It is a testament to the tradition of motor sport in La Sarthe that the main thoroughfare that joins it with Paris and connects Paris to the west of the country is closed for this spectacle.[69] It is perhaps the attempts to maintain links with ordinary cars and with ordinary people that have made the Le Mans 24 Heures the iconic race that it is. Georges Durand's initiative to launch a race that restored motor sport's links with ordinary cars was a response to the growing alienation of spectators from powerful single-seater racing cars. The 24-hour race continued to fetishize the surplus

série. C'est ce qui en faisait l'énorme popularité. Même en 1951 et en 1953, lorsque Jaguar tripla son chiffre de vente après avoir gagné au Mans, c'est parce que, pour beaucoup de gens, cette course restait une épreuve pratique, destinée à mettre en valeur des voitures normales.

En fait, cela n'était plus vrai depuis longtemps. Depuis le jour, exactement où les organisateurs acceptèrent d'engager au Mans ce que l'on appelle des "prototypes". Ce mot devrait désigner un modèle, un premier exemplaire. En fait, il désignait un monstre.' 'Plus de monstres au Mans,' 27 July 1956, *L'Express*, p. 8.
69   The closing of public roads is also practised at the legendary TT motorcycle races in the Isle of Man, as well as the North West 200 in Northern Ireland.

capacity of the car and indeed augmented this fetishizing by increasing the number of hours the car was to be used. However, as stated, through the use of more everyday cars and the incorporation of public roads, Durand had undeniably anticipated a banalization of the automobile and the consequent alienation of motor racing. Thus, the Le Mans 24 Heures provided at least a partial alternative to the over-valorization of the surplus capacity of Grand Prix cars, as it seemed that a fetishizing of speed alone was no longer universally sufficient. The next section will examine two examples of how motor sport continued to be fetishized in the post-1945 era of the increasingly banalized car.

Representations of Post–Second World War Motor Sport

In the early 20th century, motor racing constituted a form of fetishizing of the surplus capacity of the automobile, more specifically a fetishizing of speed and endurance. The Le Mans 24 Heures race expanded this fetishizing while at the same time addressing the alienation which ensued from the growth of Grand Prix cars as they moved further and further away, in both appearance and performance, from everyday cars. We will now look at how motor sport continued to be fetishized even as the automobile was becoming more mundane and thus part of Baudrillard's system of needs. Firstly, we will examine a short text written by Roland Barthes which engages with, among other sports, motor racing. Secondly, the Claude Lelouch film *Un homme et une femme* (1966) will be explored as an example of how, while banalized, motor racing continued to be fetishized for its original surplus capacity as regards speed.

What is Sport?
In 1961, Roland Barthes wrote the narrative for a documentary that Canadian author and director Hubert Aquin filmed. The film discusses six sports and sets them in different countries, with the intention of showing them as 'social and poetic phenomen[a].'[70] The

---

70 'phénomène social et poétique.' Barthes, Roland. 2004. *Le sport et les hommes.* Montréal: Les Presses de l'Université de Montréal. p. 6; Barthes, Roland. 2007. *What is Sport?* Translated by Richard Howard. New Haven, CT: Yale University Press, p. viii.

sports examined are bullfighting, motor sport, soccer, ice hockey and the Tour de France cycle race.[71] Barthes had previously written about two sports in his *Mythologies*, where he engaged with wrestling and the Tour de France.[72] This second essay on the Tour can be seen as a more sympathetic and less overtly Marxist reading of the sport. Barthes engaged with the automobile in his *Mythologies* and once again, a little later in his career (1965), when he published an article on the growing commodification of the car. The 1961 treatise on motor racing during the Trente Glorieuses is particularly worthy of examination, as it discusses how motor sport was perceived at a critical stage in French social and automotive history.

Barthes begins by describing the process undergone by a racing driver and his team to prepare for a race. This involves science and human courage with one sole aim, namely to defeat time: to be 'The victor over a much subtler enemy: time.'[73] Barthes highlights the importance of man's relationship with the automobile, stating that it is the balance of man and machine that is the difference between winning and losing and, indeed, living and dying. The power of the car over the very life of a person underlines the continued fetishizing of speed:

> By the machine man will conquer, but perhaps by the machine he will die. So that here the relation between man and the machine is infinitely circumspect: what will function very fast must first be tested very slowly, for speed is never anything but the recompense of extreme deliberation.[74]

Thus, the relationship which exists between a racing driver and his vehicle is one that must be entered into with great caution. In deciding to exploit the surplus capacity of the automobile, the racing driver

---

71   MacKenzie, Scott. 1997. 'The Missing Mythology: Barthes in Québec.' *Canadian Journal of Film Studies* 6 (2): 65–74 (p. 67).

72   Barthes, 2003 [1957], *Mythologies*, pp. 13–23; pp. 103–13.

73   'Le Vainqueur d'un ennemi bien plus subtil: le Temps.' Barthes, *Le sport et les hommes*, p. 21; *What is Sport?* p. 11.

74   'Par elle, l'homme vaincra mais peut-être aussi par elle il mourra. Aussi le rapport de l'homme et de la machine est ici infiniment précautionneux, ce qui se jouera très vite doit d'abord s'essayer très lentement, car la vitesse n'est jamais que la récompense d'une extrême lenteur.' Barthes, *Le sport et les hommes*, p. 21; *What is Sport?* p. 11.

knowingly places more pressure on the vehicle than is needed for 'ordinary' use. These precautions must also be carried onto the racetrack.

This paradoxical 'extreme deliberation' ('extrême lenteur') is further highlighted by Barthes in the next section of the documentary as we see a test session for the car on the track. In a scene that uses long shots of a single car testing, the narrator interrupts the sound of the roaring engine to remind us that:

> Next, in order to try it out, to race alone, with no other enemy but time, and to confront in this effort both the machine and the terrain together, for it is all three at once that the racer must first of all conquer before triumphing over his human rivals.
>
> Finally and above all it is the engine that must be prepared and where we find an embarrassment of riches, much like those found in an inspired brain: here twelve sparkplugs must be changed every five laps.[75]

Having taken all these precautions, we proceed to the filming of a motor race. Taking place in Sebring, Florida, the 12-hour endurance race featuring cars of different sizes and classes is depicted at length as Barthes's text continues to be narrated intermittently in the background. Filmed in 1959, it features a Le Mans-type start, as the drivers run across the racetrack to jump into their cars and drive off. Once again, this is followed by a number of long shots during which the text is narrated and in which the relationship between man and machine is explored.

More specifically, Barthes explores the relationship between man and machine as they encounter the different challenges that the circuit offers. This relationship is different on straights and in corners, and Barthes examines how the balance of the relationship ebbs and flows accordingly:

> On straight drives, it is the motor's effort that is most important, yet this effort remains human in its way: in it are deposited the

---

75 'Ensuite, l'essayer, courir seul, sans autre ennemi que le temps, et affronter à ce temps, à la fois la machine et le terrain, car ce sont eux, tous les trois à la fois que le coureur doit d'abord vaincre avant de triompher de ses rivaux humains. Il faut enfin et surtout préparer le moteur, et sa richesse comme celle d'un cerveau génial est embarrassante: ici ce sont douze bougies à changer tous les cinq tours.' Barthes, *Le sport et les hommes*, p. 23; *What is Sport?* pp. 12–13.

Figure 4 Test scene from film.
© *Le sport et les hommes*, Hubert Aquin (1961).

labor, the inventiveness, and the care of dozens of men who have prepared, refined, and checked the most difficult of equations: an extreme power, a minimal resistance, whether of weight or of wind.

But on the turns, apart from the machine's suspension, it is the racer who does everything; for here, space is against time. Hence the racer must be able to cheat space, to decide whether he can spare it … or if he will brutally cut it down; and he must have the courage to drive this wager to the brink of the impossible.[76]

76 'Dans les lignes droites, c'est l'effort du moteur qui emporte la décision, mais cet effort reste humain à sa manière, en lui sont déposés le travail, l'invention et le soin d'une dizaine d'hommes qui ont préparé, raffiné et vérifié la plus difficile des équations: une puissance extrême, une résistance minime, que ce soit celle du poids ou celle du vent.

Mais dans les virages, mise à part la suspension de la machine, c'est le coureur qui fait tout; car ici l'espace est contre le temps. Il faut donc savoir tricher avec l'espace, décider si on le ménage … ou si on le coupe brutalement;

Much of Barthes's text focuses on the relationship between the driver and his car; it does not concern how an audience perceives motor sport; thus, this text cannot be considered in the same context as his earlier mythologies. This text is a reflection on the how and why of individual engagement in this sport together with its personal and social importance. The English translation of the text of the document is 'What is Sport?' and it is this that Barthes considers here.

Barthes is also aware of the danger involved in the sport. During a shot of a particularly brutal car crash, which leaves us in no doubt that the driver has perished, the narrator explains why, although part of the sport, it is particularly tragic here:

> In this combat against time, terrible as the consequences may sometimes be, there is no fury: only an immense courage focused on the inertia of things. Hence the death of a racer is infinitely sad: for it is not only a man who dies here, it is a particle of perfection which vanishes from this world. But it is precisely because such perfection is mortal that it is human. No sooner is everything lost in one place than other men will begin again in another.[77]

The last line of this section is, perhaps, a further indication of how motor sport and speed are fetishized. Barthes suggests that while speed and motor sport are extremely dangerous, the human desire for both is such that the cyclical nature of life and death is effectively replicated in this sporting practice.

The use-value of the car, or rather parts of a car, is also referred to as Barthes explains how these vehicles are different from everyday cars. They are not equipped with a starter; the reason for this is straightforward, starters are heavy and are not needed, and anything that reduces the weight of a car can mean that it is gaining seconds on the

---

et ce pari il faut oser le pousser jusqu'au bord de l'impossible.' Barthes, *Le sport et les hommes*, p. 25; *What is Sport?* pp. 16–17.

77 'Dans ce combat contre le temps, si terrible parfois qu'en soit la sanction, il n'y a aucune fureur, rien qu'un courage immense dirigé contre l'inertie des choses. Ainsi la mort d'un coureur est infiniment triste, car ce n'est pas seulement un homme qui meurt, c'est un peu de perfection qui disparait de ce monde. Mais c'est précisément parce que cette perfection est mortelle qu'elle est humaine. A peine tout est-il perdu ici que d'autres hommes vont recommencer là.' Barthes, *Le sport et les hommes*, p. 27; *What is Sport?* p. 17.

track. However, this is also indicative of how the Grand Prix car has been alienated from the standard road vehicle. It is not necessary for an ordinary car to be designed with a view to gaining seconds; thus, in an attempt to maximize the surplus capacity of the car, the racing car has been moved further away from its original use-value. Barthes goes further with this in comparing a motor car to a bird:

> At rest, these cars are heavy, passive, difficult to maneuver: as with a bird hampered by its wings, it is their potential power that weighs them down. Yet once lined up, approaching their function, which is combat, they already become lighter, grow impatient [...] To stop is virtually to die. If the machine fails, its master must be informed of the fact with a certain discretion. For a great racer does not conquer his machine, he tames it; he is not only the winner, he is also the one who destroys nothing. A wrecked machine generates something like the sadness caused by the death of an irreplaceable being, even as life continues around him.[78]

This close association of an automobile with an animal echoes the early 20th-century discourse around animism of cars.[79] In using the verb 'to tame' ('apprivoiser') and then likening a car breaking down to a death, much like that caused by the car accident earlier in the text, the fetishizing of the car through this sport is underlined.

Barthes concludes his reflection on motor sport by suggesting what a race signifies. Once again, he highlights the importance of the relationship between man and his machine as they work in unison in an attempt to conquer the laws of physics:

> This is the meaning of a great automobile race: that the swiftest force is only the sum of various kinds of patience, of

---

78 'Au repos ces machines sont lourdes, passives, difficiles à déplacer, comme un oiseau gêné par ses ailes, c'est leur puissance virtuelle qui les fait peser. Pourtant, à peine alignées, rapprochées de leur fonction qui est le combat, elles s'allègent déjà, deviennent impatientes [...] S'arrêter c'est presque mourir, si la machine est malade il faut en informer son maître avec ménagement. Car un grand coureur ne dompte pas sa machine, il l'apprivoise; il n'est pas seulement celui qui gagne, il est aussi celui qui ne détruit rien. Une machine hors du jeu, c'est la tristesse d'un être qui meurt, et qu'on ne peut remplacer, même lorsqu'autour de lui la vie continue.' Barthes, *Le sport et les hommes*, p. 29; *What is Sport?* pp. 20–21.
79 Campbell, 'Vital Matters,' p. 161.

measurements, of subtleties, of infinitely precise and infinitely demanding actions.

What this man has done is to drive himself and his machine to the limit of what is possible. He has won his victory not over his rivals, but on the contrary *with them*, over the obstinate heaviness of things: the most murderous of sports is also the most generous.[80]

Thus, the goal of motor sport is to bring both man and machine to the extremes of what is possible in a practice that actively strives ever to expand the surplus capacity of the automobile. In the eyes of Barthes, motor sport is a rejection of the everyday car and a fetishizing of an alienated version of the automobile, with the ultimate goal of transcending the apparent limits of the machine through its intimate relationship with its driver. In the next section, and against this suggestive backdrop, we shall see how the automobile impacts on the relationship of the human protagonists in Claude Lelouch's *Un homme et une femme*.

Fetishizing Motor Sport in French Cinema

Claude Lelouch released *Un homme et une femme* in 1966. It received critical acclaim, winning the Palme d'Or in Cannes, two Oscars and a multitude of awards all over the world. It was also a financial success, saving Lelouch's film company from bankruptcy, which had threatened immediately prior to its release. This movie has motor racing as a theme, its main character being a racing driver; however, with location filming and many improvised scenes, it also incorporated several innovations inaugurated by the Nouvelle Vague movement.[81]

---

80 'Voilà ce que signifie une grande course automobile: que la plus rapide des forces n'est qu'une somme de patience, de mesures, de subtilités, d'actes infiniment précis et infiniment exigeants.
  Ce que cet homme a fait c'est se mener lui-même et sa machine à la limite du possible. Sa victoire il l'a remportée non sur ses rivaux, mais au contraire avec eux, sur la pesanteur obstinée des choses: le plus meurtrier des sports est aussi le plus généreux.' Barthes, *Le sport et les hommes*, p. 33; *What is Sport?* p. 25.
81   The Nouvelle Vague was a movement in French cinema which was charac-terized by rejection of traditional film-making in favour of new approaches

Un homme et une femme is significant as it depicts a fetishizing of speed through the automobile and through motor sport at a time when the automobile was becoming further banalized as an everyday commodity. The automobile and racing serve as the backdrop to the story; much as in Barthes's reflection on the sport, motor racing in Trente Glorieuses France was not immune to the fetishizing of speed.

Un homme et une femme introduces the audience to two widowed parents as they meet for the first time in Deauville, where their respective children are at boarding school. Jean-Louis Trintignant's character, also called 'Jean-Louis,' gives Anne, played by Anouk Aimée, a lift back to Paris as she has missed her train. Thus begins the first of many car journeys made by the protagonists. The basis for their relationship is formed in Jean-Louis's Ford Mustang. In an interview shortly after the movie's release, Lelouch said that he wanted the weather to play an important role. He wanted fog and rain to help create the atmosphere, and it is the ambience of being sheltered together from the elements that brings the two closer. We learn in flashbacks how each became widowed. Anne's husband was a stuntman; he is introduced crashing a flaming car into two others. He is killed in a work accident, dying before Anne's eyes while filming a battle scene for a movie. Anne's husband is portrayed as a loving and charismatic character, and thus the scene is set for her reluctance to enter a relationship with someone who has a dangerous profession. Later on, during another car journey in the rain, we learn how Jean-Louis's wife died. We cut to an elaborate flashback of the start of the Le Mans 24-hour race.

Using footage from the 1964 race, the entire flashback, including Jean-Louis's accident and his wife's subsequent suicide, is recounted in what seems to be a radio commentary. This form of narrative gives the depiction of the race a more authentic feel, with the viewers having the impression that they are no longer watching a movie but rather an actual event at which there has been a terrible accident; it serves to highlight the almost matter-of-fact way that motor racing is a sport in which one risks one's life. While telling this terrible tale of grief, the radio commentator interrupts himself to let the listener know that Graham Hill has gone into pit and then continues the commentary on the Ferraris leading the race, as if this suicide were merely a trivial

to editing, visual style and narrative. It was particularly popular in the 1950s and 1960s.

aside. Much like the footage of the crash in *Le Sport et les hommes*, Lelouch does not shy away from the fact that racing is dangerous; while Jean-Louis does survive this crash, he nevertheless remains in a coma after a three-hour operation. However, it is as a result of seeing him leave the operating theatre that his wife decides to take her own life. The amount of time devoted to Jean-Louis's transfer to the operating theatre and his wife's subsequent wait for any news is counterpointed by the commentator's oblique reference to her own subsequent death. The choice of Le Mans for this sequence would most likely have resonated strongly with many viewers for, as already discussed, just 11 years earlier the worst ever motor racing accident had taken place there.

The shots of the Le Mans race comprise one of three sporting clips in the movie. When choosing the racing scenes, Lelouch went for arguably the three most famous and historical arenas in France. As already mentioned, Le Mans was the scene of Jean-Louis's accident and was also the hub of motor sport in the country. Prior to this flashback, we have a testing scene set in the days immediately following Jean-Louis's first meeting with Anne. While not explicitly referred to in the film, this testing takes place at the oval test track of Monthléry just south of Paris.[82] What follows is eight continuous minutes of Jean-Louis driving two different cars around the track. This scene echoes the testing shots in *Le Sport et les hommes*, as we see the importance of precision and preparation in the relationship between driver and car. At one stage, there is a second car on the track, which runs alongside on the slope, but for the most part, it is just Jean-Louis and his machine. The very famous soundtrack for this movie is for once absent, hardly anything is said, and the only music is the sound of the Ford GT-40 revving and shifting gears. It is a homage to the racing car.

This scene is also evoked in a later short which Lelouch filmed in 1976. *C'était un rendez-vous* has become a film of mythical proportions in motoring circles.[83] This *court métrage* is an eight-minute shot taken by one camera positioned on the front bumper of what was claimed at the time to be a Ferrari, driven at high speeds through the streets of Paris.[84]

---

82   Lelouch confirmed this in an interview about the film.
83   Lelouch, Claude, dir. 2003 [1976]. *C'était un rendez-vous*. Paris, Spirit Level Film.
84   Borden, Iain. 2013. *Drive: Journeys through Film, Cities and Landscapes*. London: Reaktion, p. 20.

At times cars are overtaken as if they are not there, and the film ends at the top of the steps at Montmartre where the driver gets out to embrace a girl running up the steps to meet him. The soundtrack to this short is again the sound of the engine roaring. As no permits to drive through Paris were obtained, Lelouch was arrested shortly after the release of this movie, while a plethora of urban myths surfaced about the speed driven, the car used and whether the movie was tampered with in any way. It remains an example of what has been called *cinéma vérité*, and the scene in *Un homme et une femme* can be seen in much the same way. It is a typical testing session; at the only point where we have dialogue, it is a commentary on the revs used in completing a lap of the circuit.

The final race portrayed in the film is the Rallye de Monte-Carlo. Departing from various cities all over Europe to converge on Monaco, this rally is the oldest of its type in the world. Once again, radio-type commentary is used to introduce the competitors; however, Jean-Louis is not the driver but the co-pilot in this race. The footage shown in the movie is taken from an actual Monte Carlo rally. Lelouch entered a three-person team in the race driving a Mustang. The drivers were Lelouch himself, Jean-Louis Trintignant and a representative of the Ford company known as Monsieur Chemin. There is footage of the Mustang but also of other vehicles filmed in dry, wet and snowy conditions. We see images of Citroën DS, Mercedes, and Aston Martins skidding through corners. Lelouch entered the race so that he could film for the entire five days of the rally; in this way, he could record the progress of the race and its effects on the drivers. This race scene is different from the earlier test sequence in that it is interspersed with shots of Anne carrying on with her life. As co-pilot, Jean-Louis is required to describe the itinerary of twists and turns taken by the team. This is paralleled in Anne's profession as a scriptwriter. As Jean-Louis is barking out instructions to Monsieur Chemin, who is at the wheel, Anne is talking the film director through her script and discussing how it will work best on camera. This synchronicity between the protagonists is symbolic of the place they are now at in their relationship.

The choice of car in *Un homme et une femme* is also significant. All race cars used by the main protagonist as well as his own personal car are American: Fords. The Ford Mustang was an iconic car, but the question must be asked: why did the director not choose a French car? Ross argues that as a tool to indicate an 'object from another planet,'

Figure 5 Test scene from film.
© *Un homme et une femme*, Claude Lelouch (1966).

the use of a foreign, preferably American, car is common.[85] The Ford Mustang as an American car has an exotic element to it; the very name Mustang suggests something of the Wild West.[86] During their first encounter, Anne states that Jean-Louis does not look like someone who would be married; the fact that she is being driven home in his high-powered American sports car surely influences this assumption.

Un homme et une femme was a very successful movie with a strong motor racing current throughout. It shows scenes from three of the highest-profile circuits and races in France and devotes a large slice of its running time to each; however, it is the final sequence that is perhaps the most significant for this study. Jean-Louis is a reasonably well-known car racer but, in this film, his race, as is seen in the last scenes, is to beat the train from Deauville to Paris to win the woman he loves. Having been abandoned at the train station, Trintignant's character jumps into his Mustang and drives directly from Deauville

85   Ross, *Fast Cars, Clean Bodies*, p. 33.
86   The Mustang is replaced by a Citroën 2CV in the 2019 sequel *Les Plus Belles Années d'une vie*, which features the same two protagonists meeting once again 52 years after their first encouter in the original film. The choice of vehicle for this (second) sequel, reflects both the physical frailty of its driver and the sympathetic yet tired regard held for the 2CV.

to Paris to meet Anne as she gets off the train. There is an earlier scene that is similar to this one upon receiving a telegram from Anne at the end of the Monte Carlo saying that she loves him, Jean-Louis gets into the car in which his team has just completed the rally and drives across France to see her. In both scenes, the importance of speed is apparent. Using a specialist rally car to drive to Paris just after finishing a race underlines the affective link between motor sport and the standard road car, showing how speed is not only fetishized in racing but can also be transferred, under emotionally charged circumstances, to the public roads. However, in the last scene, when the Mustang defeats the train in a race to Paris, the fetishizing of the surplus capacity of the car is most obviously highlighted. By giving the Mustang a direct opponent in the form of the train, Lelouch's film echoes Barthes's text where he sees time as the enemy of driver and car. Thus, in a more modern France, there is still room for a fetishizing of commodities for their use-values and, more specifically, in this case, for their surplus capacities:

> Advertising is at work everywhere in *Un homme et une femme*: in the omnipresence of cars during this decade of the 'reign of the car' [...] Lelouch's universe thus appears to be that of a trendy salesgirl fascinated by consumer society as well as that of a promoter of this same society, who masters the methods of its development.[87]

In *Un homme et une femme*, motor sport facilitates the fetishizing of the motor car and, unlike in Barthes's text, this perspective is applied in everyday life, as the surplus capacity of the car is used to good effect in the *dénouement* of the film.

In both *Le Sport et les hommes* and *Un homme et une femme*, we see post-1945 engagement with motor sport. Barthes's text eulogizing five different sports devotes most attention to motor sport and the Tour

---

87 'La publicité est partout à l'œuvre dans Un homme et une femme: dans l'omniprésence des voitures en cette décennie du " règne de la bagnole" [...] L'univers de Lelouch apparait ainsi à la fois comme celui d'une midinette fascinée par la société de consommation et comme celui d'un promoteur de cette même société, qui maîtrise les méthodes de sa mise en valeur.' Frodon, Jean-Michel. 2010. *Le Cinéma français: de la nouvelle vague à nos jours*. Paris: Cahiers du cinéma, p. 225.

de France. Beautifully shot and featuring long silences during which the viewer can admire the drivers racing along the Florida circuit, and punctuated with the narration of the critic's reflections on the sport, *Le Sport et les hommes* displays how motor sport and speed were fetishized in this period. These cars and drivers are different from the DS, which Barthes discussed in his *Mythologies* a few years earlier, and also in his treatise on the role of the 2CV in modern society, both of which will be discussed later. In this text, he is concerned with the automobile as a purveyor of speed and its ability to conquer space and time. In *Un homme et une femme*, Lelouch depicts motor sport as a quest for speed that can still be fetishized in a modern France, in which the car has become more commonplace. However, we might usefully note that Ross argues that this film is almost nostalgic, as the myth of speed had already been 'waning' for a number of years when it was released.[88]

Conclusion

France has been a testing ground for motor racing from the very beginning of the sport. The first-ever races took place with Paris as their focal point, and the first attempts at motor sport events, such as an early switch from road racing to circuits, were a result of a national desire to promote this technological innovation. Early growth stemmed from the initiative taken by *familles artisanales* to adapt their work and build what they hoped would be the future of horseless transport. This desire was then adopted by the upper classes, as epitomized by the early presidents of the FIA, who embraced organizing and taking part in races in order to build the reliability and reputation of the self-propelled vehicles. The impact of Le Mans on the further advancement of motor sport is significant; its name will forever be associated with the hosting of the first international Grand Prix, but it is for its endurance race that this city is truly famous. The Le Mans race has successfully maintained its link with everyday automobile tourism and, as such, has established a much more enduring relationship with supporters. The race continues to grow despite recession and has shown an ability to adapt and change

---

88   Ross, *Fast Cars, Clean Bodies*, p. 33.

in the face of new challenges. As a result, it remains as relevant today as it was over 80 years ago.

Speed and modernity became intrinsically linked with the automobile in early 20th-century France as trials and then, shortly thereafter, city-to-city races drew hundreds of thousands of spectators. The automobile was consumed in image for capacities that were not necessarily essential to its functioning, as it covered ever greater distances at ever greater speeds. As images of speed and modernity were inscribed in and upon the automobile, it was increasingly consumed as a desired object and, thus, took on the characteristics highlighted by the Marxist concept of the commodity fetish as an object valorized for properties over and above its utilitarian-value. By fetishizing speed and the modernity associated with it, the basic properties of the car – the capacity to transport passengers to different destinations – became alienated. Motor racing played an important part in the expansion of this desire for speed. The fetishized desire for the surplus capacity of the car was not restricted to the field of motor racing, however. The automobile as a purveyor of speed and as a symbol of modernity also became the totemic embodiment of modern life for French car manufacturers of the early 20th century. It is consequently to that representation of the automobile that we shall now turn.

Chapter 3

An Object of Desire

Early 20th-Century Representations
of the Car

This chapter will extend the discussion to examine representations
of the automobile in early 20th-century France outside the domain
of motor sport. Perceptions of the automobile will be examined in
representations of the car by manufacturers. The particular impact
of Michelin and Citroën in the development of the fetishized vehicle
will be explored. These distinct representational vectors each shed
light on the ways in which the automobile was valorized during
the early 20th century. The cultural manifestations explored in this
chapter reveal how the car was consumed as an object of desire, not
only as regards the vehicles produced but also the imagery used to
promote them.

Les frères Michelin and their great rival André Citroën are renowned
for their respective roles in the development of the car and automobility. What perhaps sets their two companies apart in the early years
of their existence is how these industrialists availed of the media to
publicize their products. As the automobile was gaining popularity,
first Michelin and then Citroën utilized the media as a tool to further
their own renown. By closely aligning the automobile with modernity
and progress, these two manufacturers contributed to establishing
a collective desire for the car. Their efforts to transform French
society through the promotion of the car were portrayed as a means
of improving the country more broadly. The automobile became
popularly associated with speed and mobility, and was marketed as a
provider of properties which extended beyond its utilitarian capacity.
Thus, the early fetishizing of the automobile was crucially linked to the
cult of modernity. Philip Hadlock examines this interest in the modern
in early 20th-century France:

It would be difficult to speak of the 'modernity' of early twentieth-century French culture without considering its frenetic interest in machinery, and especially in modes of transportation. The first decade of the twentieth century in France produced numerous emblems of this craving to develop more powerful machines, to observe them at work, and to interact with them in new ways.[1]

Thus, the automobile was destined to play a larger role in a society where it was going to be possessed by some and gazed upon and desired by others. The fetishizing of the car through ostentation was a means by which ownership of an automobile served to portray class distinction, and this distinction of possession was displayed in different forms. This class distinction incarnated by the car also extended to art and mythology as it did in Bourdieu's famous work on the subject, and was applied to the car by Gartman.[2]

André Citroën

André Citroën played an extraordinary role in the early development of the automobile in France and internationally. He laid the groundwork for many innovations and left a legacy which resulted in the creation of two of the most iconic cars of the post-1945 era, the DS and the 2CV. However, as owner-manager of the Citroën company until his death in 1935, the conception and construction of the Traction Avant was undoubtedly his greatest triumph. The Traction revolutionized car production in the country; the vehicle's solid steel shell with front-wheel drive were important technological innovations, while its manufacture on a production line introduced Fordism to France.[3] Citroën's contribution to the growth in popularity of the automobile stretched beyond its construction. A charismatic man, his attempts to promote the car through various media outlets made him a singular entrepreneur. During the 1920s and early 1930s, he embarked on a series of heavily mediatized events to build his renown and that of

1   Hadlock, Philip G. 2006. 'Men, Machines, and the Modernity of Knowledge in Alfred Jarry's *Le Surmâle.' SubStance* 35 (3): 131–48 (p. 131).
2   Bourdieu, *La Distinction*; Gartman, David. 2012. *Culture, Class, and Critical Theory: Between Bourdieu and the Frankfurt School.* New York: Routledge.
3   Wolgensinger, Jacques. 1991. *André Citroën.* Paris: Flammarion, p. 48.

his cars. While overtly championing 'the car within reach of all' ('la voiture à la portée de tous'), his forays into marketing indulged in much fetishizing of the use-values of the automobile. Indeed, his proclaimed attempts to demystify the car may actually be seen as a way for Citroën to make the magical shroud that surrounded the car even denser.

André Citroën's grandfather was one of 12 children in a Jewish family that came to have business connections all over Northern Europe. His father settled in Paris, where André was born and enjoyed an upper-class education at the prestigious Lycée Condorcet, whose alumni include Henri Bergson and Marcel Proust, who was seven years his senior.[4] Citroën went on to follow in the footsteps of such scientists as André-Marie Ampère and François Arago and public figures such as Alfred Dreyfus in graduating from the École Polytechnique.[5] Having trained as an engineer, he happened to see wooden double-helical gears in operation during a family visit to Poland. He bought the patent and returned to Paris to produce a metal version of the innovation and develop it into a successful gearwheel manufacturing business. The double-chevron insignia found on the radiators of Citroën vehicles is a stylized version of the gears that launched their namesake in business.[6] This business, set up in 1904, grew steadily, and gradually Citroën developed a name for himself as not only a talented engineer but also a gifted promoter of his wares. By the time André became directly involved in the manufacturing of cars, the automobile industry was well-established in France. Better productivity and the proliferation of producers meant that, by the later 1900s, many of the original manufacturers were struggling to compete with their rivals. It was with this in mind that Émile and Louis Mors, car manufacturing brothers with a factory in the Rue du Théâtre, Paris, approached André to become part of the company in an attempt to improve its efficiency by increasing output and, crucially, by publicizing the car. The Mors brothers had an impressive sporting history, having won their first race, the Paris–Saint-Malo, in 1899, followed by the Bordeaux–Biarritz event and even the infamous

---

4   Séguéla, Jacques. 1999. *80 ans de publicité Citroën et toujours 20 ans.* Paris: Hoëbeke, p. 74.
5   Laux, *In First Gear*, p. 128.
6   Cadène, *L'automobile*, p. 115.

Paris–Madrid competition.[7] However, when the French monopoly on the racing track ended with sustained competition from Italy and Germany, coinciding with a downturn in the business, the Mors brothers decided to withdraw from motorsport in 1908 in order to concentrate on maximizing automobile production.[8] Citroën, as an advocate of mass production, was judged to be the best person to see the Mors company through this period of difficulty. Spending five years with Mors while still running his own firm, Citroën succeeded in modernizing the Rue du Théâtre factories, the production of which went from ten cars a month, each of them different, to 100 cars a month in 1913.[9] This increase was not enough to turn the tide for Mors, and when Citroën left in 1913, the company was still operating at a loss. However, this experience had given Citroën the opportunity to travel to the United States in 1912 to meet Henry Ford and learn about his system of mass production. Citroën has often been referred to as the 'Henry Ford of Europe' or the 'French Ford,' and it was his adoption of assembly line production that was to transform the automobile in France into a standardized vehicle along the lines of the Model T in the United States.

The First World War was to play a crucial role in Citroën becoming a car manufacturer. Drafted as a captain in the reserves, André quickly set about drawing up a proposal for the construction of a factory capable of building 20,000 military shells a day, using the methods and techniques already in practice in his gearwheel business. This proposal found its way onto the desk of the army's Chief of Artillery, General Baquet, who immediately had Citroën transferred in order to fulfil his promise.[10] In 1915, André Citroën purchased 30 acres of waste ground on the Quai de Javel in Paris, where he set up a state-of-the-art factory, incorporating facilities deemed necessary at the time, including not only production lines but also shops, canteens and clinics.[11] This adoption of the production line was a gamble as it had never before been used in Europe; though André had seen it in action in the United

7   Laux, *In First Gear*, p. 126.
8   Smith, Paul. 2004. 'La Place de l'automobile dans le développement des stations.' *In Situ. Revue des patrimoines* (4): 2–20 (p. 5).
9   Laux, *In First Gear*, p. 131.
10   Wolgensinger, *André Citroën*, p. 32.
11   Dumont, *Quai de Javel*, p. 5.

States, there was still no guarantee that it would be successful in France. Citroën opened his factory in 1915 with the ambitious goal of manufacturing '10,000 shells per day when the total national arsenals cannot exceed 4,000 pieces per day.'[12] Financed by the army, Citroën set about producing shells, and while production was slow at the start, with 1,500 shells per day, this output gradually grew to 10,000 the following year.

The year 1918 saw Citroën employ 18,000 workers, almost half of whom were female, and produce a maximum daily output of 35,000 shells.[13] By the end of the war, Citroën's factory had produced 20 million shells, which was more than the other major manufacturers combined.[14] Citroën had also generated enormous profits for his company,[15] which he used to convert his modern factory on the Quai de Javel into a car manufacturing plant. Such developments recall the significant linkage between war and technology in Futurist theory. In practice, the increased use of technology during the First World War served as the catalyst for a major transformation in industrial production methods, which in turn facilitated the car's development. While the war had consolidated the positions of the larger French manufacturers, with the use of their facilities for the construction of arms and, to a lesser extent, vehicles, it had at the same time sounded the death knell for the smaller producers, who were already struggling to keep up with rates of output prior to 1914.[16] These smaller businesses were requisitioned during the war and, without adequate funding, were unable to continue in its aftermath. The year 1919 saw the emergence

12   '10 000 obus par jour au moment où l'ensemble des arsenaux nationaux ne peuvent dépasser 4 000 pièces quotidiennes.' Loubet, Jean-Louis. 1998. 'Citroën et l'innovation (1915–1996).' *Vingtième siècle. Revue d'histoire* 57: 45–56 (p. 46).
13   Cohen, Yves. 1991. 'The Modernization of Production in the French Automobile Industry between the Wars: A Photographic Essay.' *The Business History Review* 65 (4): 754–80 (p. 759).
14   'Citroën: 20 millions d'obus, Renault: 8.6 millions, Peugeot: 6 millions, Berliet: 6 millions.' See Loubet, Jean-Louis. 2001. *Histoire de l'automobile française.* Paris: Seuil, p. 75.
15   Smith, Michael Stephen. 2006. *The Emergence of Modern Business Enterprise in France, 1800–1930.* Vol. 49. Cambridge, MA: Harvard University Press, p. 406.
16   Schweitzer, Sylvie. 1994. 'Rationalization of the Factory, Center of Industrial Society: The Ideas of André Citroën.' *International Journal of Political Economy* 24 (4): 11–34 (p. 27).

of intense competition between what were to become the giants of the motor industry. Citroën, Renault, Peugeot and Berliet were the firms that benefited most from the war, and the following years saw attempts to expand or, in the case of Berliet, simply to survive a series of misjudgements which saw this company go into liquidation in the early twenties.[17]

Adopting the principles of Taylorism[18] acquired during his trip to Detroit, Citroën announced that 'the car must be an instrument of work and pleasure for everyone.'[19] He accompanied this statement with the production of his Citroën A, which was released in 1919. He concentrated on the production of one car, available at a lower price than that of his competitors, as he embarked on a marketing campaign aimed at helping the public discover the delights of the automobile. He thereby portrayed himself as a liberator, highlighting his company's determination to open up the automobile market and thus boost its sales. The inauguration of the Traction Avant proved to be the culmination of Citroën's work, as it was an attractive, reliable car available to a larger market than had previously been possible. However, it is the way in which Citroën marketed his cars, and indeed automobility in general, that is most noteworthy. His stated aim to place the car within the grasp of all was based on a campaign associating the automobile with complementary aspects of a rapidly modernizing France. In the process, André Citroën commodified the car, so that he made it an object of desire for a wider audience than ever before. The automobile became fetishized by larger numbers of people who, although unable to purchase one, were surrounded by a rhetoric revolving around speed, mobility and modernity, as Citroën presented the car to the media in a series of innovative forms.

While mechanically the Type A, Citroën's first car, did not differ significantly from other cars of the time, it stood out in its accessories. Mass production meant that it was more economical to fix a lot of extras to every car rather than satisfy the whims of each individual buyer.

17 Dockès, Pierre. 1993. 'Les Recettes fordistes et les marmites de l'histoire (1907–1993).' *Revue économique* 44 (3): 485–528 (p. 504).
18 Taylorism or the principles of scientific management used scientific methods to analyse the most efficient production process in order to increase productivity.
19 'l'auto doit être un instrument de travail et de plaisir pour chacun.' Séguéla, *80 ans de publicité Citroën*, p. 69.

Electric lighting and an electric self-starter were provided, along with a soft top, a spare wheel and a host of other items at no extra charge.[20] The initially planned price of 7,250 francs was significantly lower than that of any other car available at the time and stimulated a considerable response from the public, eager to become motorized. Citroën received over 16,000 orders within two weeks of the announcement that this car would go into production; the company reached its target of 30,000 orders well before the first models were wheeled out of the factory.[21] Well-known as a gambler,[22] André decided to accept orders for a vehicle which was yet to be built, and evaluations of costs and output were at best estimates based on information received from Ford and also gleaned from experience of assembly line production throughout the war. While interest was immense, production did not go as planned. Output targets of 100 cars per day were not realized, with factories averaging only 30 cars a day for the first two years. This was still a higher output than any other French manufacturing firm, but it meant a steep rise in the price of the Type A, up to 12,500 francs in 1920, which was still viewed as reasonable considering all of the extras included.[23]

These problems notwithstanding, Citroën's sense of marketing came to the fore. The launch of the Type A had been preceded by weeks of deliberate rumour-mongering, and at the 1919 Salon de l'Automobile, he parked 50 Type As outside the gates of the Salle d'Exposition, readily available for test-driving.[24] The Salon was now not merely a means for people to discover new cars, for Citroën was using it as a veritable marketing opportunity (*support publicitaire*). A Type B and Type C followed this first foray into the automobile market and, as it was easier to improve an already established vehicle rather than build a new one, each of these models was gradually enhanced. The Fordist practice of following the alphabet was expanded to incorporate these developments; thus, a B2 emerged in 1922, which was improved upon with the B12 in 1925, and then the B14 in 1926.

20   Panhard, Jean. 1989. 'Petite histoire de l'automobile en France.' *Culture technique* 19: 29–42 (p. 3).
21   Panhard, 'Petite histoire de l'automobile en France,' p. 3.
22   Reynolds, *André Citroën*, p. 135.
23   Wolgensinger, *André Citroën*, p. 130.
24   Vantal, Anne. 1998. *Les Grands Moments du salon de l'auto*. Paris: EPA, p. 34.

The Type C or 5CV produced in 1922 was an attempt by Citroën to expand his market to include female drivers. The Type C and Type C2, which was to emerge two years later, were consequently smaller and more manoeuvrable than their predecessors. These two-seaters had an electric starter fitted as standard and were advertised as especially suitable for 'the modern woman' ('la femme moderne'). Initially only available in bright yellow, the new model gradually became known as Le Petit Citron ('the little lemon'), a nickname that André must surely have considered when deciding on the colour.[25] As he had done previously, Citroën showed a keen eye for marketing, and the C series turned out to be a considerable success, running until 1932, during which time over 360,000 cars were built.[26]

The Citroën C was replaced in 1932 by another powerful small car which had been making a name for itself on the motor testing track of Montlhéry – another means utilized by Citroën to increase interest in his vehicles.[27] Indeed, in the twenties and early thirties, he availed of an array of media to publicize his cars, thus stimulating the French public's perception of the vehicles and of Citroën, the man. The launch of each new model was preceded by a series of rumours about its maximum speed or reliability, which were all carefully allowed to 'escape' from Quai de Javel. Each launch was also accompanied by a full-page advertisement in the Parisian dailies. Thus began Citroën's attempt to create an environment within which the car would become more popular and, crucially, more desired. After-sales service became part of the automobile selling business as Citroën set up 400 car dealers throughout France.[28] Once again, this reflected his adoption of the American mass-marketing approach, which had proved successful. Payment in instalments was also promoted, as Citroën attempted to open the market to as wide an audience as possible.[29]

Citroën promoted the car and underlined its desirability through a close association with modernity, embracing the newest means of

25   Wood, Jonathan. 1993. *The Citröen*. Princes Risborough: Shire, p. 5.
26   Parissien, Steven. 2013. *The Life of the Automobile: A New History of the Motor Car*. London: Atlantic Books, p. 98.
27   Wolgensinger, Jacques. 1996. *Citroën: une vie à quitte ou double*. Paris: Arthaud, p. 54.
28   Wolgensinger, *Citroën*, p. 50.
29   Loubet, *Histoire de l'automobile française*, p. 105.

Figure 6 Citroën advertising on Eiffel Tower (1925).
Public domain image.

advertising. The name Citroën appeared in skywriting over Paris in 1922, when this new form of advertising had just been invented.[30] In 1924, Citroën famously illuminated the Eiffel tower with his name using 250,000 light bulbs.[31] It was purported that it was these lights that guided Charles Lindbergh on his pioneering transatlantic flight which was to land in Paris in 1927. Citroën seized upon this opportunity to strengthen his links to modernity by inviting Lindbergh to the Quai de Javel.[32] He also made the most of the occasion to associate himself with another modern symbol by inviting Gaumont to film his introduction of Lindbergh to his factory workers. It was the meeting of air and road travel, and also the meeting of the working classes with what the future might hold.[33] This was the conscious creation of an atmosphere in which modernity could be embraced. American ways, epitomized by Lindbergh's heroic solo flight, were welcomed as mobility in all its forms was promoted. The filming of the festive party lent itself to the atmosphere and helped create an aura of technical revolution, with an additional aura of democratization as symbols of modernity were being made more accessible. Whether this was true or not was immaterial; Citroën was creating an atmosphere in which his automobiles were symbols, symbols of modernity and of mobility. He was attempting to democratize a vehicle that remained the preserve of the upper and middle classes in the twenties, but which was gradually being seen as an attainable commodity by the lower classes too.

While his stated aim was to democratize the car, the steps taken by Citroën in its promotion suggest otherwise. By closely allying the automobile to other forms of modernity, he undoubtedly established the car as a totem of modern France; however, this representation was always inflected by considerations of class. David Gartman suggests that the emergence and continuing success of aviation had a direct impact on the growth and design of cars.[34] While Charles Lindbergh may have been popularly considered one of the 'people,' he also became

---

30   Loste, Jacques. 1949. *L'Automobile, notre amie*. Paris: L'Argus de l'automobile, p. 48.
31   Wolgensinger, *André Citroën*, p. 52.
32   Séguéla, *80 ans de publicité Citroën*, p. 10.
33   Wolgensinger, *André Citroën*, p. 54.
34   Gartman, David. 1994. *Auto Opium: A Social History of American Automobile Design*. New York: Routledge, p. 118.

associated with and admired by different classes in French society through his engagement with modernity. Michel Rachline describes Citroën's success in welcoming Lindbergh to the Quai de Javel factory as a 'masterstroke' ('coup de maître'), inscribed within a marketing process designed 'to seduce, attract, conquer, inform.'[35] Announcing that he wanted to 'satisfy everyone's fantasies,'[36] Citroën highlighted the desirability of the automobile. Paradoxically, his purporting to make the automobile more accessible actually allowed Citroën to add to its exchange-value through its systematic fetishization.

Citroën also engaged in the fetishizing of the surplus capacity of the car; more specifically, he promoted his own vehicles through widely publicized special tests, which he organized on the racetrack of Monthléry.[37] A Citroën 6 broke several speed and endurance records on 22 October 1931 and was baptized 'Rosalie' in honour of that day's patron saint.[38] The broader association with sanctity is itself suggestive of a durable fetishizing strategy that would most famously be explored by Roland Barthes in his analysis of the Citroën DS (see Chapter 6). At the technical level, and while Citroën was not an early participant in motor racing, the choice of a racetrack to showcase the performance of the new vehicle is significant. Highlighting its ability to complete a considerable number of laps at high speeds is indicative of how the use-value of the car was routinely overstated by Citroën. He furthered this valorization of the surplus capacity of the car through the inauguration of the trans-Saharan and trans-African *raids* or *croisières* ('overland cruises'), to which we now turn our attention.

In the aftermath of the First World War, André Citroën initiated a large-scale public relations exercise designed to demonstrate his vehicles' potential in the colonies. The timing of this decision was particularly significant. Having emerged victorious yet devastated from the war, France sought to increase awareness within the *métropole* of its overseas possessions. The reasons for this decision were twofold

---

35   'séduire, attirer, conquérir, informer.' Rachline, Michel. 1992. *La Genèse d'une automobile*. Paris: Albin Michel, p. 63.

36   'satisfaire les fantaisies de chacun.' Reiner, Silvain. 1958. *Des moteurs et des hommes*. Paris: Fayard, p. 63.

37   Wolgensinger, *André Citroën*, p. 54.

38   This might also be considered an example of the link between the automobile and the divine.

Figure 7 Advertising poster for the Citroën Petite Rosalie (1925).
© Archivart/Alamy Stock Photo.

and contradictory as France decided to celebrate its accession to the position of a major imperial power. For, on the one hand, the French Empire had reached new heights in terms of the number and extent of its colonies in the wake of the Versailles Treaty, and this was something to be celebrated in l'Hexagone.[39] However, the war had also provided glimpses of a new world power in the form of the United States, whose entry into the war defined its outcome. In the face of this new force, France took steps to strengthen its links with its colonies by making its citizens more aware of its territories outside Europe. This process culminated in the Paris Colonial Exhibition of 1931, which, as Ellen Furlough suggests, 'came at a moment in France of heightened attempts by pro-empire individuals and groups, along with the French government, to represent the colonies as an essential part of Greater France (*la plus grande France*).'[40] Thus, in deciding to launch his cars on highly mediatized trips into Africa and Indochina, Citroën was taking advantage of the political situation to associate his vehicles with the nation's consciously colonial vision of its post-war modernization.

The impetus for Citroën's interest in colonial expeditions came in 1920 with the acquisition of the patent for the half-track caterpillar system designed by Russian-based engineer Adolphe Kégresse, who had worked for Tsar Nicholas II from 1906 to 1917.[41] This involved attaching a rubber belt to a set of two wheels on each side of the rear axle of Citroën Model A and Model B cars. The Citroën *autochenille* was thus equipped to brave the harshest territory in North Africa, which included sand dunes and rocky terrain. Citroën's first assault on the desert saw a team of ten companions led by Louis Audouin-Dubreuil and Georges-Marie Haardt, director-general of the Citroën factories at the time. They were accompanied by military personnel, geographers and a film crew as they embarked on an expedition scheduled to leave Touggourt in Algeria in December 1922 and arrive in Timbuktu, in the French Sudan, some 20 days later in January 1923.[42]

---

39 Dine, Philip. 2012. *Sport and Identity in France: Practices, Locations, Representations.* Oxford: Peter Lang, p. 177.

40 Furlough, Ellen. 2002. '*Une leçon des choses*: Tourism, Empire, and the Nation in Interwar France.' *French Historical Studies* 25 (3): 441–73 (p. 441).

41 Pociello, Christian, and Daniel Denis. 2000. *À l'école de l'aventure: pratiques sportives de plein air et idéologie de la conquête du monde, 1890–1940.* Voiron: Presses universitaires du sport, p. 149.

42 Wolgensinger, Jacques. 1974. *Raid Afrique.* Paris: Flammarion, p. 59.

André Citroën ensured that the expedition's preparation and its subsequent success were extensively covered in the national media. Citroën carried out well-publicized testing of the system in the sand dunes of Arcachon near Bordeaux, which culminated in the successful ascent of the Dune du Pyla. A short film of the Citroën *autochenille* was also released. Entitled *Arcachon, le tourisme de l'avenir avec les voitures Citroën* ('Arcachon, the future of tourism with Citroën cars'), the film by Pathé-Gaumont shows two Citroën Half-Tracks emerge from the Hotel Régina in Bordeaux, each carrying five passengers and a driver. The two cars proceed to descend the steep steps leading to the street. An intertitle explains the scene:

> Tourism of the Future
> CITROËN cars fitted with the KÉGRESSE HINSTIN propellant, having come by road from Paris to Arcachon, delight tourists at the 'HOTEL RÉGINA,' who can take a trip in an unprecedented way in the lovely landscapes of PYLA.[43]

The cars are filmed taking their passengers to the Arcachon dunes, driving in the countryside, climbing and descending sand dunes, driving into the water from the beach before returning to the city, going back up the steps and entering the hotel. A picture of one of the Citroën *autochenilles* also appears on the front page of the local newspaper, *La Petite Gironde*, with the title 'Une maison qui voyage' ('A House That Travels'). The picture shows the Citroën pulling a large trailer parked in front of the Grand Théâtre.[44]

The 'Première Traversée du Sahara' consisted of five vehicles. It left Touggourt on 17 December 1922 and arrived in Timbuktu on 6 January 1923. Upon its triumphant arrival at its destination, the Citroën team symbolically handed over the mail, an act that strengthened the link

---

43   'Le Tourisme de l'Avenir
Des voitures CITROËN munies du propulseur KÉGRESSE HINSTIN, venues par la route de Paris à Arcachon, font la joie des touristes de "l'HOTEL RÉGINA" que peuvent excursionner d'une façon inédite dans les ravissants paysages du PYLA.' Citroën, *Arcachon, le tourisme de l'avenir avec les voitures* (Bordeaux: Pathé-Gaumont, 1921), film. http://villegiature.gironde.fr/?id=072-regina-chenilles (accessed December 2013).
44   *La Petite Gironde*, 11 September 1921. http://villegiature.gironde.fr/?id=072-regina-chenilles&pattern=cms_viewer_v2.xml&img_num=1 (accessed December 2013).

between the expedition and the state. By carrying out this function, the Citroën team was, in effect, acting in France's name. At the same time, the expedition was also seen to embody the values of industrial rationality, as its vehicles travelled through African communities, in the process offering an image of renewed national dynamism.[45] Thus, the automobile had a central role in the imperial project, as its surplus capacities – in this instance, the speed and endurance which enabled it to cross the barren territory of the Saharan desert – were portrayed as a means of 'civilizing' the colonies. These capacities, which had earlier been so crucial in motor racing, were now to serve further as they were viewed as values that could help France recover some of its prestige in the post-war era.

Earlier French forays into the Saharan desert had typically been conceived as military exercises, not infrequently carried out in the wake of attacks by local tribes on colonial forces. The successful half-tracks were accordingly militarized, each carrying a heavy machine gun. Several members of the Citroën expeditions had military backgrounds, including Lieutenant Louis Audouin-Dubreuil, the joint leader of the three *croisières*, and Commander Bettembourg. They functioned as military advisors on the first two expeditions. Indeed, it was their experience with automobile-led military detachments that led to their selection. The choice of Georges-Marie Haardt as joint leader of the expeditions with Audouin-Dubreuil was also significant. As director-general of the Quai de Javel factory, Haardt was an example of how an executive could be promoted to take part in such a pioneering initiative.[46]

The success of the mission had a double resonance: it proved the ability of automobiles to cross hostile and previously inaccessible terrain; and it did so in a Citroën, thereby promoting this brand over and above the others. The triumph of the expedition had a strong commercial impact, with Citroën's sales rising by 50 per cent in 1923.[47] In the cultural sphere, the expedition was supported by a short documentary film that was shown throughout France, while a written account of the voyage by Haardt and Audouin-Dubreuil was published. André Citroën is presented in *La Première Traversée du Sahara en automobile: de Touggourt*

45   Bloom, *French Colonial Documentary*, p. 74.
46   Séguéla, *80 ans de publicité Citroën*, p. 32.
47   Wolgensinger, *Raid Afrique*, p. 122.

à Tombouctou par l'Atlantide (1923) as a groundbreaking pioneer whose goal was the promotion of the French nation and its technology. In the preface, written by Citroën himself, he references the colonies and how his automobiles as purveyors of technology are capable of replacing their traditional mode of transport, namely the camel. He also refers to his own role in this process as a 'duty,' suggesting that the French presence in the colonies was of such importance that it was necessary for him to undertake this expedition:

> Where a car with a 10 HP motor passed easily thanks to the caterpillar tracks, it was necessary to give a normal car a much more powerful motor to face these same obstacles and still it could only overcome them with the help of a camel or men, which proved that the caterpillar tracks could be considered, for the moment, as the only practical, economical and safe means of Saharan transport.
>
> It was then that colonials, soldiers and explorers posed the problem of crossing the Sahara to us.
>
> The value of such an experience seemed to me so great that I considered it a real duty to attempt it. The Touggourt-Timbuktu expedition was decided; it remained to prepare it.[48]

This automotive mission turned an exploration of France's African territories into an effective advertising tool. While Citroën used the expedition to boost his company's profile, the government welcomed a privateer's efforts to facilitate access to the colonies. With the shared political goal of consolidating *la plus grande France*, the government welcomed Citroën's demonstration that not only was it possible for

---

48   'Là où une voiture avec un moteur de 10 HP passait facilement grâce à la chenille, il fallait mettre sur une voiture à roues un moteur beaucoup plus puissant pour affronter ces mêmes obstacles et encore n'arrivait-elle à les vaincre qu'avec l'aide du chameau ou des hommes; ce qui prouvait que la chenille pouvait être envisagée, pour l'instant, comme le seul moyen pratique, économique et sûr pour les transports sahariens.

C'est alors que des coloniaux, des militaires, des explorateurs nous posèrent le problème de la traversée du Sahara.

L'intérêt d'une telle expérience me parut si grand que je considérai comme un véritable devoir de la tenter. L'expédition Touggourt-Tombouctou était décidée; il restait à la préparer.' Haardt and Audouin-Dubreuil, *La Première Traversée du Sahara en automobile*, pp. 13–14.

citizens to traverse the colonies but that it was only feasible using French innovations. This mutually beneficial partnership between the state and Citroën had been anticipated in the highly publicized lead-up to the event when André Citroën personally accompanied the expedition leaders to the Palais de l'Élysée, announcing: 'The camel is dead, it has been replaced by Citroën.'[49] There, Haardt recollects, they explained the route to be taken by the group to the President of the Republic, Alexandre Millerand:

> I go over my memories of the last days. On 1 December, my visit, accompanied by Mr. André Citroën, to the President of the Republic who, in a very long audience, carefully inquired, map in hand, about all the details of the organization of the expedition and addressed its members his warmest wishes.[50]

La Première Traversée du Sahara en automobile is a 343-page publication that describes in detail the expedition and the return journey across the Sahara. While much of the book deals with the daily events and obstacles to be overcome in such uncharted territory, a colonial undertone runs throughout the work as reference is regularly made to France's civilizing mission in its African territories. As the journal highlights the beauty of this apparently untamed land, it also refers to the modernizing aspect of the expedition. The beauty of the scenery is in the foreground, but this is, first and foremost, the context within which the vehicle functions at its optimum level. This explicit valorizing of the modern, of the technical, implicitly draws attention to the colonial aspect of the journey, as the sound of progress echoes through the desert:

> It would be unfortunate if the scenic side of the trip alone captured the reader's attention. With the splendour of the sites glimpsed, of the memories encountered, the noise of our engines

---

49 'Le chameau est mort, la Citroën la remplace.' Deschamps, Eric. 1999. *Croisières Citroën: carnets de route africains.* Boulogne-Billancourt: ETAI, p. 84.
50 'Je repasse mes souvenirs des derniers jours. Le 1er décembre, ma visite, accompagné de M. André Citroën, au Président de la République qui, dans une audience très longue, se renseigna minutieusement, carte en mains, sur tous les détails d'organisation de l'expédition et adressa à ses membres les vœux les plus chaleureux.' Haardt and Audouin-Dubreuil, *La Première Traversée du Sahara en automobile*, p. 28.

must constantly mingle. This too has its beauty; it is the song of progress, it is the rhythm of human effort affirming its victory over the elements. Our great desire is that the story of our trip be included in the *livre d'or* of French industry.[51]

While there is little or no overt use of the word 'colony' in the text, the imperial aspect of the mission is evident throughout, as when the authors note the support received from the Ministry for the Colonies. By the same token, the foregrounding of the expedition's modernity serves to assert the centrality of the French *Patrie* ('fatherland') in the development of these less fortunate regions and, crucially, to legitimize its own expansion: 'The caterpillar-tracked car got the better of the desert. Thanks to her, the plane and the rail will come. Their triple and fruitful alliance will push beyond the Equator, to the Congo, the borders of the fatherland.'[52]

References to the 'natives' ('indigènes') encountered in the course of this expedition are imbued with the self-promoting attitude of the colonial *mission civilisatrice*. Interaction is seen as a novelty, as an experiment in introducing technological modernity to a people heretofore uncivilized. This depiction reinforces the impression that this colonial mission was being carried out also for the good of the lands crossed. At times, the resulting interaction is evoked in terms of colonial clichés, such as the age-old exchanging of trinkets *à la* Columbus: 'The Tuaregs surround us. Distribution of gifts to these great looters of the desert who find what we offer them very natural. Long ago, before we were masters of the land, they would have massacred us to take them themselves.'[53] The use of words such as 'looters' ('pillards')

51   'Il serait injuste que le seul côté pittoresque du voyage sollicitât l'attention du lecteur. A la splendeur des sites entrevus, des souvenirs rencontrés, doit se mêler sans cesse le bruit de nos moteurs. Cela aussi a sa beauté; c'est le chant du progrès, c'est le rythme de l'effort humain affirmant sa victoire sur les éléments. Notre grand désir serait que le récit de notre voyage puisse prendre place au livre d'or de l'industrie française.' Haardt and Audouin-Dubreuil, *La Première Traversée du Sahara en automobile*, p. 6.
52   'L'auto-chenille a eu raison du désert. Grace à elle l'avion et le rail vont venir. Leur triple et féconde alliance va pousser au-delà de l'Équateur, jusqu'au Congo, les frontières de la patrie.' Haardt and Audouin-Dubreuil, *La Première Traversée du Sahara en automobile*, p. 307.
53   'Les Touareg nous entourent. Distribution de cadeaux à ces grands pillards du désert qui trouvent très naturel ce que nous leur offrons. Autrefois, avant

and 'massacre' serves to highlight the beneficial impact of the French presence in Africa. Since the colonizers have become 'the masters of the land' ('les maîtres du pays'), the natives have not only acquired the civilization to appreciate the gifts bestowed upon them by their masters but have also ceased to be a threat to the latter.

Similarly, the film of the *raid* indulged in clichés to emphasize the modernizing effort of the expedition. The opening intertitles of *La Traversée du Sahara* thus begin with the following statements:

> From the dawn of antiquity, communication across the desert could only be assured by camel-driven caravans … Which slowly crossed the immense desert landscape … The vast French colonial domain in Africa requires more rapid communication … This is being made possible by courageous men, with the help of the *auto-chenilles*.[54]

These seemingly authoritative statements are accompanied by a series of shots incorporating camels and vast expanses of desert, penetrated by the half-track vehicles. The ability of the half-tracks to cross the desert easily and efficiently is contrasted with the slow, meandering progress of camel-powered transit. The beneficial impact of the automobile, particularly on the promotion of a modern way of life, is also highlighted.[55] *La Traversée du Sahara* proved a box office success. It introduced the cinemagoing public to the North African colonies, presenting the civilizing work carried out there as well as the indelible mark left by the automobile. The latter thus served as a powerful vehicle to sell this modern image of the colonizer. Its ability to reach these untamed territories and 'civilize' them was vital as it strengthened France's actual and symbolic role in Africa.

In February 1923, André Citroën triumphantly travelled to Africa to welcome the expedition as it arrived back in Touggourt. There he greeted them with a congratulatory telegram from the French president.[56] The written account of the expedition, published in

---

que nous soyons les maîtres du pays, ils nous auraient massacrés pour les prendre eux-mêmes.' Haardt and Audouin-Dubreuil, *La Première Traversée du Sahara en automobile*, p. 97.

54 Bloom, *French Colonial Documentary*, p. 75.
55 Bloom, *French Colonial Documentary*, p. 75.
56 Wolgensinger, *Raid Afrique*, p. 68.

1923, constitutes an invaluable primary source for the investigation of prevailing attitudes. Fittingly, it concludes with the statement that one of the cars, the 'Scarabée d'or,'[57] has been housed in the Army Museum at the Invalides, thereby underlining the military nature of the expedition and its aspiration to triumphal national *grandeur.* The memory of the First World War still fresh, this commemorative investment places Citroën's expedition on a par with military successes historically achieved by the nation. With his privately financed caterpillar tracks, this astute entrepreneur had made the most of contemporary politics to promote the colonies as well as himself, and thus received ample support from the authorities. The government, in turn, having observed that the Citroën expedition effectively crossed and symbolically united the French African territories, made the most of the publicity this garnered to promote overseas France within the Hexagon.[58] The success of the military expedition was enough to persuade Citroën to attempt to promote the automobile in the colonies in a civilian context. Moreover, this patriotically commercial engagement was itself part of a broader societal awakening to the colonies at this time.

In much the same vein as the first trans-Saharan mission, the Croisière Noire, which lasted from October 1924 to June 1925, was used by Citroën to promote automotive travel and technology. What distinguished it from other *raids* into the desert was the public acclaim it garnered, in contrast to, among others, successful attempts by Renault to negotiate this inhospitable terrain. Renault's six-wheelers traversed the Sahara and did so in comparable times to those of Citroën.[59] However, a lack of publicity ensured that these early Renault

57   'The cars each had a name: all five are, in fact, emblazoned as once were the palfreys of knights leaving on crusade, as were planes, cars and even artillery during the war. The first was the "Golden Scarab," the second the "Silver Crescent," the third the "Flying Turtle," the fourth the "Bull Apis" and the last the "Crawling Caterpillar"' ('Toutes les cinq sont, en effet, blasonnées comme l'étaient jadis les palefrois des chevaliers partant pour la croisade, comme le furent pendant la guerre les avions, les autos et même les pièces d'artillerie. La première porte au "Scarabée d'or," la seconde au "Croissant d'Argent," la troisième à la "Tortue Volante," la quatrième au "Bœuf Apis," et enfin la dernière à la "Chenille Rampante."' Haardt and Audouin-Dubreuil, *La Première Traversée du Sahara en automobile*, p. 50.
58   Murray, 'Le Tourisme Citroën au Sahara,' p. 106.
59   Rouxel, Marie-Christine. 2003. *Renault en Afrique: croisières automobiles et raids aériens, 1901–1939.* Boulogne-Billancourt: ETAI, p. 8.

expeditions would remain little-known.[60] The Croisière Noire, on the other hand, constitutes an important chapter in the history of French colonialism. Its running was accompanied by daily accounts in the national newspapers and radio broadcasts; it was also followed up by a well-received book. Finally, and perhaps most importantly, it led to a film entitled *La Croisière Noire*, released in 1926.[61] André Citroën's Expédition Centre-Afrique, as the project was also known, was the next step in the scheme to modernize the colonies. It was organized in the wake of the successful trans-Saharan crossing, and its aim was to link France's North African colonies to those in West and Central Africa, as well as Madagascar. It served to mask the difficulties experienced by Citroën's other African project, CITRACIT,[62] and became the most successful African expedition mounted by Citroën, not only because it succeeded in reaching its stated goal, but also because of the very positive publicity garnered by the 'mission.' As with his two previous projects, Citroën energetically sought state support for this venture. In a letter to the president, he highlighted the national interest of his project: 'from a national point of view, the success of this second mission will demonstrate internationally the leading role of the French automobile industry in the world.'[63]

The Croisière Noire left Colomb-Béchar in Algeria on 24 October 1924 and arrived at its destination of Tananarive, Madagascar, on 26 July 1925. Of all the trans-African expeditions carried out in this period, it is this voyage that most clearly captured the imagination of the public at the time, and it has also continued to do so up to the present day, with the film version of the expedition still being screened on national television.[64] The film premiered with a live orchestra at the Opéra de

---

60   Bordes, François, ed. 1988. *L'automobile à la conquête de l'Afrique (1898–1932)*. Aix-en-Provence: Centre des Archives d'Outre-Mer, p. 55.
61   Poirier, Léon, dir. 1926. *La Croisière noire. Film de l'expédition Citroën Centre-Afrique*. France, Gaumont.
62   The CITRACIT (Compagnie transafricaine Citroën) project envisaged the creation of a tourist network of cars and hotels. It was cancelled once deemed unviable. See Murray, 'Le Tourisme Citroën au Sahara,' p. 95.
63   'au point de vue national, le succès de cette deuxième mission montrera une fois de plus à l'étranger la place prépondérante prise par l'industrie française automobile dans le monde.' Qtd. in Hargreaves, Alec G. 2005. *Memory, Empire, and Postcolonialism: Legacies of French Colonialism*. Lanham, MD: Lexington Books, p. 84.
64   Hargreaves, *Memory, Empire, and Postcolonialism*, p. 92.

Paris on 2 March 1926, significantly, with President Gaston Doumergue in attendance.[65] It presented Africa as an infinitely large continent of exotic primitiveness through which the Citroën vehicles forged a way. It depicted the unifying action of the automobile, linking north to south and east to west. Gilbert Meynier has referred to colonial conceptions of the empire as a body needing to be activated, incapable of action without the ability of the supposedly superior French mind.[66] In successfully crossing the African continent, the Citroën expedition demonstrated the capabilities of the automobile and technology as a whole to a public who saw a continent still in darkness but now ready to be shown the light of civilization. Indeed, in a twist on both Conrad's classic formulation of the African 'heart of darkness' and Meynier's metaphor of the body, French technology was now bringing light to the continent's heart and thus promoting life itself. By forging a way through the colonies, the automobile was improving the functioning of that heart and thus the whole African continent. This image was apparent in the advertisements used to promote the expedition. A map of the African continent aerated by arteries spreading to all areas highlighted the life-bestowing nature of the civilizing mission. This is one of the first images to appear in the film *Croisière Noire*, with the arterial routes travelled by the automobile in the course of the expedition. Reference to the continent in terms of the human body had earlier been made by a French-Moroccan entrepreneur, Gaston Gradis, in his 1924 account of Renault's crossing of Africa, where he stated that the plan was to 'look for the axis to form the backbone of the Empire.'[67]

The public success of the Croisière Noire was nurtured by a series of events throughout 1926, culminating in the exhibition held at the Musée des Arts Décoratifs in the Louvre. The Scarabée d'or took pride of place and was surrounded by stuffed animals and other items collected along the journey. In an adjoining room, a constant projection of images from the expedition served to place all objects found in context. Also associated with the expedition were glamorous galas, at which Josephine Baker was a noted regular.[68] The mutual admiration

65   Wolgensinger, *Raid Afrique*, p. 91.
66   Qtd. in Bloom, *French Colonial Documentary*, p. 91.
67   'chercher l'axe pour former la colonne vertébrale de l'Empire.' Gradis, *À la recherche du grand-axe*, p. 5.
68   Baker was a black American who moved to France in 1925 and became

between André Citroën and Baker originated in Citroën presenting her with a B14 Sports Cabriolet in appreciation of her work. In response, Baker updated the lyrics of her most celebrated song, 'J'ai deux amours,' singing that the two loves of her life were her country and Citroën.[69] She wore a hat and hairstyle that made a direct reference to a marketing poster for the Croisière which used the image of a Mangbetu woman with a distinctive headdress. This celebrated fashion statement resonated strongly in affluent circles in Paris, the Mangbetu hairstyle being featured in *Vogue* magazine in 1926, and becoming fashionable, with Parisian designer Madame Agnès developing it for her wealthy clientele.[70] Baker came to embody African culture, although she herself had no direct link to it.[71] Thus African exoticism as perceived through Josephine Baker and Citroën's adopted civilizing mission were linked as both became popular in 1920s Paris.

Such was the success of the repeated expeditions into North Africa that G. Arnaud announced in a paper written for the *Annales de Géographie* in 1927 that 'one can therefore confirm that the conquest of the Saharan desert by automobile has been achieved.'[72] Not only had automobiles conquered the Sahara, the mechanical progress of the car was such that it was no longer necessary to resort to half-tracks or six-wheelers. Arnaud proudly claimed that 'in January, Lieutenant Estienne covered Paris–Chad–Niamey in ten days in a simple 6 CV Renault.'[73] Even the safety question on desert roads seemed to be fading, as 'they have little to fear from dissidents.'[74]

The Citroën expeditions were symbolic of the French automobile industry, the emerging tourist industry and the state's geopolitical and

linked to all forms of exoticism due to the frenetic nature of her dancing. Cf. Sheringham, Michael. 1996. *Parisian Fields*. London: Reaktion, p. 46.

69   Wolgensinger, *André Citroën*, p. 55.

70   Bloom, *French Colonial Documentary*, p. 93.

71   Sweeney, Carole. 2004. *From Fetish to Subject: Race, Modernism, and Primitivism, 1919–1935*. London: Praeger, p. 48.

72   'On peut donc confirmer que la conquête du désert saharien par l'automobile est réalisée.' Arnaud, G. 1927. 'La Conquête automobile du Sahara.' *Annales de Géographie* 3: 173–76 (p. 176).

73   'en janvier dernier le lieutenant Estienne a couvert en dix jours Paris – le Tchad – Niamey sur une simple 6 CV Renault.' Arnaud, 'La Conquête automobile du Sahara,' p. 175.

74   'elles n'ont guère à redouter les dissidents' Arnaud, 'La Conquête automobile du Sahara,' p. 176.

geostrategic ambitions. The Croisière Noire, which traversed central Africa to finish in Madagascar, was followed by the Croisière Jaune, which was an expedition to French possessions in Indochina. The fact that each expedition set more distant colonies as its goal was evidence of the ever-improving quality of automotive transport. The geostrategic importance of the colonies in Africa and Indochina ensured that they became fertile advertising grounds for the Citroën brand as representations of the 'civilizing' expeditions were widely distributed in France.

André Citroën, through his innovative marketing and close association with modernity, fostered a strong desire for the automobile, which was transferred to a broader public than previously. While his stated aim was to bring the car to all, by publicizing it through the most expensive and outlandish means, he actually increased its fetishization. It was this penchant for opulence and for taking risks that eventually brought an end to André Citroën's tenure as the owner of the car brand. Citroën went bankrupt in 1933, and he died shortly thereafter. His ailing company was bought by the Michelin brothers, who quickly set about completing many projects initiated by Citroën, most notably the production and marketing of the Traction Avant, which went on to become one of the bestselling cars of the interwar era. Originally tyre producers, the Michelin brothers had played an essential role in the growth of the automobile in early 20th-century France and it is to this company and its innovations that we now turn.

Les Frères Michelin

The titles of the books dedicated to Michelin are striking in how they differ from the studies of most other protagonists in the story of the car. Terms such as 'adventure,' 'saga,' 'secret' and 'magic' are examples of this.[75] They are revealing as they suggest that Michelin was remarkable in its drive to publicize and sell tyres. An aggressive marketing campaign nurtured this dynamic image of the company. Its innovations, seen as

75 Jemain and Hanon, *Michelin*; Michelin. 2004. *La Saga du Guide Michelin: de 1900 à aujourd'hui, un formidable voyage à travers le temps*. Clermont-Ferrand: Manufacture française des pneumatiques Michelin; Darmon, Olivier. 1997. *Le Grand Siècle de Bibendum*. Paris: Hoëbeke; Dumond, Lionel. 2002. *L'épopée Bibendum: une entreprise à l'épreuve de l'histoire*. Toulouse: Privat.

being for the good of the car and of tourism as a whole, put Michelin at the forefront of travel in France. Bibendum, the rotund Michelin Man, is one of the world's most recognizable corporate symbols today; the Michelin guide remains the point of reference for French tourists; the Michelin star system in gastronomy is the pinnacle of *haute cuisine*.[76] More recently, a new culinary award has been added. Entitled the Bib Gourmand, this award is for restaurants that do not reach Michelin star standards of cooking yet achieve a consistently high level.[77] The title of the award is a further reference to the Michelin Man. All of this, and we still have not mentioned the pneumatic tyre, the invention which set this process in motion. The Michelin company had played a significant role in the birth and nurturing of the car before taking over Citroën, one of France's largest manufacturing companies, to oversee production of arguably the most iconic cars France has ever produced. The growth of Michelin, first as a commercial enterprise and then as a household name in France and throughout the world, will be explored here. Analysis of the various marketing endeavours undertaken by the firm will show how Michelin gained a foothold in what was, at the turn of the century, a precarious industry. *Les frères* Michelin set in motion a train of events and marketing models that were to assure the company's future and to place it firmly in the public eye.[78] These various approaches will be analysed along with the relationship established between Michelin and its competitors, between Michelin and the government, and between Michelin and the public. Finally, the effects of the central role played by Michelin in transforming and modernizing the perception of the physical geography of France will be examined.

Michelin's most famous marketing creation was conceived in the late 19th century and exemplified one of the key tropes associated with fetishizing a commodity, as it instilled life into the company's tyres to create an anthropomorphic creature. Michelin's Bibendum was born just before the turn of the century and has become such an iconic character that the actual details of how he came into being are now unclear. The *famille* Michelin was eager to claim its conception for themselves, as was

---

76 Dumond, *L'épopée Bibendum*, p. 5.
77 Lottman, Herbert. 2003. *The Michelin Men: Driving an Empire*. New York: I.B. Tauris, p. 270.
78 Ribeill, Georges. 1991a. 'From Pneumatics to Highway Logistics: André Michelin, Instigator of the Automobile Revolution, Part I.' *Flux* 3: 9–19 (p. 14).

the cartoonist employed by the brothers to design posters. Michelin claimed that, at the Universal and Colonial Exhibition in Lyon in 1894, the entrance to the Michelin stand was decorated with two columns of tyres, a sight that prompted Édouard Michelin to remark to his brother: 'Hey, if it had arms and legs, it would be a man!'[79] This version of events has largely been accepted by the general public in that it romanticizes the conception of this icon. However, the cartoonist Marius Roussillon, who worked under the pen name 'O'Galop,' and who was to be the chief designer of Michelin marketing posters throughout the early 20th century, contended that it was from his various sketches presented to Michelin in 1898 that Bibendum was born.

O'Galop's conception, based on the story of Gambrinus, a mythical king said to have invented the art of brewing, would be the source of the slogan. Gambrinus holding up a pitcher of beer and exclaiming *Nunc es bibendum*, a Latin verse from the poet Horace meaning 'now is the time to drink,' was suggested by André Michelin as an addition. The first in a series of *Nunc es bibendum* posters appeared in April 1898. The slogan, from which the character derived his name, is liberally translated as 'To your health, any obstacle is meat and drink to the Michelin tyre.'[80] This is accompanied by an image of a nice, plump Bibendum smoking a cigar and giving a toast with a champagne glass full of nails, glass shards and other miscellaneous items capable of puncturing a tyre. Alongside Bibendum are 'Pneus X et Y,' both of which have been punctured. They appear old, worn and unstable, apparently unable to deal with the obstacles overcome by the Michelin. The Michelin character earned his name in a highly mediatized incident when a reputed racing driver, Léon Théry, upon making his triumphant arrival in the Amsterdam–Paris race, and seeing André Michelin, announced, 'Here comes Bibendum.'[81] Michelin was able to make the most of this opportune moment to baptize his character. This personification of the company's tyres has become one of the most recognized trademarks the world over.

79   'Dis donc, s'il avait des bras et des jambes, ça ferait un bonhomme!' Gonzalez, *Bibendum*, p. 32.
80   'Á votre santé, le pneu Michelin boit l'obstacle.' Champeaux, Antoine. 2003. 'Bibendum et les débuts de l'aviation (1908–1914).' *Guerres mondiales et conflits contemporains* 209: 25–43 (p. 26).
81   'Et voilà Bibendum.' Gonzalez, *Bibendum*, p. 33.

Figure 8 Advertising poster portraying Bibendum (1898).
Public domain image.

As the owner of one of the world's most identifiable logos, André Michelin set about using his mascot at every available opportunity. From his relatively modest beginnings in poster form in 1898, Bibendum was to be drawn by a number of cartoonists. Although essentially the same character, his form moved with the times to make him relevant to and popular with each changing generation. Thus, he effectively replaced André Michelin in the public's mind as a tall, portly, smiling, bespectacled *bonhomme*, who was always there, always willing to lend a hand. In using Théry's nickname, Michelin had transposed the image of their jovial character onto their own public image. In 1901, André Michelin began a process to make the name of Bibendum readily familiar; he took out a weekly slot in the newspaper *L'Auto-Vélo*, which was later to become *L'Auto*. He used it to acquaint the public not only with his latest products but also his mascot, who appears in all manner of guises in marketing rubber-based products.[82] Very often presented in the form of an editorial, this marketing innovation was used to keep the public up-to-date with the development of automobile travel and the obstacles it faced. In presenting itself as a provider of information and as a conveyor of public opinion, the column pushed people to consider and think about automotive transport. The portrayal of Bibendum in comical settings served as a tool to appeal to a wider audience, attracting the curious eye to the segment, then engaging the reader with broader issues. Michelin decided on a Monday slot, and in so doing, he tapped into a much larger reading market than during the week: Mondays are traditionally the day when readers buy a newspaper to catch up on events over the weekend, including sports news and various spectacles.[83] 'Le Lundi de Michelin' began on 11 March 1901 and was to continue for 13 years, up to the First World War. This regular slot was also a new venture in the field; up to then, advertising had been carried out on an ad hoc basis, slots being allocated on demand and often without any real method or message to portray. 'Le Lundi de Michelin' appeared for over a decade over 690 editions, providing a strong platform to promote Michelin. This sociocultural embedding, whereby Bibendum was portrayed in various guises with which the French public could identify, allowed Michelin's mascot to

---

82   Jemain and Hanon, *Michelin*, p. 54.
83   Darmon, *Le Grand Siècle de Bibendum*, p. 44.

become more recognizable and thus accepted. The fact that not only Michelin's competitors, the British company Dunlop and the German firm Continental, but also various car manufacturers, such as De Dion and Peugeot, adopted similar marketing strategies is testament to the effectiveness of 'Le Lundi de Michelin' as a mechanism for informing the public about its products.

'Le Lundi de Michelin' was novel in its format and also in its content, featuring the company's mascot in a plethora of different incarnations.[84] By this means, Michelin marketed more than tyres. They advertised the phenomenon of automobility itself, in what was the first in a long line of innovations aimed at marketing the car and, if not actually making it a commonplace commodity, at least making it familiar to all. Subsequently the full weight of Bibendum was thrown into far-reaching activities, from the creation of signposts and campaigning for the numbering of roads to the creation of tourist guides and a tourist office in Paris.

While 'Le Lundi de Michelin' continued until the First World War, it was not the only source of publicity for Michelin. From 1911, Bibendum also began to appear in *Théâtre illustré du pneu*, a supplement to the popular newspaper *L'Illustration*, which had never before allowed any form of advertising.[85] In this series, Bibendum would engage with a theatrical theme to transmit the particular message that Michelin had in mind. Very often, what appeared were forms of advice for the Michelin user, presented from a different angle on a weekly basis. So, for instance, 'To be or not to be … non-slip' and 'Tartuffe or the multiplication of … breakdowns' show Bibendum assuming the persona of the main character in these celebrated works and explaining how to get the best out of the Michelin tyre.[86] There was a moral to be found in each Michelin story. These little cartoons sought to explain any perceived deficiencies in the Michelin tyre. Thus, as any problem was encountered on the roads, Bibendum would address this fault and explain what the client needed to do to avoid further difficulties. The use of well-known classics also pushed the audience to identify with Bibendum. Bibendum's

---

84   Michelin, *La Saga du Guide Michelin*, p. 31.
85   Darmon, *Le Grand Siècle de Bibendum*, p. 47.
86   'Être ou ne pas être … antidérapant'; 'Tartuffe ou la multiplication des … pannes.' Michelin. 1908. *Recueil. Documents techniques et publicitaires*. Clermont-Ferrand: Michelin et cie, p. 2.

Figure 9 Advertising poster for Michelin (1912).
© Classic-Ads/Alamy Stock Photo.

Figure 10 Cover of *Théâtre illustré du pneu* (1911).
Public domain image.

role in *Théâtre illustré du pneu*, much like that in *L'Auto*, drew to a close on the eve of the First World War but not before providing over 40 different morals to be drawn from the tragedy of a Michelin puncture.[87]

Apart from these two weekly spots in the press, Michelin also made use of more irregular appearances in the media. The company notably issued at various times what were called 'technical documents.'[88] Ostensibly aimed at informing the public about the latest innovations to come from the Clermont factories, these were another means for Michelin to place Bibendum and the company's product firmly in the public eye. One such document dating from before the First World War and dedicated to transport and trucking, shows Bibendum, on the back cover, supporting the globe on his shoulders *à la* Atlas.[89] These documents were issued to meet a need in the market; they supported the role played by the more regular media slots of reassuring the public as to the reliability of the company's tyres. In 1912, another *document technique* was issued to inform the public about the availability of tools which were to be used in the changing of tyres; these 'Michelin levers' ('leviers Michelin') meant that changing a tyre was so easy that a 14-year-old boy could do it.[90] Proof of this was supplied in an account of an experiment carried out at the 1912 Salon de l'Automobile. During this spectacle, various children of the age of 14 were asked by Michelin to change a tyre. This report is supported by a series of photographs in which a young-looking man, wearing a chauffeur's uniform and hat, carried out the task with apparent ease. Astute use was made of the politics of the day to penetrate the market further. In 1916, at the height of the war, a *document technique* was brought out as a homage to the steel-rimmed wheel.[91] We see Bibendum wearing the jacket and helmet of the French army and holding a steel-rimmed wheel aloft on the cover. In the background, there are a number of army trucks, all shod with steel-rimmed wheels, and also the outline of a plane, the wheels of which are visible.[92] In the foreground, at the feet of this triumphant Bibendum, lies a broken German helmet. The next logical step for

87   Darmon, *Le Grand Siècle de Bibendum*, p. 47.
88   'documents techniques.' Michelin, *Recueil*, p. 3.
89   Michelin, *Recueil*, p. 5.
90   Michelin, *Recueil*, p. 6.
91   Michelin, *Recueil*, p. 6.
92   Michelin, *Recueil*, p. 6.

Michelin was to bring out a series of guides dedicated to the visiting of First World War battlefields, which the company duly did in 1917.[93] From 19 April 1919, *L'Illustration* began carrying Michelin marketing material, with the result that 'Le Lundi de Michelin' was transformed into 'Le Samedi Touriste.'[94]

Through the association of the Michelin Man with its many publicity ventures, Bibendum became the mascot of the brand. By instilling life into a set of tyres, the Michelin brothers created an identifiable character that would be used to increase interest in and desire for the car. Bibendum would appear in magazines and newspapers, helping stricken cars by producing fresh tyres from the ample supply in his physical make-up. Initially a drawing, a physical incarnation of the Michelin Man began to appear at the firm's publicity events, where a man dressed up in a suit of tyres would stand beside André Michelin to embody the jovial, progressive image put forward by the firm.[95] This character would go on to play an important role in the advancement of tourism, as Michelin sought to further automobility through its capacity to help the public discover France, an effort which encouraged patriotism especially before and after the First World War.

The Michelin company had an important early impact on the promotion of tourism in France. In encouraging the discovery of the French countryside, Michelin was developing a strong link between automobile travel and pleasure tourism, thus publicizing a further reason to obtain a car, which increased the demand for and thus the exchange-value of the car. Much as Citroën had promoted the car in tandem with modernity, this linking of it to pleasure tourism served to increase desire for the car as the public was made aware of destinations and monuments deemed worthy of visiting. The creation of driver's guides, of tourist guides, and of a tourism office in Paris, as well as the company's public campaigning for better road markings, all served to increase the visibility of the car.

The year 1912 saw Michelin bring out a publicity brochure entitled *Ce que Michelin a fait pour le tourisme*.[96] It mentioned 'la carte

93   Mom, *Atlantic Automobilism*, p. 251.
94   Moulin-Bourret, *Guerre et industrie*, p. 706.
95   Gonzalez, *Bibendum*, p. 34.
96   *Ce que Michelin a fait pour le tourisme: guides Michelin, bureaux de tourisme, plaques indicatrices, cartes Michelin.* [no place: no publisher], 1912.

Michelin,' 'les itinéraires gratuits' and 'le guide Michelin.' All of these innovations were conceived by André Michelin to widen his company's market base. A campaign for the numbering of roads and another to add *bornes kilométriques* ('milestones') were to follow. This seven-page *document publicitaire* informed the reader of all the steps taken by Michelin to promote automobility since the advent of the new technology. This ensured that the public was in no doubt as to who was responsible for the modernizing of the nation's transport systems and infrastructure. In assuming this 'quasi-institutional' role, the Michelin brothers were attempting once again to embed their reputation in automobility.[97]

In 1908, at 105 Boulevard Pereire in Paris, the company opened the first in a network of 'Bureaux de Tourisme Michelin,' in which staff helped car owners establish the best way to reach a given destination in France and beyond. Bibendum explains the process thus: 'All you need to do is indicate to one of the Michelin Tourist Offices the outline of the planned trip to receive a free detailed itinerary giving all information on the route to follow.'[98] The objective of the Bureau de Tourisme Michelin was to free the motorist of any trepidation before a journey. The lack of road signage and consequent difficulties in reaching one's destination were major obstacles to the expansion of early car travel. By providing the driver with an in-depth, detailed itinerary to be followed, Michelin attempted to eliminate any such uncertainty, thereby promoting tourism. Not only did the driver receive the complete itinerary, he – or, more rarely, she – also got details of any site in the vicinity of the itinerary which, in a phrase that was to become famous, may be 'worth a detour.'[99] Thus, in the creation of tools for the physical mapping of the French landscape, the Michelin office was also contributing to its mental mapping. The growing reliability of the car in an increasingly technological age strengthened the link with modernity, just as it cut links with old

---

97   Darmon, *Le Grand Siècle de Bibendum*, p. 44.

98   'Il suffit d'indiquer à l'un des Bureaux de Tourisme Michelin les grandes lignes du voyage qu'on projette pour recevoir gratuitement un itinéraire détaillé donnant tous renseignements sur la route à suivre.' *Ce que Michelin a fait pour le tourisme*, p. 2.

99   'vaut un détour.' Rowland, Michael. 1987. 'Michelin's *Guide vert touristique*: A Guide to the French Inner Landscape.' *The French Review* 60 (5): 653–64 (p. 654).

France. Weber refers in *Peasants to Frenchmen* (1976) to the impact of the machine in this broader rejection of traditional French values: 'Just as the schools and the skills they taught created a new breed of children, so the machines when they came introduced a different relationship between man and nature. The earth lost its sacredness, the gods their divinity, magic its power.'[100] The office was also a good *centre de recherches* for this new initiative as it provided material resources for the establishment of maps. From a single person in 1908, the 'bureau des itinéraires,' as it became known, grew to employ 120 people in 1925, who together provided carefully constructed itineraries for 155,000 requested routes.[101] Carefully compiled, each itinerary was later to be used as the basis for the company's regional guides, the forerunner to the Michelin *Guide vert.*

While *Le Guide rouge Michelin* in its early life did incorporate some town plans and smaller maps, it was not until 1910 that 'les cartes routières Michelin' were established commercially. The roads sketched on these maps were sourced through the French ministries of War and of the Interior, and use was made of information collected by the Bureau des Itinéraires in adapting these official details to the needs of the motorist.[102] The distances between towns and the numbers of routes were added to the list; these were followed by converting the map from a simple tool to get from A to B into a tourist-oriented document that proved a helpful supplement to the *Guide rouge.* An eight-colour code scheme was used to distinguish the various roads from those that are 'regularly maintained' to those, at the other extreme, that are 'not surfaced or too narrow.'[103] Each area became linked with tourism; picturesque roads were bordered in green, while forests, churches, castles and other such features were highlighted. The *cartes Michelin* were conceived with the motorist in mind;[104] the way they were folded facilitated consultation while the driver was at the wheel. This newest

100   Weber, Eugen. 1976. *Peasants into Frenchmen: The Modernization of Rural France, 1870–1914.* Stanford, CA: Stanford University Press, p. 484.
101   Karpik, Lucien. 2000. 'Le Guide rouge Michelin.' *Sociologie du travail* 42 (3): 369–89 (p. 13).
102   Francon, Marc. 2001. *Le Guide vert Michelin: l'invention du tourisme culturel populaire.* Paris: Economica' p. 41.
103   'régulièrement entretenue(s) [...] non empierré(es) ou trop étroit(es).' Darmon, Olivier. 2004. *La route autrefois.* Paris: Hoëbeke, p. 19.
104   Gonzalez, *Bibendum*, p. 44.

tool to expand tourism was essentially a combination of information that was already available but which was now presented in a manner that made it accessible to even the most ill-at-ease driver.[105] The first map to be issued was that of the Clermont-Ferrand area; this was followed by Marseille-Cannes-Nice, then the Paris area, culminating in a foldable 47-page map of the whole of France issued in 1913.[106] Bibendum announced the creation of these maps in the 1909 edition of the *Guide Michelin*: 'This new document is recommended to drivers for the accuracy and precision of its information.'[107] In this announcement, the words 'exactitude' and 'précision' are once again indicative of how new 'certainties' are being fetishized; the Michelin maps represented a further proof that modern France, which was cutting links to its past, was a more scientific and rigorous country. In the Michelin guides over the following years, numerous references to the maps were made in order that the user would consider purchasing one before going on a journey. The maps, after the guide and the Bureau des Itinéraires, were another way of opening up the country to its citizens. All were linked, and all had the same goal of stimulating tourism; indeed, the creation and evolution of these guides have been identified with the invention of 'popular tourism.'[108]

The creation and expansion of Michelin maps of France went hand in hand with a concerted campaign to establish numbering of French highways and byways. 'What would it take to revolutionize automobile tourism?' asked 'Le Lundi de Michelin.' 'Simply that all the roads have a number which is used on maps and the roads themselves.'[109] Roads at the time were classified into four groups by the Ministère des Ponts et Chaussées.[110] However, these details were very rarely transferred

---

105   Darmon, *La route autrefois*, p. 19.

106   Michelin, *La Saga du Guide Michelin*, p. 73.

107   'Ce nouveau document se recommande aux chauffeurs par l'exactitude et la précision de ses renseignements.' Michelin. 1909. *Guide Michelin*. Clermont-Ferrand: Michelin-Guide, pp. 648–49.

108   For a detailed account of how the maps were conceived, refer to Francon, *Le Guide vert Michelin*, pp. 51–54.

109   'Que faudrait-il pour révolutionner le tourisme automobile? Simplement que toutes les routes aient un numéro qui soit reporté sur les cartes et les routes elles-mêmes.' 'Le Lundi de Michelin de 1912', qtd. in Darmon, *La route autrefois*, p. 14.

110   Beyer, Antoine. 2004. 'La Numérotation des routes françaises. Le sens de la nomenclature dans une perspective géographique.' *Flux* 55: 17–29 (p. 20).

to signage on the roads and, more often than not, roads were devoid of any information. If distances in kilometres were made available, it was unclear what they related to and made little sense to anyone but ministerial officials. Having publicly helped an Englishman drive from Geneva to Clermont-Ferrand in 1911, André Michelin immediately began a new campaign to have the numbering on his maps and that on the nation's roads match up.[111] His original approaches to the government having been rejected, Michelin initiated a petition at the 1912 Salon de l'Aviation, during which he obtained the signature of Armand Fallières, the President of France at the time. It is uncertain whether Fallières knowingly signed a petition for something that his government had recently refused.[112] Alain Jemain suggests that the president thought that he was signing the visitor's book for the Salon.[113] Michelin created a poster calling on people to follow their head of state in signing the petition: a picture of Fallières leaning over to sign and bordered by the French colours made it appear as if this petition was a matter of national interest. Within a month, 200,000 signatures were collected and sent to the Ministre des Travaux Publics, Jean Dupuy.[114] The latter confirmed his approval for the numbering of the country's roads just months later.[115] Sponsored by the 'Touring Club de France,' the first road to be numbered was the route between Paris and Trouville, the shortest route between the capital and the seaside, Trouville having already become one of the country's first seaside resorts thanks to its rail connection. This growth in leisure tourism in France will be examined in Chapter 4.

Another ingredient in Michelin's recipe for the expansion of tourism was the creation and distribution of town signs. In 1910, André Michelin commissioned the conception of a sign which would indicate the name of the town being traversed. These were placed at the entrances and exits of towns throughout France. It was another step towards the brand recognition to which Michelin aspired. Each sign comprised the name of the relevant *commune* and the number of the road. They also had two

---

111   Gonzalez, *Bibendum*, p. 88.
112   Ribeill, Georges. 1991b. 'From Pneumatics to Highway Logistics: André Michelin, Instigator of the Automobile Revolution, Part II.' *Flux* 5: 5–19 (p. 8).
113   Jemain and Hanon, *Michelin*, p. 60.
114   Bonnet and Gazagnes, *Sur les traces de Michelin*, p. 234.
115   Qtd. in Gonzalez, *Bibendum*, p. 88.

pieces of advice for the safety of the town's inhabitants: 'Please slow down' and 'Watch out for children.'[116] In so doing, Michelin contributed to the broader processes of homogenization and codification which had been enshrined in the Third Republic, as discussed by Weber.[117] Placed above all this information were the words: 'Don de Michelin' ('A gift from Michelin'). The fact that these signs were a self-serving ploy is referred to also in the previously cited brochure *Ce que Michelin a fait pour le tourisme* (1912), in which Bibendum proudly announced that these 'Plaques Michelin' are 'offered free of charge to municipalities.'[118] This was a relatively cheap way of introducing the name Michelin to urban and rural settings alike.[119] Thus, Michelin had succeeded in culturally embedding its name into early automobility. By taking up an almost institutional role in the codification of the automobile network, it ensured strong visibility in this 'obligatory landscape for drivers' ('paysage obligatoire des automobilistes'). Through different forms of fetishizing, with Bibendum as a totem, Michelin succeeded in investing additional value in the car as, in the changing society before the First World War, new beliefs regarding technology and modernity were being espoused and the nation was gradually turning its back on 'old France.' The design and creation of maps and later itineraries by Michelin served to further the impression that the country was becoming increasingly 'known.' This process was enhanced with the inception of the Michelin travel guides, as we shall see in the next section.

In the early years of its existence, Michelin spent more on advertising than was actually earned by the company, but this was seen as necessary to gain a firm foothold in the emerging market. While all of the above measures promoted the motor car and motor tourism, they essentially consisted of the creation and expansion of that market, in which Michelin would have a larger role to play. The Michelin Guides, initially intended to introduce drivers to the mechanics of cars and to give them a helping hand in their travels, were transformed into a comprehensive tourist guide, complete with reviews of restaurants and hotels. Bernard

---

116   'Veuillez Ralentir' and 'Attention aux enfants'. Séguéla, *80 ans de publicité Citroën*, p. 28; Darmon, *La route autrefois*, p. 16.
117   Weber, *Peasants into Frenchmen*, p. 303.
118   'offertes gratuitement aux Municipalités.' *Ce que Michelin a fait pour le tourisme*, p. 4.
119   Jemain and Hanon, *Michelin*, p. 60.

Lerivray's 1975 review[120] of the various tourist guides historically made available in France, shows that Michelin Guides were aimed at a different customer from others as the company attempted to make its guides less austere and more accessible to broader sections of the public. The constant promotion of everyday tourism, which was to continue well into the Trente Glorieuses, amounted to a very cost-effective way of promoting automobility and thereby boosting tyre usage. All attempts to improve and modernize roads can essentially be seen as a means of heightening public and state awareness of the reality that the car existed but the infrastructure to accommodate it did not. Michelin and Bibendum together built a France that was very well informed about the capacities of automobiles. Lucien Karpik, in his analysis of *Le Guide rouge*, sees the steps taken as a form of seduction.[121] Thus, in order to increase collective desire for the car and automobility, it was first necessary to eradicate uncertainty, any reluctance felt by the potential driving public not only with regard to the vehicles themselves but also, as we have seen, concerning the discovery of the country. Through the technology offered by the car, the public could feel assured that it was increasingly possible to turn one's back on the past and embrace a new future in a modern nation. In 1900, Michelin produced the first example of *Le Guide rouge*, which was designed to promote the automobile across the country. Its goal was stated as follows: 'The present work wishes to give all the information which may be useful to a driver travelling in France, to kit out his automobile, to repair it, to enable him to find accommodation and food, to correspond by post, telegraph or telephone.'[122] The timing was well-judged. The guide was launched the year after the first Tour de France Automobile and made the most of the aura of modernity established at the 1900 Exposition Universelle in order to establish a foothold in France. Initially, the red guide was more a professional aid than an out-and-out guide for tourism. This was to change as the automobile

---

120 Lerivray, Bernard. 1975. *Guides bleus, guides verts et lunettes roses*. Paris: Le Cerf, p. 11.
121 Karpik, 'Le Guide rouge Michelin,' p. 5.
122 'Le présent ouvrage a le désir de donner tous les renseignements qui peuvent être utiles à un chauffeur, voyageant en France, pour approvisionner son automobile, pour la réparer, pour lui permettre de se loger et de se nourrir, de correspondre par poste, télégraphe ou téléphone.' Michelin. 1900. *Guide Michelin, offert gracieusement aux chauffeurs*. Paris: Albouy, pp. 5–6.

became more popular. However, it would be accurate to say that *Le Guide rouge* was a technical guide in its infancy before gradually assuming the role of tourist guide. The reasons for this are apparent; in the early years of the 20th century, it was as important to have a driver who also fulfilled the duties of a mechanic as it was to know where one was going. The first *Guide rouge* was 'offered free of charge to drivers' ('Offert gracieusement aux Chauffeurs'), so it was the driver, not the person being driven, who used the guide. The guide consequently comprised practical advice, including notes on spare parts, and a 'Decree regulating the circulation of Automobiles'[123] – in other words, information to facilitate the job of the *chauffeur* in transporting his employer.

In a further attempt to demystify the French countryside, a large section of the first *Guide rouge* was dedicated to the 'List of towns in alphabetical order and maps.'[124] This litany of towns was not arbitrarily chosen; nor is it insignificant that the towns were classified alphabetically. In fact, the taxonomy proposed in *Le Guide rouge* constituted an attack on the monopoly of the railway system in transporting French citizens. During the second half of the 19th century, the national rail network had gone some way towards opening up the country, but in alphabetizing a list of towns, Michelin was making a statement: no longer were towns simply to be considered as stations on a railway line. Rather, all towns featured in the *Guide rouge* were accessible to the car owner, and the list was a symbol of the freedom which was now the prerogative of any motorist. It created a new France for the traveller, a France that was not restricted to the compass of the railway. This list provided a taste of what the future was to hold for the country; the railway network had initially promoted travel, but now it was the turn of the motor car to expand personal mobility.

The choice of towns in this 'nomenclature' is also significant. We are told in a 'note explicative' that this is not merely a list of towns; rather it is a repository of the towns capable of sustaining the motor car: 'If there is a petrol station in a city or town, a mechanic who can intelligently repair it, that city or town is included on this

123 'Décret portant règlement relatif à la circulation des Automobiles.' Michelin. *Guide Michelin, offert gracieusement aux chauffeurs*, p. 6.
124 'Nomenclature des villes par ordre alphabétique et plans.' Michelin. *Guide Michelin, offert gracieusement aux chauffeurs*, p. 54.

list.'[125] Michelin thus prioritized towns, not according to the values of conventional tourism but from the more practical point of view of the motorist. This was the filter that was applied to the choice of towns before any other factors were considered. Michelin created a hierarchy of places to visit, the first criterion being the ability to support the automobile. Thus, this hierarchy broke from older ways of imagining the national space, as it constructed a new social and cultural reality that depended on the possession of a car. Once this basic necessity was established, the Guide would furnish extensive details about each town. It described hotels using a three-star system, promoted restaurants (going so far as to say whether or not they were recommended by the Automobile-Club de France) and gave details as to the presence of a train station and post office. These details were provided for all towns once they satisfied the most basic criterion of all, namely, the availability of motor fuel.

The street plans of 13 cities, from Agen to Tours, are also presented to accompany this nomenclature. While Paris is mentioned in the guide, no details of its hotels or of places to refuel are supplied; nor is there a plan of the capital. Paris appears on the list but only as a source of automobiles. The aim of the Guide is not to facilitate the exploration of Paris; instead, Paris is the centre from which all exploration is to be initiated. Moreover, this is first and foremost a traveller's guide, and as such its aim is systematically to promote the use of the car. From 1901, the attractiveness to the tourist and the practical utility of the nation's roads are classified. The mention of the distance in kilometres from Paris of each town included in the 1900 nomenclature tells us much about the orientation of the guide; it was an aid to those venturing from the known (Paris) into the unknown ('Province'). The Michelin guide was not the first tourist guide. But it was innovative in that it was aimed at a new audience, not considered by the assortment of guides available at the turn of the century.[126]

Lucien Karpik classifies the development of the *Guide rouge* into three distinct time frames: 1900–08 for 'Le Guide Technique,' 1908–33 for

125   'Du moment où il existe dans une ville ou un village un vendeur d'essence, un mécanicien susceptible de faire intelligemment une réparation, ce village ou cette ville se trouve inscrit dans la présente liste.' Michelin. *Guide Michelin, offert gracieusement aux chauffeurs*, p. 54.
126   Francon, *Le Guide vert Michelin*, p. 193.

'Le Guide Touristique' and 1933–98 for 'Le Guide Gastronomique.' This evolution has a clear parallel in the progression of the automobile. Michelin developed its guide over the years to match the progress made by the car. Initially a breakdown and technical manual for the chauffeur, the creation of the Bureau des Itinéraires coincided with the change in the approach adopted in the *Guide*. The itineraries provided by the Bureau were to be used extensively in an attempt to introduce tourism to a wider audience.[127] The guide was gradually becoming more human-focused than machine-oriented, and this was reflected in the addition of listings of sites of tourist interest. In 1908, spas are added, 1910 sees the addition of seaside resorts and in 1912 ski resorts make it into the guide. Monuments are classified using a star system and, while these monuments are not actually described, this is another step towards the creation of a country in which automobile ownership is both desired and even required, as places beyond the reach of the railway are now shown to be readily accessible. Hotels were classified first by price, then by quality. All of these changes reflected the fact that the France portrayed in the Michelin guide had, albeit arbitrarily – as Karpik suggests – evolved as a country and specifically as a social and cultural reality. It was no longer a vast land stretching out into the distance but rather a national space comprised of picturesque routes, important monuments and tourist resorts. 'Unseen France' ('La France non-vue') was evolving into a France 'to be seen' ('à voir'), and *Le Guide Michelin*, with all of its accessories, was providing the key information on how to access it.

Le Guide vert was born in 1934, and from the outset, the target audience was broader than the previous Paris-centric guides. Michelin expanded the scope of the guide to make it more accessible to this wider audience. In Bernard Lerivay's comparative study[128] of the *Guide vert* and *Guide bleu*, and similarly in Marc Francon's critical study[129] of the *Guide vert*, the approach taken by Michelin is seen to be different from other guides available at the time. Central to this process was the construction of the selected sites as readily accessible, both geographically and conceptually. Catherine Bertho-Lavenir speaks of 'the

127   Karpik, 'Le Guide rouge Michelin,' p. 14.
128   Lerivray, *Guides bleus, guides verts et lunettes roses*, p. 11.
129   Francon, *Le Guide vert Michelin*, p. 46.

dramatization of the visit to the monument,' by which she means the recounting of the history of a monument in theatrical terms.[130]

In what was effectively an early exercise in cultural democratization, *Le Guide vert* discussed the history of each town and each monument in a more anecdotal manner than that adopted by other guides. While all accounts were fact-based, the emphasis was placed on the extraordinary. There was scene-setting that involved dialogues between historical figures who explained the history of the area. The style and tone used were similar to *Le Tour de la France par deux enfants* (1877), the reader that had been used in classrooms throughout the land during the Third Republic. It described France through the eyes of its two young protagonists as they travelled through the country, providing accurate historico-geographic accounts to the book's young audience.[131] In similar fashion, the *Guide vert* began to breathe life into history, making it more accessible, using everyday language while at the same time maintaining historical accuracy. The level of language employed is also revelatory of the projected audience of the guide.[132] The *Guide vert* took a step back from the aloofness apparent in other guides and tried to make France accessible to all its readers. Less detail is used in descriptions of monuments in the *Guide vert*, which suggests the ability to travel to, and see, a large number of monuments in a short period of time.[133] The automobile driver was the target, capable of travelling from town to town and discovering monuments which were beyond the reach of the railway network without having to learn the entire history of each attraction.

The *Guide vert* thus developed from the *guides régionaux* to become a popular tourist guide for motorists. It was aimed at a motorized public from the outset and hence did not suffer from any transitional issues, unlike the *Guide bleu*, which was an updated version of the *Guide Joanne*, a tourist aid for well-to-do train travellers. By reducing the price of the guides, animating the histories with heroes such as Joan of

130 'La Théâtralisation de la visite du Monument.' Bertho-Lavenir, Catherine. 2004. *La Visite du monument*. Clermont-Ferrand: Presses universitaires Blaise Pascal, p. 154.
131 Bruno [Augustine Fouillée], G. 1877. *Le Tour de la France par deux enfants: devoir et patrie*. Paris: Belin.
132 Lerivray, *Guides bleus, guides verts et lunettes roses*, p. 83.
133 Francon, *Le Guide vert Michelin*, p. 17.

Arc and Napoléon, and using uncomplicated and everyday language, Michelin succeeded in creating a tourist guide capable of reaching a broad audience. Selling 86,000 copies in 1912,[134] and going on to adapt itself to the growing tourist public, the creation and evolution of the various Michelin guides had an early impact on the discovery and exploration of a new, more open France. In reducing ongoing fears, initially with regard to the reliability of the car and later about travelling into the unknown, the guides played a crucial role in increasing the desire for possession of a car. The promotion of the country as a tourist destination encouraged a nationalism that was in turn fostered by 'commercial patriotism' ('patriotisme commercial'), of which the guides to the First World War battlefields are perhaps the most famous example.

The valorization of automobile use through Michelin's regular advertising of the progress being made in the field served to heighten demand. As reliability improved, moreover, a strong association with tourism was fostered through a Michelin campaign to modernize the road network and road markings. This, as well as the inauguration of the tourist guides, further heightened the visibility of, and thus demand for, the automobile. By foregrounding the pleasures that could be experienced through the use of the car, the company increased public interest. This was reflected in the strong linkage established between Michelin and automobility, which culminated in its acquisition of Citroën in 1934. Michelin owned Citroën until 1975, overseeing the construction of three of the most iconic cars in French automotive history: the Traction Avant, the 2CV and the DS. This history was founded on a legacy of marketing the automobile and the company's own related products, all of which had a profound impact on the company's early growth.

Conclusion

André Citroën and André Michelin both established clear links between the automobile and modernity as they endeavoured to market their products. The close association with progress was highlighted by

---

134   Francon, *Le Guide vert Michelin*, p. 54.

both companies as they promoted the automobile in order to make it available to the maximum number of people. However, the means by which they engaged in the marketing of the car, by promoting it as an object of desire, added prestige-value to the automobile. In spite of the efforts of these two companies to democratize it, the automobile in early 20th-century France became fetishized for its exchange-value. A close association with modernity ensured that the automobile remained an object of desire. These companies also valorized the surplus capacity of the automobile. Both participated in early motor racing to prove their products, and this was extended to the racetrack at Montlhéry. The creation of the Michelin guides and tourist offices was a further step to boost desire for the automobile, as these initiatives attempted to reduce ignorance and enhance knowledge about travelling in France. The Citroën *croisières* combined these techniques with the decision to extend testing of its vehicles to sub-Saharan Africa. Through the application of science and technology, the *croisières* and the resulting documentaries, which were screened throughout mainland France, ensured that the automobile remained a symbol of modernity. The examination of the role of the automobile in North African tourism will now be extended to wider consumption as we see the automobile gradually becoming more attainable and having a strong impact on the development of mass tourism.

Chapter 4

Vers le Midi

The Automobile Discovered and as a Vehicle of Discovery

My name is Laurent Patrick Fignon and I was born on a Friday in the heart of the Trente Glorieuses, which was then at its peak. It was 12 August 1960, at 3:10 a.m. [...] At the time, even in the streets of our big cities, pride in speed became a sure bet, an aspiration for everyone, a proof of freedom. Renault, Citroën and Peugeot competed for innovations to offer 'modern' couples the thrill of the road and of escape. Going fast, always going faster.[1]

This chapter will examine how the car was to have a substantial impact on post-1945 holidaymaking as the effects of the Trente Glorieuses were increasingly apparent. Cyclist Laurent Fignon's[2] parents experienced this change. The automobile was to be central in

1 'Je m'appelle Laurent Patrick Fignon et je suis né un vendredi au cœur des Trente Glorieuses, qui connaissaient alors leur apogée. C'était le 12 août 1960, à 3 h 10 du matin [...] A l'époque, jusque dans les rues de nos grandes villes, l'orgueil de la vitesse devenait une valeur sûre, une aspiration de chacun, une preuve de liberté. Renault, Citroën ou Peugeot rivalisaient d'innovations pour offrir aux couples 'modernes' le grand frisson de la route et de l'évasion. Aller vite, toujours plus vite.' Fignon, Laurent. 2009. *Nous étions jeunes et insouciants*. Paris: Librairie générale française, p. 43.
2 Laurent Fignon won the cycling Tour de France in 1983 and 1989 and, perhaps most famously, lost the 1989 edition to the American Greg LeMond. This loss was perceived by many to be a changing of the guard from the traditional cyclist to a more modernized, streamlined, time trial–oriented era.

the growth of mass tourism, coming to incarnate the 'modern,' and specifically modern ways of escape.[3]

Le Viaduc de Millau is a supreme example of the tradition in France of travelling to the sea on holiday. Opened in 2004, it was built in order to cater, particularly, for the traffic flows during the peak two months of the year (i.e. July and August). The large number of cars heading south and later returning for *la rentrée* cross this bridge on their way to and from the sea during the summer holidays. Spanning the Tarn Valley, the Viaduc de Millau is the highest road bridge in the world and is a modern-day testament to the number of car-driving holiday-makers.[4] In 2010, it was the fifth most visited 'non-cultural' monument in France.[5] Another reminder of the social significance of holidaying occurred in 2006 in the small town of Lapalisse, which hosted a *fête de l'embouteillage* to commemorate the traffic jams caused by those going on holiday in Trente Glorieuses France.[6] It was a nostalgic commemoration of the period when the Route Nationale 7 was the main road to the Côte d'Azur.[7] These two locations serve as 'lieux de mémoire,' as Pierre Nora might put it,[8] that is to say, as monuments to the roles played by the automobile and the road in the explosion of mass tourism, and thus in a tradition of holidaymaking that is still alive today. This evolution in holidaying emerged as a result of a number of factors, amongst which the transformation in the perception of the car in all classes was central, particularly after the Second World War.

The recorded progression of the number of French holidaymakers indicates a history of mass motorized tourism, which emerged during the late 1940s and early 1950s. Patterns of automobility established at that time have been substantially maintained into the present. Thus,

3   See Rojek, Chris. 2005. *Leisure Theory: Principles and Practice.* London: Palgrave Macmillan.
4   Millau is also symbolic as the town in which José Bové destroyed a McDonalds in an attack on globalization in France.
5   Direction Générale des Entreprises. 2006. *Mémento du tourisme.* Ivry-sur-Seine: Observatoire National du Tourisme, p. 8.
6   *La Vie de l'auto,* 9 November 2006.
7   In a further commemoration of this *lieu de mémoire,* in summer 2021, La Poste issued a collection of stamps in honour of the Nationale 7 and its popularity in Trente Glorieuses France.
8   Nora, *Les Lieux de mémoire.* 'Le front de mer' and 'La forêt' are two relevant essays in this collection.

Figure 11 Le pont de Millau, Aveyron, France.
© Éamon Ó Cofaigh (July 2007).

of the two-thirds of the population currently taking holidays, 85 per cent do so between 1 July and 30 August, and 80 per cent of these holidaymakers remain in France.[9] The third interesting statistic is that more than 50 per cent of holidaymakers spend their time on the beach. In order to investigate these figures, it is necessary to examine the factors that influenced the genesis and evolution of holidaymaking before and during the Trente Glorieuses. The interwar holidaymaker can be seen as a distinct entity from those who left *en masse* for the beaches during the economic upturn of the Trente Glorieuses. Having remained a largely upper-class activity until it became a political priority in the 1930s with the rise of the Front Populaire, the practical ability to go on holidays stayed largely out of reach for the majority of workers before the Second World War. It was not until the 1950s that what has been called mass tourism began to take hold when a series of factors, including the growth in car ownership, came into play. We will examine how the evolution of holidaymaking played a role in the change in perception of the automobile. The object of desire became an object of desired mundanity, and, later, it came to fit into an expanded epistemological system, as has been theorized by Baudrillard and Urry.[10] The fetishized car as commodity continued to be desired but as a commodified mundanity. The properties associated with the automobile in the pre-war era were replaced by those of a social need as the car became more commonplace.

Holidaying Distinction

The advent of *congés payés*, as paid holidays are called in France, in 1936 allowed all workers two weeks of paid holidays during the summer each year. The trend of escape from the urban space and the discovery of the beaches of the Riviera reflected a new desire on the part of the worker to indulge in the pleasures and leisure activities hitherto

9   Anderson, Susan C., and Bruce Tabb. 2002. *Water, Leisure and Culture: European Historical Perspectives*. Oxford: Berg, p. 224. See also Pompl, Wilhelm, and Patrick Lavery. 1993. *Tourism in Europe: Structures and Developments*. Wallingford: Cab International, p. 211.
10   Baudrillard, *Le Système des objets*; Urry, 'The "System" of Automobility,' p. 27.

perceived as the preserve of the wealthier classes. The post-war obsession with Saint-Tropez and its glamorous lifestyle was indicative of the evolution of this desire. In *La Distinction*, Pierre Bourdieu examines the need of certain classes to imitate others in an attempt to bridge the perceived gap between them.[11] The social group that Bourdieu and others have referred to as the new 'petite bourgeoisie'[12] was a significant segment of this holidaying trend. Bourdieu's portrait of an archetypal new petit bourgeois was a 29-year-old draughtsman in an engineering firm, married to a secretary.[13] This Bordelian 'need' to emulate the traditional upper classes on the Côte d'Azur mirrored how the automobile was beginning to be seen as part of a broader system of needs as the appeal of beach holidaying grew after 1945, a phenomenon characterized by Jean Baudrillard and explored in our Introduction.

Going on holiday became an expression of the capacity of the *petit bourgeois* and later the working classes to engage in the practices of the upper classes, as Rauch explains:

> While the holidays of the French masses are changing destinations and mentalities, they are often repeating inherited savoir-faire. Visiting places that have borne the dreams of past generations [...] is a must, that is 'to do' the Côte d'Azur, the English Promenade at Nice, the port of St. Tropez in [the] Var, the coves of Cassis near Marseille, etc.[14]

The automobile had previously facilitated escape from industrialized cities and enabled wealthy factory owners to run their industries yet still indulge in seaside holidays. As this process was observed by others lower down the social ladder, the car became a coveted commodity as its flexibility and usefulness became more understood. Initially, a commodity consumed by the wealthier classes, the car was transformed

---

11   Bourdieu, *La Distinction*, p. 8.
12   Defined by Crossick as 'the world of small retail, artisanal and manufac-turing enterprise.' Crossick, Geoffrey. 1994. 'Metaphors of the Middle: The Discovery of the Petite Bourgeoisie 1880–1914.' *Transactions of the Royal Historical Society* 4: 251–79 (p. 251).
13   Bourdieu, *La Distinction*, p. 387.
14   Rauch, André. 2002. 'Vacationing on France's Côte d'Azur, 1950–2000.' In *Water, Leisure and Culture: European Historical Perspectives*, edited by Susan C. Anderson and Bruce Tabb. Oxford: Berg, pp. 223–38 (p. 224).

into an attainable product as the working classes came to acquire the financial benefits of the Trente Glorieuses. Thus, it became viewed as a means of liberation, symbolizing the ability to imitate better-off members of society. It was an integral part of an era in which a broader range of social classes would come to acquire this symbol of opulence and modernity, and its possession would signify social progression.[15] Car ownership signified reaching a world of mobility hitherto the domain of the upper classes. The purchase of an automobile, and the associated ability to engage more easily in holiday tourism, enabled workers to experience pleasures previously unknown to them.

The desire to indulge in the leisure practices of the upper classes is reflected in Joffre Dumazedier's landmark 1962 examination of the evolution of French leisure, in which he critiques the inability of facilities in traditionally popular holiday resorts to accommodate the greater numbers travelling in the 1950s: 'We know the success of the Côte d'Azur. Saint-Tropez is a curious example: there are 360 hotel rooms and around 500 furnished rooms [to rent]; however, according to official figures, around 20,000 people come to spend their holidays there.'[16] These figures highlight the growing number of holiday-makers in these traditional resorts. However, the noted lack of facilities suggests an unsympathetic attitude to these masses of workers from an upper-class perspective. The refusal or inability adequately to cater for the arrival of such large numbers may suggest an unwillingness to accept this new form of tourism. André Rauch, in terms which echo Bourdieu, characterizes this growth in mass tourism as an attempt to imitate a privileged lifestyle, and one which the upper classes wanted to keep to themselves:

> Sun, sea, sand and crowds are most suitable for vacationers at the bottom of the social ladder; but this promiscuity is less appreciated by the well-to-do classes among whom the taste for

15 See Ross's discussion of French movie *La Belle Américaine*, in Ross, *Fast Cars, Clean Bodies*, p. 30. In this 1961 film, possession of an opulent American car is all that is necessary to accede to a higher class in society.

16 'On connaît le succès de la Côte d'Azur. Saint-Tropez en est un curieux exemple: on y compte 360 chambres d'hôtel et environ 500 chambres meublées; or, selon les chiffres officiels, 20 000 personnes environ viennent y passer leurs vacances.' Dumazedier, Joffre. 1972 [1962]. *Vers une civilisation du loisir?* Paris: Seuil, pp. 132–33.

solitude is considered a sign of distinction, especially when they are afraid of being around 'people who are not from the same background.'[17]

In consequence, the choice of destination as a sign of distinction played a crucial role in holidaymaking in early Trente Glorieuses France as the impact of the automobile became more apparent.

The automobile played different roles before and after the Second World War. As we have seen, the car was portrayed and perceived in a context that revealed it as a definer of social class. With their right to annual *congés payés* now a decade old, the working classes began to desire the car for its ability to provide freedom. The automobile took on a new image, one which signified liberty for the factory workers engaged in its construction in the huge Parisian factories owned by Citroën and Renault, amongst others. The French capital brought together many of the richest people in the country, who coexisted with those who worked in the city's factories. The latter's engagement in popular holidaying developed alongside the growth in the reliability and the accessibility of the motor car.[18] This was most obviously embodied in what has become known as 'Le tourisme bleu' – seaside vacationing – and the development of this form of holidaying rather than any other stemmed from a need for the Parisian population first and foremost to escape from the city. As Urry states in *The Tourist Gaze* (1990): 'Resorts were believed to be extraordinary because concentrated there were the sea, the sand, sometimes the sun, as well as the absence of the manufacturing industry that was present in almost all other substantial towns and cities.'[19] Holidaymaking came to be perceived as 'escaping' from everyday life and was promoted and desired accordingly. At a more fundamental level, the belief in the regenerative power of sun, sea and sand led to the development of a need for this characteristically modern form of escape.

---

17 'Soleil, mer, sable et foule conviennent le plus souvent aux vacanciers situés au bas de l'échelle sociale; cette promiscuité est en revanche moins appréciée des classes aisées où le goût de la solitude est tenu pour un signe de distinction, surtout lorsqu'elles redoutent de côtoyer "des gens qui ne sont pas du même milieu".' Rauch, *Vacances en France*, p. 149.
18 Rojek, Chris, Susan M. Shaw, and Anthony J. Veal. 2006. *A Handbook of Leisure Studies*. London: Palgrave Macmillan, p. 482.
19 Urry, John. 2002 [1990]. *The Tourist Gaze*. London: Sage, p. 32.

A growing interest in holidaying did not make itself felt statistically until the late 1940s and early 1950s. The mass tourism which ensued led to the creation of the perceived 'need' for a holiday. Jean Baudrillard's reading of the creation of need-value and also that of kitsch,[20] both of which he associates with consumer society, is that 'large layers of the population proceed along the social ladder, reach a higher status and at the same time the cultural demand, which is only the need to manifest this status by signs.'[21] The broad social need for holidays – and, more specifically, the need to go to the beach – was a motif that figured widely in the media in the Trente Glorieuses.

Tourism was highlighted particularly in French magazines with early accounts of Paris being abandoned to non-French tourists as its population headed for the beaches: 'In the streets of Paris, Parisians who leave Paris for the holidays feel like they are leaving a city empty. It's pure presumption on their part, because Paris is full. Tourism in Paris shows a significant increase compared to last year.'[22] This was echoed in *Paris Match* in August 1950: 'In Paris without Parisians.'[23] Holidays took up a lot of magazine space during the summer months of the 1950s and 1960s. On 4 July 1955, the front cover of *Elle* was adorned with a woman bathing in the sea with the caption reading, 'Have a great holiday!' ('Bonnes vacances!'). In August of the same year, a woman in a white dress walks along the beach, while the caption underneath has a quotation from designer Alice Chavanne: 'The tanned woman is in fashion!'[24] Spending time on the beach in order to get a tan is highlighted here as it shows how the image of the human body can reflect social status. More broadly, the steady growth in the popularity

20   Baudrillard refers to 'kitsch' as the equivalent of 'cliché' in Baudrillard, Jean. 1986 [1970]. *La Société de consommation: ses mythes, ses structures*. Paris: Gallimard, p. 165; Baudrillard, Jean. 1998. *The Consumer Society: Myths and Structures*. Translated by C.T. London: Sage, p. 109.

21   'de larges couches de la population procèdent le long de l'échelle sociale, accèdent à un statut supérieur et en même temps à la demande culturelle, qui n'est que la nécessité de manifester ce statut par des signes.' Baudrillard, *La Société de consommation*, p. 166; *The Consumer Society*, p. 109.

22   'Dans les rues de Paris, les Parisiens qui abandonnent Paris pour les vacances ont l'impression de laisser une ville vide. C'est pure présomption de leur part, car Paris est plein. Le tourisme à Paris accuse une augmentation importante par rapport à l'année dernière.' *Elle*, 15 July 1952, p. 13.

23   'A Paris sans Parisiens.' *Paris-Match*, 26 August 1950, p. 36.

24   'C'est la femme brune qui est à la mode!' *Elle*, 22 August 1955, cover.

of holidaying in the sun began to signify a social need to get away and avail oneself of the beneficial properties of the beach.[25] The importance of the sun rather than the sea is stressed by Urry, as he claims that: 'The ideal body has come to be viewed as one that is tanned.'[26] The physical benefits of seaside holidaying correspond to the notions of pleasure and the importance of the body advocated by 'the new petite bourgeoisie' as explored by Bourdieu. The physical emancipation of the body was of primordial importance in the quest for freedom, as it was important to 'substitute relaxation for tension, pleasure for effort, creativity and freedom for discipline, communication for solitude.'[27] What became mass tourism presented the opportunity for such physical expression, replacing work in an office with exercise and relaxation under the sun and in the sea; the tanned body represented a welcome contrast to Parisian life. The Côte d'Azur was the region in which such outlets primarily existed for the working classes. While the Normandy beaches were much closer geographically to Paris and many of the northern industrialized cities, the image and perception of wealth and decadence associated with resorts such as Cannes and Saint-Tropez meant that the tourist gaze moved south to these resorts throughout the Trente Glorieuses.[28]

The growth in popularity and accessibility of the automobile also led to an evolution in the way it was perceived. As the Trente Glorieuses progressed, the place of the automobile in working-class society evolved. While it remained an object of desire, a commodity to be acquired, it had evolved additionally into a Baudrillardian need, possession of which signified belonging to a more modern society. This crossover between desire and need has been highlighted by Leiss, who asks: 'Is it possible to draw a line of demarcation between needs

---

25   See also Andrieu, Bernard. 2007. 'Du teint hâlé honni au bronzage de rigueur.' *Cerveau et psycho* 22: 54–65; Rutsky, Robert L. 1999. 'Surfing the Other: Ideology on the Beach.' *Film Quarterly* 52 (4): 12–23; Rainis, Michel. 2000. 'French Beach Sports Culture in the Twentieth Century.' *The International Journal of the History of Sport* 17 (1): 144–58; Pinçon, Michel, and Monique Pinçon-Charlot. 1994. 'L'aristocratie et la bourgeoisie au bord de la mer: la dynamique urbaine de Deauville.' *Genèses* 16 (1): 69–93.
26   Urry, *The Tourist Gaze*, p. 38.
27   Bourdieu, *La Distinction*; Bourdieu, *La Distinction*, p. 426.
28   Vincendeau, Ginette. 2000. *Stars and Stardom in French Cinema*. London: Continuum, p. 102.

and wants?'[29] However they may be characterized, as houses were in the process of modernizing, the demand for consumer 'essentials' such as a fridge and later a television emerged and intensified. These items became inscribed as needs and were coveted in order to allow their possessors to engage in everyday life. Thus, a household needed these commodities to fit into the new culture of modernity and hygiene which, as Ross posits, became prevalent in the postcolonial era.[30] The automobile became essential in this expansion; although it remained an object of desire, this object can be seen to have evolved from a mysterious purveyor of power and prestige into a constituent part of the household. The car continued to be desired and fetishized. However, this was different to what had occurred before the Second World War or indeed during the early Trente Glorieuses.

Holidaying before the Second World War

Having the closest resorts to Paris, early seaside vacationing in France began in Normandy in the 19th century. The English upper classes, as the beneficiaries of an Industrial Revolution which took place first in England and then in continental Europe, took to vacationing before many of their European counterparts. This began on the south coast in resorts such as Brighton and Newhaven, but, in the 1820s, spread to the other side of the Channel, to the beaches of Normandy and, more particularly, to the resort towns of Dieppe, Cabourg, Trouville and Deauville.[31] The French upper classes also made these resorts their summer destination primarily for their proximity to Paris.[32] It was becoming easier to reach the sea from the capital, and the construction of the rail line to the region in 1848 meant that it was possible to reach Normandy's golden beaches within five hours. Hotels and particularly casinos began to spring up in these towns as the wealthy classes established their habits there. In the 1850s, the town of Trouville was the preferred holiday retreat of Napoléon III's court. It was his half-brother, the Duc de Morny, who identified the marshland across

29   Leiss, *The Limits to Satisfaction*, p. 61.
30   Ross, *Fast Cars, Clean Bodies*, p. 155.
31   Urry, *The Tourist Gaze*, p. 27; Bertho-Lavenir, *La Roue et le stylo*, p. 30.
32   Bertho-Lavenir, *La Roue et le stylo*, p. 169.

from Trouville as the perfect location for a new town specifically to serve increasing tourism to the area.[33] This new town, Deauville, was constructed with upper-class holidaymaking in mind.

The growth in popularity of the automobile among the wealthier classes in the early 20th century gave the so-called Côte Fleurie a new lease of life following the economic downturn which had occurred in the aftermath of the Franco-Prussian War.[34] With the advent of the automobile, members of the upper classes enjoyed further autonomy as their latest purchase duly made its way to the nearest *station balnéaire*, which was evolving to become the famous and glamorous resort of the day. In 1911, the Count Le Marois redeveloped the surroundings of the racecourse at Deauville-La Touques in the image of Longchamp.[35] Coco Chanel opened her second boutique in Deauville in 1913, and Printemps also opened its first shop outside of Paris there.[36] The resorts were places in which the wealthy wished to be seen, and a number of artists and writers also made this area their summer home. Marcel Proust was among them, being chauffeur-driven to Cabourg and spending every summer from 1907 to 1914 in the Grand Hôtel; he used the town as a model for the town 'Balbec' in his epic novel *À la recherche du temps perdu*.[37] André Citroën became emblematic of the type of wealthy Parisian who brought his family to stay in a rented villa and to stroll along the Promenade des Planches.[38] Thus, the perception of the town of Deauville is critical; Catherine Bertho-Lavenir refers to the importance of its image in the press and also, crucially, to its role as the standard-bearer for automobile-oriented tourism.[39]

Leisure activities were of particular importance to the upper classes. In consequence, these resorts incorporated the facilities to

---

33 Hébert, Didier. 2012. 'Deauville: création et développement urbain.' *In Situ. Revue des patrimoines* 6: 1–13 (p. 4).
34 Smith, 'La Place de l'automobile,' p. 2.
35 De Villiers, Marc. 1921. 'Comte Le Marois.' *Journal de la Société des Américanistes* 13 (1): 129–30 (p. 129).
36 Madsen, Axel. 2009. *Coco Chanel: A Biography*. London: Bloomsbury, p. 28.
37 Karlin, Daniel. 2007. *Proust's English*. Oxford: Oxford University Press, p. 122.
38 Aubenas, Sylvie, and Xavier Demange. 2007. *Elegance: The Séeberger Brothers and the Birth of Fashion Photography, 1909–1939*. San Francisco, CA: Chronicle, p. 35.
39 Bertho-Lavenir, *La Roue et le stylo*, p. 169.

host events that would amuse their clientele.[40] Horse racing was seen as the principal sport in the social calendar, and with the emergence of Deauville as a resort, horse races began to be held there. The Grand Prix de Deauville (originally called the Coupe de Deauville), a prestigious flat race first run in 1866, still exists today.[41] The nascent motor industry also invested in this area with the running of one of the first automobile trials from Paris to Trouville in 1897.[42] This race was a resounding success that attempted to exploit the established interest in equine sport and transfer it to the automobile as it was gaining currency as a means of transportation. The prominent journalist Pierre Giffard was even quoted as saying at the time: 'We are on the threshold of a century which will see man separate from the horse. This will be the end of a collaboration that has spanned thousands of years.'[43] The choice of route for the race was by no means arbitrary, as it showed the possibility to reach the sea outside the constraints of the train timetable. Motor racing was to remain popular in the region as Dieppe vied with Le Mans to host the first-ever motor racing Grand Prix and the inaugural Grand Prix Automobile de France.[44] Although unsuccessful in securing this pioneering race, Dieppe went on to host the following four Grands Prix de France in 1906, 1908 and then, after a three-year break, in 1911 and 1912.[45] A speed trial was held at Deauville in 1901 and again the following year, the success of which was lauded by the specialist newspaper *La Locomotion*:

> The Deauville kilometre, inaugurated in 1901 by *Auto-Vélo*, will take place on August 26, 1902 for the second time. This race, which was a great success last year, can be assured of no less this year. It enjoys, in fact, the favour of the public as well as

40   Huggins, Mike. 1994. 'Culture, Class and Respectability: Racing and the English Middle Classes in the Nineteenth Century.' *The International Journal of the History of Sport* 11 (1): 19–41 (p. 19).
41   Pinçon and Pinçon-Charlot, 'L'aristocratie et la bourgeoisie au bord de la mer,' p. 73.
42   Ribémon, Jean-Luc, and Ray Toombs. 2010. *Deauville 1936: un grand prix près des planches*. Mulsanne: ITF, p. 11.
43   'Nous voici au seuil d'un siècle qui verra l'homme se séparer du cheval. Ce sera la fin d'une collaboration vieille de plusieurs milliers d'années.' Pierre Giffard, qtd. in Studeny, *L'invention de la vitesse*, p. 339.
44   Bonté, Hurel, Ribémon and Bruère, *Le Mans*, p. 19.
45   Ribémon and Toombs, *Deauville 1936*, p. 3.

automobile constructors, for very simple reasons. Competitors do not have to pay much to take part in the event, many even go by road. On top of this, with the season in full swing on the pretty beaches of Trouville and Deauville, spectators are naturally very numerous there and are further increased by a good number of Parisians who take advantage of this opportunity to spend a day or two at the seaside.[46]

Three decades later, Deauville welcomed the Grand Prix de France in 1936, when the race was run in the streets of the town in an imitation of Monaco, where the first street race had taken place in 1929.[47]

The importance of leisure activities in the region was highlighted in 1933 by the *Michelin Guide*:

This elegant resort, which has grown dramatically in popularity, attracts the most aristocratic of the world. Its refined luxury, its choice entertainment, its races, its regattas, its polo and golf courses, its pigeon shooting rank it among the most popular resorts for the most select clientele. On the days of races and international tournaments, huge crowds gather there.[48]

Early tourism in Normandy was fuelled by the upper classes as they sought a form of *dépaysement* from Paris. Initially linked via train and later by car, the Côte Fleurie was the initial seaside destination of choice of the wealthier Parisian classes and remained so until advances

---

46 'Le kilomètre à Deauville, inauguré en 1901 par l'Auto-Vélo aura lieu le 26 août 1902 pour la deuxième fois. Cette course qui a remporté un grand succès l'année dernière, peut être assurée d'un non moins grand cette année. Elle jouit, en effet, de la faveur du public et des constructeurs, cela pour des raisons bien simples. Les concurrents n'ont pas grands frais à faire pour aller prendre part à l'épreuve, beaucoup même y vont par route. D'autre part, la saison battant son plein sur les coquettes plages de Trouville et de Deauville, les spectateurs y sont naturellement fort nombreux et sont encore augmentés de bon nombre de Parisiens qui profitent de cette occasion pour aller passer un jour ou deux au bord de la mer.' *La Locomotion*, 9 August 1902, p. 1.
47 Jacob, Jean-François. 1973. *Monte-Carlo: 60 ans de rallye*. Paris: Laffont, p. 66.
48 'Cette élégante station, dont la vogue s'est accrue avec éclat, attire à elle ce que le monde compte de plus aristocratique. Son luxe raffiné, ses distractions de choix, ses courses, ses régates, ses terrains de polo et de golf, son tir au pigeon la classent parmi les centres de séjour les plus appréciés de la clientèle la plus select. Aux jours de courses et de tournois internationaux, une affluence énorme s'y presse.' Michelin Guide, qtd. in Darmon, *La route autrefois*, p. 56.

in the road network and the car itself allowed for the possibility of reaching the Côte d'Azur with relative ease. The emergence of the Côte Fleurie as a tourist destination at the turn of the 20th century was closely linked to that of the car; this was evidenced by the number of automotive events staged in the area.

In the decades following the First World War, the first signs of a larger public taking an interest in holidaying were beginning to appear as part of a broader social evolution that would see the question of the everyday become a key theme in the 1930s.[49] There were indications that more widespread leisure time would be availed of by all citizens, as highlighted by Bertho-Lavenir: 'The 1930s represented a sharp acceleration in this regard. What the pioneers of 1900 dreamed of, their successors achieved on a large scale. And the spirit of 1936 is above all the highlighting of the profound changes that have affected the whole of society for several decades.'[50]

The belief spread that a certain amount of leisure time would not only increase productivity but give people a sense of worth and a sense of working towards a specific objective. In Italy, in 1925, Mussolini's Fascist state established the Opera Nazionale Dopolavoro (OND, the National Organization for Recreation).[51] This body was to 'see to the constitution and the operationalization of institutions capable of raising up skilled and manual workers physically, intellectually and morally during their free time.'[52] Leisure time was seen to be of benefit both to the previously mentioned petite bourgeoisie and the working classes. One section of the OND was dedicated to 'excursionism' and promoted tourism, increasing a feeling of belonging to Italy and encouraging patriotism. This initiative was mirrored in Nazi Germany

---

49   Sheringham, Michael. 2010. *Everyday Life: Theories and Practices from Surrealism to the Present*. Oxford: Oxford University Press, p. 121.
50   'Les années 1930 représentent une brusque accélération à cet égard. Ce que les pionniers de 1900 avaient rêvé, leurs successeurs le réalisent à grande échelle. Et l'esprit de 1936 est surtout la mise en évidence de changements profonds qui travaillent toute la société depuis plusieurs dizaines d'années.' Bertho-Lavenir, *La Roue et le stylo*, p. 343.
51   Boyer, Marc. 2007. *Le Tourisme de masse*. Paris: L'Harmattan, p. 145.
52   'veiller à la constitution et à la mise en service d'institutions capables d'élever physiquement, intellectuellement et moralement les travailleurs intellectuels et manuels pendant leurs heures de liberté.' Corbin, Alain. 1995. *L'avènement des loisirs: 1850–1960*. Paris: Aubier, p. 381.

in 1933, when Robert Ley created Kraft durch Freude ('Strength through Joy').[53] This new initiative was apparently decreed by Hitler:

> I want sufficient leave to be granted to the German worker and for everything to be done to ensure that this leave, as well as other leisure time, is a real relaxation for him. I wish it, because I want a people with strong nerves; because it is only with a people in control of their nerves that one can truly engage in great politics.[54]

Much like the OND, Kraft durch Freude aimed at providing fulfilling leisure time for citizens; its promotion of tourism also aimed at dissipating any rivalries that existed between regions in Germany at the time.[55]

Thus, workers in Europe were discovering that free time could be available not only to enrich their lives but also to discover their countries and engage in a form of tourism heretofore unknown to the working classes. The emergence of the Front Populaire in France was to prove the catalyst for the creation of paid holidays. However, its roots originated in a pan-European growth in interest in leisure time. *Les congés payés* have nostalgically been linked to the development of mass tourism. They have also been popularly associated with a growth in personal wealth and freedom. While they hold a certain amount of validity, these popular memories are largely overstated as increases in personal wealth among the working classes were not apparent until after the Second World War, but accompanied the reconstruction of France during the Trente Glorieuses.[56] However, the paid holiday law itself and its background are significant as they laid the foundation for the unprecedented democratization of automobile ownership in the 1950s and 1960s.

Paid holidays became law in France in June 1936, a month after the left-wing coalition of the Front Populaire, under the leadership of Léon

---

53 Robin, Régine. 1991. *Masses et culture de masse dans les années trente*. Paris: Ouvrières, p. 116.
54 'Je veux qu'un congé suffisant soit accordé au travailleur allemand et que tout soit fait pour que ce congé, de même que les autres temps de loisirs, soit pour lui une vraie détente. Je le souhaite, parce que je veux un peuple aux nerfs solides; car ce n'est qu'avec un peuple maître de ses nerfs que l'on peut vraiment faire de la grande politique.' Corbin, *L'avènement des loisirs*, p. 388.
55 Rauch, *Vacances en France*, p. 108.
56 Boyer, *Le Tourisme de masse*, p. 103.

Blum, came to power. The appointment of Léo Lagrange as a junior minister in charge of the Secrétariat d'État aux Loisirs demonstrated the Front Populaire's commitment to the promotion of this aspect of workers' lives. In the creation of this department, the government showed that it was interested in 'improving both the moral and physical health of the population at large.'[57] This was to be achieved by affording workers the time, and the means, to leave the city and spend time in healthy activities such as cycling or hiking. Reduced rates for Sunday trips on the national railway network and the two-week paid holiday decree were signed into law by the Front Populaire government on 11 June 1936.[58] Anybody who had completed two years' continuous work was entitled to these holidays with one condition: holidays had to be taken during the summer months.[59] This allowed for children to be taken on holidays and thus promoted the family unit. The creation of paid holidays was accompanied by reductions in the price of a train ticket to be used during the summer period, which promoted the positive use of free time.[60]

While 1936 remains symbolic for the creation of free time for French citizens, it would be untrue to say that all eligible citizens seized this opportunity immediately. Generally seen and commemorated as the beginning of mass tourism, the numbers travelling during the summer period remained broadly the same as previous years, paid holidays and train ticket reductions notwithstanding.[61] The reality of the situation was that the working classes simply could not afford to indulge in tourism during the early years of paid holidays; instead, they used the time to carry out necessary house repairs, while some even worked clandestinely in order to boost their salaries.[62] Thus, the inauguration of paid holidays in 1936 was essentially a symbolic gesture. Many workers viewed it with suspicion and even fear that there might no longer be a job for them when they returned to work. As Rauch puts it, 'It is also true that in public opinion a liberal conception remained

---

57   Kelly, Michael. 2001. 'Holidays.' In *French Culture and Society: The Essentials.* London: Arnold, p. 125.
58   Mom, *Atlantic Automobilism*, p. 339.
59   Corbin, *L'avènement des loisirs*, p. 375.
60   Corbin, *L'avènement des loisirs*, p. 375; Boyer, *Le Tourisme de masse*, p. 116.
61   Rauch, *Vacances en France*, p. 100.
62   Corbin, *L'avènement des loisirs*, p. 375.

latent: tourism, luxury consumption, is situated, by definition, outside any intervention. In working-class circles in 1936, "no one can believe that we are going to be paid for doing nothing".[63] The ability to leave on holiday remained an unfulfilled desire in interwar France as workers continued to fantasize about escape rather than actually experience it.

The effects of the introduction of *congés payés* were not seen until a number of years after the Second World War. The war delayed any increase in holidaymaking until the 1950s, when the Trente Glorieuses and the growth they brought introduced the possibility for the working classes to benefit sufficiently from the economic expansion in the country in order to go on holiday. Two million people did so in 1947. This figure rose to 8 million in 1951, and by 1966, 20 million French people were going on holiday.[64] The emphasis of these first holidays was on the outdoors, on mountain hiking and most notably on the sea. Caravanning and camping became very popular as a cost-effective way of spending time away from home. In order to understand the full impact of these later changes in mass automobility, it is necessary to develop our understanding of the period from 1918 to 1939.

Personal automobility typically remained accessible during the interwar period, mainly to the upper classes, as the lower classes were still unable to afford a car. Private car production rose from 41,000 in 1921 to 212,000 in 1929,[65] while the number of inhabitants per motor vehicle was slashed from 318 in 1913 to 28.5 in 1930 and dropped to 18.5 inhabitants per motor vehicle in 1938.[66] Interest in acquiring an automobile grew during this period with the introduction of a number of cars aimed at a wider market than many of the luxury vehicles produced before the First World War. As we have seen, André Citroën's productions, perhaps more than those of any other company, targeted mass ownership as he adopted many of the marketing techniques and strategies developed by Henry Ford. This growing widespread interest

63 'Il est vrai par ailleurs que dans l'opinion une conception libérale reste latente: le tourisme, consommation de luxe, se situe, par définition, hors de toute intervention: dans les milieux ouvriers en 1936, "personne ne peut croire que l'on va être payé à ne rien faire".' Rauch, *Vacances en France*, p. 99.
64 Kelly, *French Culture and Society*, p. 125.
65 Laux, James Michael. 1992. *The European Automobile Industry*. New York: Maxwell Macmillan, p. 74.
66 Laux, *The European Automobile Industry*, p. 130.

was also encouraged by political regimes of the time in an attempt to foster greater self-worth and to encourage national unity.

The growing interest in smaller, more affordable cars originated in Fascist social policy. In 1933, Hitler gave the order to Ferdinand Porsche to create a 'people's car,' a *Volks-wagen*.[67] The original requirements were that it be capable of carrying two adults and three children at a top speed of 100 km/h.[68] This vehicle was to be made available to citizens of the Third Reich through a savings scheme, which was not only intended to make the car affordable, but also to give the working class something to which it could aspire.[69] Originally called the KDF-wagen, an indication that the aims of the Kraft durch Freude movement extended to the mass automobilization of the German people, the Beetle did not go into production before the outbreak of war, and its factories were soon redirected towards military vehicles. The idea of the people's car did not go unnoticed in France. Smaller firms decided to take a chance on this concept and began designing cars that would be both affordable and practical for a wider consumer base.[70] Here, too, the advent of the Second World War meant that plans to produce and commercialize an inexpensive car were postponed, and thus the growing demand for a more affordable car was not met until after 1945.

Nevertheless, the first significant French attempt to build a people's car was made before the Second World War in the Quai de Javel factory. The Citroën company, having been bought by Michelin in 1935, was placed under the control of Pierre Boulanger, who immediately launched 'projet TPV' (*toute petite voiture*, the 'Very Small Car Project'). Boulanger had specific demands: 'carry a basket of eggs through a tilled field without breaking them.'[71] This criterion, as Forsdick states, reflects the utilitarian expectations of the Citroën 2CV.[72]

---

67   Gunthert, André. 1987. 'La Voiture du peuple des seigneurs: naissance de la volkswagen.' *Vingtieme siecle. Revue d'histoire*: 29–42 (p. 36).
68   Stein, Ralph. 1964. *Automobile*. Paris: Flammarion, p. 185.
69   Cadène, *L'automobile*, p. 240.
70   Cadène, *L'automobile*, p. 241.
71   'transporter à travers un champ labouré un panier d'œufs sans les casser.' Pierre Boulanger, qtd. in Forsdick, Charles. 2005. *Travel in Twentieth-Century French and Francophone Cultures: The Persistence of Diversity*. Oxford: Oxford University Press, p. 112.
72   Forsdick, *Travel in Twentieth-Century French and Francophone Cultures*, p. 112.

Work began on this TPV, and 250 examples of the 2CV were built and delivered to be exhibited at the 1939 Salon de l'Automobile. But the Salon never took place due to the war, and the cars were quickly taken apart and returned to the Quai de Javel factory. It was not until after the hostilities ended that the 2CV was eventually placed on the market. There was a three-year waiting time to acquire one, as the low-budget, mass production market saw the greatest development in the post-war era.

The conception and design of the Volkswagen and the 2CV in Germany and France may be seen as examples of efforts both political and social to strengthen the mobility of the lower classes. While neither car went into production before the war, the decision to invest in their development was indicative of the growing wish to possess an automobile. The massive success of the Beetle and the 2CV, and then of the Renault 4CV, and the Fiat 500 in Italy, in the 1950s and 1960s, was a reflection and a vindication of this aspiration.

Early Post-War Automobility

The Second World War was, in fact, a decisive break in the history of the invention of free time and in that of the modalities of mass leisure. In the mid-1950s, the 'summer revolution' won out over the militant dream of workers' regeneration through paid holidays. The emergence of the methods of leisure professionals ensured the victory of collective leisure, certainly organized and even subtly disciplined – you only have to think of holiday clubs – but totally subject to the quest for profit and openly designed according to individual desires for a change of scenery and free physical activity.[73]

---

73 'La Seconde Guerre mondiale constitue, en effet, une coupure décisive dans l'histoire de l'invention du temps libre et dans celle des modalités du loisir de masse. Au milieu des années cinquante, la "révolution estivale" l'emporte sur le rêve militant d'une régénération ouvrière par les congés payés. L'irruption des méthodes des professionnels du loisir assure la victoire du loisir collectif, certes organisé voire subtilement discipliné – il n'est que de songer aux clubs de vacances – mais totalement soumis à la quête du profit et ouvertement dessiné en fonction des désirs individuels de dépaysement et de libre activité corporelle.' Corbin, *L'avènement des loisirs*, p. 375.

As part of national reconstruction after 1945, which focused on infrastructure and, more specifically, housing, the French government was also aware of the critical new role the automobile was to play. The Plan d'Équipement National or ten-year plan and the Tranche de Démarrage (a shorter plan), both drafted by the Vichy administration, were used by the provisional government as they designed their own programme for economic expansion.[74] In the late 1940s, the government nationalized the coal, gas and electricity industries in an effort to strengthen post-war productivity.[75] While nationalizations took place for both economic and punitive reasons (companies accused of collaboration, for example), the acquisition of the Renault company, in 1945, was effected for economic reasons as much as any other.[76] The increasing importance of the automobile and, more specifically, Renault's 4CV, which was to rival the 2CV in popularity, meant that the automobile industry was of strategic importance to the state. Charles de Gaulle, as President of the Republic, was significant in this new stance, as he made a number of public appearances in which he was seen to support the French automobile industry. The promotion of the automobile was, perhaps for the first time, perceived as an avenue for growth as the car became a constituent part of the Trente Glorieuses, with production growing from 2,000 vehicles in 1945 to 357,000 in 1951; this progression was to peak at 3,596,000 in 1973.[77]

Having been accused of collaboration, Renault was nationalized in 1945 and became the Régie Renault.[78] This gave the state a more important role in the automobile industry, and consequently a greater incentive to relaunch its activity. The number of cars on French roads had dropped significantly as many automobile factories had been

---

74   Kuisel, Richard F. 1983. *Capitalism and the State in Modern France: Renovation and Economic Management in the Twentieth Century.* Cambridge: Cambridge University Press, p. 147.
75   Bliss, Brian. 1954. 'Nationalisation in France and Great Britain of the Electricity Supply Industry.' *The International and Comparative Law Quarterly* 3 (2): 277–90 (p. 278).
76   Frerejean, Alain. 1998. *André Citroën, Louis Renault: un duel sans merci.* Paris: Albin Michel, p. 298.
77   Laux, *The European Automobile Industry*, p. 178.
78   Loubet, Jean-Louis. 1990. 'Les Grands Constructeurs privés et la reconstruction. Citroën et Peugeot 1944–1951.' *Histoire, économie et société* 9 (3): 441–69 (p. 442).

converted to the wartime manufacturing of arms and were unable to recommence production immediately after the war.[79] Nevertheless, with the end of the conflict in 1945, a new interest was born in the automobile. This was illustrated within the post-war government, which made car manufacturing a strategic industry and thereby encouraged its development. In an attempt to maximize output and rebuild the automobile industry, the government decided that the largest automobile manufacturers would each focus on a different sector of the market. Renault was allotted the low-end market, Peugeot was assigned the mid-range sector and Citroën the upper-end or luxury market.[80] This division was at the heart of the Plan Pons. In this way, the government aimed to consolidate the existing automobile companies and relaunch what, prior to the war, had been a prosperous sector of the economy. By allotting a different sector to each company, the government envisaged higher production as each company would be producing fewer models. Theoretically, less competition between the companies would serve to promote overall production across the range of vehicles produced. This would provide the public with fewer choices but at least a minimum number of vehicles to ensure availability.[81] Named after Paul-Marie Pons, the deputy director of mechanical and electrical industry in the Ministère de la Production Industrielle, this state-managed approach was greeted with equal measures of welcome and hostility.[82]

By prioritizing the largest manufacturing companies and by recommending their absorption of smaller firms, the Plan Pons immediately sounded the death knell for many of the traditional family carmakers who were then struggling for their very existence. Amalgamation into a small number of super-companies consolidated these larger firms and strengthened their hold on their respective sectors of the industry. Peugeot, as the middle-range producer,

---

79   Fridenson, Patrick. 1989. 'La Question de la voiture populaire en France de 1930 à 1950.' *Culture technique* 19: 205–10 (p. 208).
80   Sabatès, Fabien. 1980a. *100 ans d'automobile: les coulisses du salon*. Neuilly-sur-Seine: L'Automobile, p. 89.
81   Barjot, Dominique. 1999. 'Introduction.' In 'La Reconstruction économique de l'Europe (1945–1953).' Special issue of *Histoire, économie et société* 18 (2): 227–43 (p. 242).
82   Bardou, Jean-Pierre, Jean-Jacques Chanaron, Patrick Fridenson, and James M. Laux. 1977. *La Révolution automobile*. Paris: Albin Michel, p. 194.

absorbed the enterprises of Saurer, Hotchkiss and Latil in a concerted effort by the government to make it as strong an entity as Renault and Citroën.[83] Citroën, as the receiver of the higher-range market, where it had almost no competition, was unhappy to have been so hamstrung by a government directive.[84] Seen traditionally as a Jewish company (André Citroën was the son of a Jewish diamond merchant), there may have been an anti-Semitic motive behind this decision; as Loubet suggests, claiming that this absorption was first proposed by the same department in 1942 under the Vichy regime.[85] Indeed, François Allain lends weight to this argument, positing that Paul-Marie Pons was fortunate to have the position of assistant director still, having been a member of the Pétainiste administration.[86] The decision to award the recently nationalized Régie Renault the low-end market was also met with opposition as this sector was increasingly seen as the area within which most growth was possible. While there was a certain need for a top-of-the-range car, the interest of the lower classes in the car, fuelled by the *congés payés*, suggested that the numbers looking for affordable cars would grow. Hence, when the Plan Pons was decreed, this directive to Citroën was met not only with hostility but with strong opposition. It was becoming clear that the sector in which there was going to be the most development in the post-war era was the economy sector. Citroën met with the ministry on a number of occasions to discuss the possibility of building a product that had already been researched for a number of years. The ministry eventually allowed Citroën to enter into direct competition with the Renault 4CV, which was seen by the government as the French answer to the Beetle.

In October 1946, General de Gaulle decided to open personally the Salon de l'Automobile in the Grand Palais.[87] This first post-war Salon, after a gap of seven years, was attended by 809,000 people compared with 440,000 visitors in 1938.[88] The French people, now led by their

83   Loubet, 'Les Grands Constructeurs privés et la reconstruction,' p. 444.
84   Loubet, Jean-Louis. 1999. 'L'industrie automobile française: un cas original?' *Histoire, économie et société* 18 (2): 419–33 (p. 426).
85   Loubet, 'Les Grands Constructeurs privés et la reconstruction,' p. 451.
86   Allain, François. 2002. *Citroën 2 CV*. Boulogne-Billancourt: ETAI, p. 15.
87   Rizet, Dominique. 1998. *100 ans de passion automobile: le salon de l'automobile, 1898–1998*. Paris: Mazarine, p. 71.
88   Loubet, *Histoire de l'automobile française*, p. 245.

wartime 'saviour,' were urged to forget the dark days of the war and to embrace a new future in which access to these vehicles and, hence, to all of France was being prioritized. At the 1946 Salon, the Renault 4CV was exhibited for the first time, as was the Dyna Panhard.[89] The harsh reality of a country in the aftermath of a war was disguised as much as possible, yet it could not be wholly avoided. While there were 671 exhibitors in 1946 as opposed to 526 in 1938,[90] the cars themselves were not available for purchase, and waiting lists ranging from 12 months to five years reflected the reduction of the nation's *parc automobile* from 800,000 vehicles in 1938 to less than a third of this figure in 1946.[91] Meanwhile, having received permission to produce its TPV, Citroën was encountering problems with the 2CV and failed to exhibit it in 1946. Consequently, the acronym TPV gained another meaning – 'toujours pas vue' ('still not here').[92] The 2CV was eventually exhibited at the 1948 Salon; however, the waiting list that grew for it meant that customers would be unable to benefit from its low price or well-publicized reliability until the 1950s.[93] Nonetheless, the decision taken in the 1930s to promote the development of such a car, a decision which coincided with the election of the Front Populaire, laid the foundation for vacationing in the years following the Second World War.

The two cars that defined the early period after the Second World War were the Renault 4CV and, particularly, the Citroën 2CV. These two cars, alike in terms of specifications and target buyers, according to Loubet, turned out to complement one another rather than actually to compete.[94] The 4CV became popular in cities, with the Deuch, as the 2CV was affectionately called, remaining in the countryside. Upon its first appearance at the Salon de l'Automobile in 1948 and in response to subsequent marketing from 1950, the Deuch was roundly criticized by motoring journalists. While they had accepted the similarly low-budget 4CV's launch in the immediate aftermath of the

---

89   Huchet, Isabelle. 1995. *50 ans à toute vitesse: l'automobile, les français et la société*. Paris: Hintzy Heymann, p. 8.
90   Loubet, *Histoire de l'automobile française*, p. 245.
91   Rizet, *100 ans de passion automobile*, p. 72.
92   Loubet, *Histoire de l'automobile française*, p. 245.
93   Loubet, *Histoire de l'automobile française*, p. 279.
94   Loubet, *Histoire de l'automobile française*, p. 254.

Figure 12 Citroën 2CV in French rural surroundings.
© Shawshots/Alamy Stock Photo.

war, they now deplored the cheap, minimalist image associated with the 2CV. This 'umbrella on four wheels'[95] initially had no radio, and no power steering, while the windows did not wind down but rather flipped out. In its earliest days, the 2CV had just one headlight; it was air-cooled and hence had no need for a radiator. It was equipped with a tiny two-horsepower engine that took 30 seconds to reach 60 km/h. For all of this, the Deuch boasted exceptional build quality, it was economical to run and it seemed never to break down. Because of these virtues, the Deuch quickly became an integral part of French lives. It was the incarnation of early mass motorization and, as such, was different from the vehicles which had been fetishized to date. Acquiring a 2CV was not seen as an indicator of class distinction, and it was not desired as such. Bertho-Lavenir suggests that the acquisition of a 2CV was, in fact, a choice of personal lifestyle, and while following the *route des vacances* in one was not recommended, in popular memory the role of this car in the expansion of Trente Glorieuses holiday-making remains undisputed.

95   'parapluie sur quatre roues' Wolgensinger, *La 2 CV*, p. 21.

The first car acquired by many families in the 1950s, the 2CV tended to remain in the family, so becoming its second car, and frequently the car that French youth inherited in the 1960s when more than one-third of the population was under 20.[96] Due to its simplicity, the Deuch rarely broke down, complicated parts were at a minimum and repairs, if necessary, were thus minor and relatively cheap. The 2CV entered society at a time when the level of car ownership was expanding. In 1938, one household in ten owned a car; by 1957, a quarter of all households possessed at least one automobile, and in 1968 some 69 per cent of households owned a car.[97] As the car that was bought by the masses, the 2CV has often been referred to as the Ford Model T of France.[98]

The early Trente Glorieuses saw the emergence of more economical cars as the four remaining large automobile companies sought to make advances into a previously untapped market. The 2CV, the 4CV and, to a lesser extent, the Panhard Dyna became the new popular vehicles.[99] In the process, the car came to be viewed and desired to fulfil the possibility of escape on holiday. Nevertheless, increasing automobile consumption remained linked to fetishization, as the car and motorized holidaymaking were desired as signs of distinction and thus a means of acceding to a higher social class. The distinction had been removed from the physical appearance of many cars, however, to be transposed onto another Marxian exchange-value, the ability to facilitate independence and, specifically, independent mobility. This transformation coincided with and helps to explain the rise of the Route Nationale 7, the road by which these new tourists travelled to the sea.

---

96 See Barthes, *Œuvres complètes*, pp. 1137–38.
97 Bardou, Chanaron, Fridenson and Laux, *La révolution automobile*, p. 224.
98 Forsdick, *Travel in Twentieth-Century French and Francophone Cultures*, p. 112.
99 Boltanski, Luc. 1975. 'Les Usages sociaux de l'automobile: concurrence pour l'espace et accidents.' *Actes de la recherche en sciences sociales* 1 (2): 25–49 (p. 36).

Direction Côte d'Azur

> I left Paris [...] Troubled by the emotion of our farewells, I went round in circles in the suburbs before heading out onto the Nationale Sept, happy to have in front of me this long ribbon of kilometres to allow me remember and to imagine.[100]

Discussed by Simone de Beauvoir, amongst others, the Route Nationale 7 has become a *lieu de mémoire* as it is popularly perceived as the site upon which the holidaying public made its way to the Côte d'Azur. However, the Nationale 6 was actually busier than its more illustrious counterpart during the summer months,[101] in a further example of how a site of memory may be invested with more nostalgic importance than it had at the time. Much like the popular perception of the 1936 inauguration of paid holidays, the Nationale 7 has become closely associated with the development of summer tourism until its replacement by the motorway network.[102]

The Trente Glorieuses, a period of unprecedented economic expansion, coincided with the beginning of a tradition of mass migration by the French during their holidays.[103] Reaching the Mediterranean, the ultimate symbol of freedom and opulence, was about to become a possibility. The Nationale 7 is the primary road that goes from Paris through Lyon and finishes in the Côte d'Azur town of Menton.[104] It is a road that originally dates back to Roman times, and that saw major development during the 1920s and 1930s, during which time La Route Bleue emerged to promote tourism along a road that was being increasingly used by bicycle, by coach and also by car.

---

100   'Je quittai Paris [...] Égarée par l'émotion des adieux, je tournai en rond dans les banlieues puis je filai sur la nationale sept, heureuse d'avoir devant moi ce long ruban de kilomètres pour me souvenir et pour imaginer.' Simone de Beauvoir, qtd. in Bertho-Lavenir, *La Roue et le stylo*, p. 366.
101   Dubois, Thierry. 2012. *L'automobile populaire.* Issy-les-Moulineaux: Le fil conducteur, p. 73.
102   Rioux, Jean-Pierre, and Jean-François Sirinelli. 1999. *La France, d'un siècle à l'autre.* Paris: Hachette, p. 349.
103   Seven million tourists in France in 1951 compared with 2 million in the period 1936–39. See Boyer, *Le Tourisme de masse*, p. 151.
104   Jacobs, Peter, Erwin De Decker, and Isabelle Vanmaldeghem. 2009. *Nationale 7: la route des vacances. Le guide pour flâner de Paris à Menton.* Paris: Hachette, p. 28.

This growth in use for pleasure purposes resulted in the establishment of tourist-based industries along the route. Garages, filling stations, post offices, hotels and restaurants appeared along the Route Bleue, all hoping to make the most of this new culture of movement. The Nationale 7 was the fastest way from Paris to the Mediterranean and was among the first roads to be repaired in the wake of the war.

Places such as Cannes, Nice and Saint-Tropez became the primary holiday destinations. These resorts formed part of the broader social construction of a dream of tourism, as Urry puts it:

> Places are chosen to be gazed upon because there is an antici-pation, especially through daydreaming and fantasy, of intense pleasures, either on a different scale or involving different senses from those customarily encountered. Such anticipation is constructed and sustained through a variety of non-tourist practices, such as film, TV, literature, magazines, records and videos, which construct and reinforce that gaze.[105]

The regular representations of the Mediterranean in magazines during the Trente Glorieuses was instrumental in this construction. To the Paris-based press, mass tourism was, in effect, Parisian tourism. It was the Parisian worker's attempts to find an escape in his or her time off. As such, tourism was essentially the discovery of the south by Parisian workers, first and foremost, and cultural references to holidaymaking had Paris as their starting point.

Nineteen fifty, the year of the first Salon du Tourisme, was also the year in which special funding was approved for the redevelopment of the French road network.[106] This move prioritized automobile travel over rail as the primary means of reaching holiday destinations. Hence, the Nationale 7 was redeveloped and, once this more comprehensive set of roadworks was completed, the Trente Glorieuses expansion led to the building of a network of motorways leading from Paris to different destinations throughout France. In 1970, the Paris–Nice motorway was officially opened, and the Nationale 7 was no longer necessary for tourists to reach the Mediterranean. The relative anonymity of the motorway meant that the symbolic nature of the Nationale 7, although

---

105   Urry, *The Tourist Gaze*, p. 6.
106   Lefebvre, Véronique. 2001. *Paris–Rhin–Rhône: histoires d'autoroutes*. Paris: Le Cherche Midi, p. 7.

no longer the main route south, remained intact.[107] The Nationale 7 as a site of memory persists as the means by which the travelling masses of the 1950s and 1960s liberated themselves from the city to reach their goal: 'the beach, bathing, partying and sociability.'[108]

The role of the automobile in the development of mass holidaying was closely linked to the nostalgic image of the Nationale 7 as it came to symbolize a means of escape from the urban environment to the sea. This link was strengthened as the car began to figure more regularly in contemporary popular in a close association with the summer holidays. Print media carried advertisements highlighting the strong relationship between the two; they also made use of the image of the car during the summer months as it came to define individual mobility. The Nationale 7 consequently became a *lieu de mémoire* celebrated in songs and magazines as the automobile gained impetus in the late 1940s and 1950s.

When Charles Trenet released what would become one of his most famous songs, 'Nationale 7,' in 1956, the government was in the process of increasing the *congés payés* by a week to three weeks. France had overcome the post-war rationing of the late forties, a period during which this continuing hardship had also seen a growing interest in a more modern nation.[109] Holidaying itself was becoming emblematic of what was perceived to be authentic modernity. Urry posits that 'To be a tourist is one of the characteristics of the "modern" experience. Not to "go away" is like not possessing a car or a nice house. It is a marker of status in modern societies and is also thought to be necessary to health.'[110] The baby boom was another indicator of growing public confidence that one could enjoy the comforts that had been promised and were now gradually becoming available.[111] In visiting the Salon de l'Automobile in the immediate aftermath of the war, General de Gaulle was also seen to promote self-improvement and self-modernizing. The growing interest in holidaying and individual mobility tapped into this

107   Jacobs, De Decker and Vanmaldeghem, *Nationale 7*, p. 30.
108   Anderson and Tabb, *Water, Leisure and Culture*, p. 223.
109   Boyer, *Le Tourisme de masse*, p. 152.
110   Urry, *The Tourist Gaze*, p. 4.
111   Neupert, Richard John. 2002. *A History of the French New Wave Cinema*. Madison, WI: University of Wisconsin Press, p. 6; Furlough, Ellen. 1998. 'Making Mass Vacations: Tourism and Consumer Culture in France, 1930s to 1970s.' *Comparative Studies in Society and History* 40 (2): 247–86 (p. 272).

broader mood and was reflected in popular culture, particularly the magazines of the early Trente Glorieuses.

Trenet is possibly best known for his song 'La Mer,' which he penned in 1943 and which was translated into English as 'Beyond the Sea' for Bobby Darin. Trenet reputedly wrote 'La Mer' in ten minutes on the train from Paris to the town of his birth, Narbonne.[112] It speaks of the beauty of the sea to which he is travelling as it symbolizes for him a whole vision of the south of France. The sea is once again referred to in 'Nationale 7,' which similarly alludes to the journey from Paris to the Mediterranean. The two songs also mention 'un ciel d'été' and are both firmly rooted in the summer months when holidaymakers can make the most of the weather and other pleasures that the seaside offers. It is interesting, however, to see the evolution in both Trenet's and French society's approach to the sea and the south of France through these two songs.

While 'La Mer' can be seen as an ode to the beauty of the sea under the summer sun, 'Nationale 7' refers instead to the possibility of making the most of the sea and the summer weather. The sea is no longer a far-off place about which people can only dream. In 'Nationale 7,' the sea is the destination, it is the goal of holidaymakers and it is this road that makes it attainable. Trenet refers to seaside resorts that can be reached by taking this road but, more importantly, he describes the evolution that has taken place as a result of the democratization of automobility. The 'route des vacances' has had the effect of transforming Paris into a 'Faubourg of Valence' and a 'Banlieue of Saint-Paul de Vence.' By referring to Paris as a *faubourg*, traditionally an industrial suburb of a city, and a *banlieue*, Trenet, far from removing the centralist bias that is associated with the capital, reinforces it. In essence, he underlines the fact that without a Paris, there would be no Nationale 7, and that the wish to engage in tourism would no longer exist. In fact, Paris has been left behind only temporarily, and all eyes are on the 'ciel d'été,' which can 'fill our hearts' and 'chase away the bitterness of life in the big city,' at least for a while.

In a 1959 video associated with this song, a tanned Trenet, wearing only a swimsuit, idly fixes a sail on his yacht. He is the epitome of joyful insouciance, something which, it appears, can only be accessed by distancing oneself from the working world and the 'malheur' associated

---

112 Darmon, *La route autrefois*, p. 50.

with living in a large city. While lounging on a yacht is an upper-class activity, the lyrics of this song constitute an ode to mass tourism rather than that practised by an elite few. In the opening lines, as Trenet describes the Nationale 7 as the road that leads to the Mediterranean, he states that one can get there by driving or by hitchhiking, and he later evokes the image of the entire family climbing into one vehicle, 'que l'on soit deux trois quatre cinq six ou sept.' The Nationale 7, the 'route des vacances' is the means by which workers in France's capital can now avail themselves of the beauty of the sea spoken of in such dreamy terms by Trenet in his earlier hit. It echoes the nostalgic Popular Front mood, which, as previously noted, created a rose-tinted view of the early days of the *congés payés*. 'Nationale 7' reflects a historical moment when workers demonstrated the will for the freedom to enjoy themselves and forget the routine of city life and work. The French word *dépaysement* describes this need; coming from the word 'pays,' it describes the changing of scenery, getting away from what one is used to in order to make a total break from the everyday routine. In his song 'Nationale 7,' Trenet alludes to the places crossed by holidaymakers in their quest for *dépaysement*. This *dépaysement* is explored by Urry when he states that 'Tourism results from a basic binary division between the ordinary/everyday and the extraordinary. Tourist experiences involve some aspect or element which induces pleasurable experiences which are, by comparison with the everyday, out of the ordinary.'[113] By extension, those who are unable to escape the constraints of their workaday existence are deemed to fall short in the expression of their underlying humanity. Corbin thus refers to holidaymaking as a social norm and a mark or sign of civilization: 'Today leisure is the foundation of a new morality of happiness. Whoever does not or cannot take advantage of free time is no longer quite a man, he is an "underdeveloped" man, an intermediary between man and beast of burden.'[114] As a sign of civilization, the act of going on holiday can be compared to the Baudrillardian need to possess an automobile or other commodity as outlined in *Le Système des objets*.[115]

113   Urry, *The Tourist Gaze*, p. 11.
114   'Aujourd'hui le loisir fonde une nouvelle morale du bonheur. Celui qui ne profite pas ou ne sait pas profiter du temps libre n'est plus tout à fait un homme, c'est un homme "sous-développé," intermédiaire entre l'homme et la bête de somme.' Corbin, *L'avènement des loisirs*, p. 388.
115   Baudrillard, *Le Système des objets*, p. 165.

This socially created 'need' occurred as the car became increasingly visible in popular cultural representations.

The Nationale 7 led to the Côte d'Azur and, more specifically, to tourist destinations such as Saint-Tropez, Nice and Cannes, which had long been associated with a more affluent milieu. The expansion in mass tourism resulted in the facilities at these resorts becoming saturated and additionally in the loss of their allure for wealthier tourists. The appeal of the resorts was also the result of film and music stars who made these towns their summer homes and were happy to be shot by the growing photo media indulging in the pleasures that the *côte* had to offer. These images appeared in popular magazines, and tourists travelled there in the hope of enjoying such activities.[116] This uneasy mixture of stars and their followers led to a clear hierarchy in resorts, as the elite hoped to maintain a certain distance from 'ordinary' holidaymakers. Saint-Tropez became synonymous with such an image, with Brigitte Bardot and Roger Vadim particularly adding to the allure of the port town. It was his film *Et Dieu créa … la femme*[117] that launched not only the career of Bardot as sex kitten but also that of the seaside resort as a primary destination on the Côte d'Azur. In this film, released in 1956, we see Bardot living in the town, which had become a haven for the rich and trendy. It shows the development of a village into a tourist destination, with Saint-Tropez itself becoming much like the town portrayed on screen. In the aftermath of the film's release, the resort welcomed an influx of visitors intent on catching glimpses of its more prestigious visitors and, perhaps, indulging in the hedonistic activities enjoyed by Bardot on screen.[118] This growth in tourism was parodied by the cartoonist Sempé in *Sauve qui peut*, where we see the employees of a small town's tourist office sending a letter to Bardot and Françoise Sagan in which they state that all travel expenses and hotel rooms will be paid for, should they wish to visit.[119] Following the film's success, Bardot became a worldwide star and was sold as France's answer to Marilyn Monroe. As Simone de Beauvoir

116 Brigitte Bardot was regularly photographed at her Saint-Tropez holiday home, La Madrague, as she cultivated an image of her need to return to nature. See Vincendeau, *Stars and Stardom in French Cinema*, p. 100.
117 Vadim, Roger, dir. 1956. *Et Dieu … créa la femme*. France, Cocinor.
118 Jacobs, De Decker and Vanmaldeghem, *Nationale 7*, p. 176.
119 Sempé, Jean-Jacques. 1964. *Sauve qui peut*. Paris: Denoël.

stated in a 1956 article for *Esquire* magazine: 'BB is now considered to be as important an export product as Renault automobiles. She is the new idol of American youth.'[120]

Et Dieu ... créa la femme confirmed Bardot as the foremost star of Saint-Tropez. This link was solidified with her subsequent purchase of La Madrague, a beach-front estate in the area, and was evoked subsequently by Renault in the marketing of the company's latest automobile. The Floride was launched in 1958 as a small rear-engined convertible. It was designed to target the wealthier tourists intent on heading to the beach resorts. It used the floor plan and engine of the Dauphine, itself the follow-up to Renault's hugely successful, but 'economy,' R4. This latest conception was designed with owner image as a primary concern. By updating an older, lighter car, the Floride was left woefully underpowered and, hence, referred to as 'a sheep in wolf's clothing' by the media in its early years.[121] This, however, was immaterial to Renault, as the aesthetics of the car were of more importance. This vehicle was intended to exploit the newfound interest in leisure in the country. In a commemorative brochure, Renault stated:

> At the end of the 1950s, France returns to the joy of living and prosperity. First presented as the 'Dauphine GT' at the 1958 Geneva Motor Show, the Floride appears in its final version on the Renault stand in Paris in October of the same year. She will perfectly embody this era of carefree cheerfulness.[122]

---

120 'BB est considérée à présent comme un produit d'exportation aussi important que les automobiles Renault. Elle est la nouvelle idôle de la jeunesse américaine.' Simone de Beauvoir, 'Brigitte Bardot et le syndrome de Lolita.' In *Les Écrits de Simone de Beauvoir*, edited by Claude Francis and Fernande Gontier. Paris: Gallimard, 1979, pp. 363–76 (p. 363) [originally published in *Esquire*, August 1959, pp. 32–38].

121 Ashmead, H. DeWayne. 'History and Articles: The History and Development of the Renault Caravelle.' http://renaultcaravelle.com/the-history-and-development-of-the-renault-caravelle/ [accessed 28 May 2009].

122 'A la fin des années 1950, la France renoue avec la joie de vivre et la prospérité. D'abord présentée comme "Dauphine GT" au Salon de Genève 1958, la Floride apparaît dans sa version définitive sur le stand Renault à Paris, en octobre de la même année. Elle va incarner à merveille cette ère d'insouciance et de gaieté.' Commemorative brochure, Renault. http://www.renault.com/passionsport/les-vehicules-historiques/pages/renault-floride.aspx [accessed 28 May 2009].

Figure 13 Exhibition celebrating the 50th birthday of the Renault Floride in the Renault Showroom on the Champs Elysées, Paris. © Éamon Ó Cofaigh (April 2009).

Initially designated a GT, for *grand tourisme*, Renault made the link with tourism even more explicit by rebranding the car as the Floride. The contextual irony of the timing of this brochure is striking as the 'era of carefree cheerfulness' referred to coincided with an intensification in hostilities in the Algerian War, which led to the collapse of the Fourth Republic.

Renault based its marketing campaign for its new Floride on Bardot and the image she embodied. In an iconic illustration of the time, Bardot posed as an elegant yet casually dressed young woman sitting barefoot on the boot of the Floride, feeding her dog against a backdrop of palm trees and deck chairs. The image is suggestive of the relaxed, leisurely and, above all, desirable atmosphere that Renault was trying to create. This was an aesthetically pleasing car, which gave the opportunity not only to relax but to look good while doing so. Another picture showed Bardot hanging out of the convertible, this time looking much more like the cheeky, seductive blonde in *Et Dieu … créa la femme*. The palm trees and deckchairs are replaced by the sea and what appears to be a summer house on its shore. The link between Bardot, the sea and the car was highlighted in this advertisement. The aim was to encourage the viewer to imagine Bardot looking beautiful and sensual and at ease in her Renault parked near the port that brought her much of her fame, Saint-Tropez. In its commemorative brochure, Renault confirmed the nature of the link with Bardot: 'Doesn't she have a choice godmother with Brigitte Bardot? Hair in the wind, tanned faces, the happy smiles of all those who drive the Floride along the paths to the sun and the great outdoors … The joy of escape behind the wheel of a young, shiny, refined car ….'[123] The rhetoric of the brochure attempted to emulate the carefree air associated with the sixties, during which time the Floride was marketed.

The name of the car is an indication of the intentions of its manufacturer. Renault was associating itself with the American ideal of travelling to the sun. Car dissemination at this time in the United States was far higher than in France; it was a market that Renault was interested in entering.[124] In naming their sleek convertible the 'Floride,' however, the company was also attempting to enhance an American trend growing in France, that of reaching the sun, sea, and sand through automotive transport.[125] In an advertisement published in 1961, Renault uses the name to underline this link with holidays. Entitled 'The holidays count double in a Floride [literally "in Florida"],'[126] a woman and a child are at the beach and the car is in the background with its top down. This wordplay with the name strengthens the association between the automobile and the seaside location of French summer holidays, while also reflecting the broader process of Americanization that characterized the evolution of popular culture in France in the post-war period.

Beyond its innovations in production and marketing, Renault was also pioneering in its commitment to the expansion of paid holidays;

123   'N'a-t-elle pas une marraine de choix avec Brigitte Bardot? Cheveux au vent, visages halés, sourires heureux de ceux qui prennent en Floride les chemins du soleil et du grand air … Joie de l'évasion au volant d'une voiture jeune, brillante, raffinée.' Commemorative brochure, Renault.
124   Loubet, 'L'industrie automobile française,' p. 430.
125   Renault was not the only company to choose names that invoked holidaying and free time. Simca brought out versions of their cars in the 1950s and 1960s which they called Week-End, Océane and Plein Ciel. Indeed, they gave a Week-End to Bardot as a present.
126   'Les Vacances comptent double en Floride.' *Elle*, 23 June 1961, p. 11.

the nationalized company granted their aforementioned extension by one week for its employees in 1955.[127] This was a full year before the government decided universally to extend paid holidays to three weeks. Renault was also ahead of its time when it approved a fourth week for its employees in 1965, a full four years before this benefit was extended to all workers.[128]

In an intriguing twist, the growth of beach vacationing and its link to the car were furthered by the advent of a revolutionary two-piece swimsuit which enabled women to obtain a better tan than was possible in a conventional one-piece. The bikini, as it is known today, was designed and marketed by a Paris-based Renault engineer who left the Billancourt factory in 1946 to take over his mother's lingerie shop.[129] His invention, consisting of four triangles made from only 30 square inches of fabric, was claimed to be the smallest swimsuit in the world. Louis Réard named his invention after Bikini Atoll in the Pacific, where nuclear testing was being carried out at the time. It was Réard's hope that reaction to his invention would be as atomic as the tests going on so far away but being heard of all over the world.[130]

The bikini was not launched on the Côte d'Azur, which Réard was targeting as its market, but in the Piscine Molitor in Paris; a decision that probably had much to do with logistics since Réard's boutique was in the capital. The Paris launch was also linked to the fact that many of those expected to go to the Mediterranean coast would do so from the French capital. The launch itself was threatened when Réard was unable to find a model willing to wear it. Eventually, he was forced to enlist the services of Michelle Bernardini, an exotic dancer from the Casino de Paris, to model the bikini for photographs.[131] While it would prove popular, the new swimsuit was rejected initially by some parts of fashionable society, with *Vogue* stating in 1951: 'Our readers dislike the bikini, which has transformed certain coastlines into the backstage of music halls and which does not embellish women.'[132] Its

127   Boyer, *Le Tourisme de masse*, p. 98.
128   Boyer, *Le Tourisme de masse*, p. 98.
129   Rutsky, 'Surfing the Other,' p. 19.
130   Rutsky, 'Surfing the Other,' p. 19.
131   Farrell, James J. 1987. 'The Crossroads of Bikini.' *Journal of American Culture* 10 (2): 55–66 (p. 55).
132   Quoted in 'From Boom to Bust: The Bikini is 60.' *Independent*, 24 June 2006.

gradual acceptance was helped by Brigitte Bardot in her defining role as the bikini-clad protagonist of *Et Dieu créa ... la femme*. Bardot, as an icon for the modern French woman, comfortable in her near-nudity, and willing to be part of a pleasure-seeking Mediterranean existence, modernized the image of holidaymaking youth. Seeking out the sea was not only about breaking out of the routine of *métro, boulot, dodo*; for French youth, the seaside became a place where the body was worshipped. It was a time when sun, sea and sex, and the development of a youth culture of holidays were together taking hold in the Mediterranean.[133] The popularity of the Côte d'Azur and its ability to influence the fashion of the time was underlined by *Elle* in 1950 with the statement, 'I saw beach fashion being born at Cannes.'[134]

It follows from the above that the capacity of the car to provide independent mobility was very desirable, particularly as its strong links with holidaying were highlighted in popular culture. The close association of Renault's marketing with holidaying was an example of the use of stars to promote the company's products. The linking of celebrities, their cars and holidays was already common during the early Trente Glorieuses, Renault's decision to employ Bardot as the face of their marketing campaign for the Floride being an explicit indication of the importance of this popular association. In the later 1960s, however, we see a dilution of this linkage as the importance of holidaying was maintained in magazines but the impact of its increasing numbers on the roads led to a questioning of the role of the car.

The increase in post-1945 holidaying ultimately led to an explosion of mass tourism and mass automobilization in late Trente Glorieuses France. The two phenomena were intertwined as one facilitated the other. It is ironic, however, that this mutual stimulation would increasingly be perceived in terms of its negative consequences. The expansion in car use, particularly for leisure purposes, meant greater competition for road space, thus limiting both mobility and speed, and in turn was regarded as a physical deceleration and a psychological disenchantment. As the Trente Glorieuses drew to a close and the baby boom generation came to criticize and finally to reject many aspects of modernity, the fact that the automobile had become an obstacle to, rather than a purveyor of, liberty figured largely in this discontent.

133   Furlough, 'Making Mass Vacations,' p. 276.
134   'A Cannes j'ai vu naître la mode de la plage.' *Elle*, 19 June 1950, p. 8.

Rauch broke down the holidaymaking habits of the French nation into four distinct periods. His third phase, the 'Tourisme de Masse (1950–1975),' in which city-dwelling workers become summertime tourists, invading seaside resorts all along the Mediterranean, does not begin until 1950, coinciding with the removal of fuel rationing in France.[135] This third period is the focus for an examination of the democratization of holidays for the typical worker. The euphoria experienced at the possibility of making an extended visit to an area that can often be quite far from home is discussed by Rauch.[136] Tourist destinations frequented by the rich evolved into destinations within reach of all and had consequently to cater for a new type of tourist. Thus began the newly intensive commodification of the tourist space. The ability to reduce unit costs while boosting profit margins by selling less to larger numbers, much like the philosophy of massification behind the development of the people's car, meant that what was once the exclusive reserve of the rich came to be considered a place for all. The *côte* was a destination where Parisian workers met during their summer holidays, and relaxed and participated in activities made available for this new market. Rauch highlights the importance of the influence of American consumer culture on French vacationing tastes: 'family budgets, market offers and the evolution of living conditions are bringing profound transformations in concepts and practices.'[137] These transformations and how they were accepted will be explored in detail over the next two chapters.

Conclusion

The democratization of tourism can be linked to a number of contributory factors. The rise to power of the Popular Front and the passing of the law granting two weeks of paid holiday to all workers has often been marked as the birth of holidaying *en masse*. The baby boom and the growth in wealth due to the Trente Glorieuses are also important

135   The four sections are: 'Nouvelles Distinctions: Santé et Loisir (1830–1918),' 'Les Années Folles et Les Congés Payés (1920–1950),' 'Les Vacances de Masse (1950–1975)' and 'Les Vacances de Crise (1975 à nos jours).' Rauch, *Vacances en France*, pp. 310–11.
136   Rauch, *Vacances en France*, pp. 129–56.
137   Rauch, 'Vacationing,' p. 223.

events to consider. The rise of people's cars also must be considered. The development first of the Beetle in Germany, to be followed by the Renault 4CV and, perhaps more importantly, the Citroën 2CV were watershed moments in the early stages of mass tourism.[138] The complementary process by means of which the mass production of automobiles led to their increasing availability to the industrial workforce resulted in a large increase in the numbers of people travelling to the Mediterranean to indulge in sea, sun and other forms of leisure.[139]

The Route Nationale 7 from Paris to Menton on the Côte d'Azur became closely associated with holidays and escape from the everyday routine. The practical implementation of paid holidays proved a watershed moment and *le grand départ* that marks the summer vacation and *la rentrée* at its end are etched into the public memory. In due course, this evolution would also see the end of the holiday association of the Nationale 7. In 1970, President Georges Pompidou officially opened the 'Autoroutes 6 et 7' motorways, thus marking the end of the Nationale 7 as the Route des Vacances and principal means of access to the Mediterranean by car.[140] This new motorway link, 'l'Autoroute du Soleil,' as it was officially called, greatly reduced the journey time from Paris to the Riviera. While it facilitated what remained essentially the same process, as an Augéan *non-lieu*[141] it has not been invested with the same meaning that is still nostalgically associated with the Nationale 7. The great history of one of the most iconic roads in France thus drew to a close. The Nationale 7 is now used mainly for local traffic between towns along the route south. However, it remains an iconic site, a name that resurfaces in public memory whenever the theme of holidaymaking is evoked.

138   Boyer, *Le Tourisme de masse*, p. 100.
139   Carsalade, Yves. 1998. *Les Grandes Etapes de l'histoire économique*. Paris: Ellipses, p. 288.
140   Lefebvre, *Paris–Rhin–Rhône*, p. 7. Georges Pompidou was seen as an autophile and was also popularly associated with an attempt to make Paris more conducive to car driving, however both of these ideas have been questioned. See: Archambeau, Olivier, and Romain J Garcier. 2001. *Une géographie de l'automobile*. Paris: Presses universitaires de France. Also Flonneau, Mathieu. 1999. 'Georges Pompidou président conducteur et la première crise urbaine de l'automobile.' *Vingtieme siecle. Revue d'histoire* 61: 30–43.
141   Viard refers to a motorways as a 'no man's land' which facilitates 'l'aller-retour' as trains do, as opposed to roads which permit 'rayonnement.' See Viard, Jean. 2007. *Penser les vacances*. La Tour-d'Aigues: L'Aube, p. 128.

Chapter 5

Three Ages of the Car in French Post-War Magazines

> Generally understood as one of the components of the written press media, the magazine press can also be studied as a specific medium. The importance of the visual, its periodicity and the imperative of creativity, the segmentation of the public and the reading contract, the internationalization and the weight of the groups constitute five of its dominant features which combine to make it a medium very much in tune with its time.[1]

Mentioned briefly in the context of tourism, the societal impact of French popular magazines in their interaction with the car will be examined more fully in this chapter. As suggested by the foregoing quotation from Charon, magazines are contemporary cultural artefacts that have to be closely in touch with their public. The abundant use of images in such publications is particularly interesting as a marker of the evolving perception of the automobile in post-1945 France. In order to trace this process, I examine three news magazines published over the Trente Glorieuses. These publications recorded the implied attitude of the French population as their spending power increased and as they

---

1   'Généralement appréhendée comme l'une des composantes du média presse écrite, la presse magazine peut aussi être étudiée comme un média spécifique. L'importance du visuel, sa périodicité et l'impératif de créativité, la segmentation du public et le contrat de lecture, l'internationalisation et le poids des groupes constituent cinq de ses traits dominants qui concourent à en faire un média en très grande adéquation avec son époque.' Charon, Jean-Marie. 1999. *La Presse magazine*. Paris: La Découverte, p. 124.

began to take advantage of the nation's economic prosperity. Gartman has argued that the perception of the automobile, particularly in the American context, can be understood in terms of three 'ages.' Using Bourdieu's theory of class distinction, he posits that the car shifted from being status symbols in the early part of the 20th century to become a symbol of mass culture. Gartman's final phase is a rejection of mass mobility with a move towards more specialized car brands.[2] These three ages are broadly replicated in the three overlapping periods of interaction with the automobile observed in the news magazines of the Trente Glorieuses. These move from continued fetishizing, with the car maintaining its aura of unattainability, through to a rapidly modernized society in which the automobile has been accepted and then has become needed. The third period occurs in the years immediately prior to the 1973 oil crisis and is defined by a growing rejection of the ubiquity, and the apparent indispensability, of the car.

The Selected Magazines

The weekly magazine *Paris Match*, founded in 1949, was originally news-focused while also making abundant space available for advertising. With a strongly photo-oriented style, *Paris Match* maintained its editorial policy until the civil unrest of May 1968 led it to push for a younger audience, one more interested in the emerging cult of the celebrity. *Paris Match* famously interviewed the gangster Jacques Mesrine in 1977[3] and President Valéry Giscard d'Estaing in 1979,[4] showing that while it now valorized celebrity, in line with an increasingly sensationalist French press, it still maintained the reputation to attract a more serious readership. In terms of its audience, the magazine was at its most successful in the late 1950s and early 1960s with its mixture of photo

2   Gartman, David. 2004. 'Three Ages of the Automobile: The Cultural Logics of The Car.' *Theory, Culture & Society* 21 (4–5): 169–95.
3   Jacques Mesrine was a glamourous criminal who was Public Enemy No. 1 for several years until his death in 1979. He published an autobiography in 1977 in which he claimed to have killed over 40 people. Mesrine, Jacques. 1977. *L'instinct de mort*. Paris: Lattès.
4   Valéry Giscard d'Estaing was a centrist politician and President of the French Republic from 1974 until 1981. The TGV was inaugurated during his presidency.

reporting, news items and showbiz news.[5] The advent of *Télé 7 Jours*, which grew with the mass acquisition of the television, spelled the end of the golden age of *Paris Match*. During its most successful period, it averaged sales of 1.5 million copies per issue, peaking in November 1955.[6] *Paris Match* lay at the heart of the Trente Glorieuses, and reflected the effects of the modernization of society as France became more prosperous.

Elle appeared for the first time on 21 November 1945. It was created by Hélène Lazareff,[7] with Françoise Giroud joining as editor from 1946 until 1953, when she left to set up *L'Express*. Ross calls Giroud 'one of the key figures behind the proliferation of women's magazines in the 1950s'[8] and describes the audience targeted by these two women: 'The reader envisioned by the staff at *Elle* was most likely young, between 25 and 35, tired of wartime deprivation, in need of frivolity, and she lived in Angoulême [i.e. a medium-sized provincial city].'[9] *Elle* quickly introduced regular slots intended to build a strong and loyal readership. In 1946, 'Le courrier du cœur' (the agony aunt column) and the horoscope appeared for the first time. In 1947, its readers were given the opportunity to win prizes, while 1948 saw the introduction of coupons. Initially dealing with perceived female interests, such as knitting patterns and cooking, *Elle* soon started to discuss broader social issues. Sex education was debated, as was premarital sex, divorce and religious education. In 1956, birth control was discussed. Highlighting modern values, *Elle* sold an image of female readers who were not happy simply to remain in the home, yet took the time to look after their appearance. While traditional in nature, the magazine tried to promote female emancipation. From its very beginning, *Elle* was extremely popular, selling 700,000 copies of its first edition. It broadly promoted a consumer-oriented and 'American' way of life: '*Elle* was to participate fully in the reconstruction of the country, to make a contribution to this exhilarating rebuilding by providing

5   Charon, *La Presse magazine*. p. 39.
6   Jamet, Michel. 1983. *La Presse périodique en France*. Paris: Colin, p. 140.
7   Hélène Lazareff was a journalist who, having spent the Second World War working in America for the *New York Times*, returned to France in 1945 intent on promoting American ideals in her homeland.
8   Ross, *Fast Cars, Clean Bodies*, p. 1.
9   Ross, *Fast Cars, Clean Bodies*, p. 1.

women – who, for the first time in history, had suffered as much from war as men – the long-awaited sunshine in order to rediscover the pleasures of consumption, seduction and frivolity.'[10]

The evolution of advertising in *Elle* is of particular interest for this study as it reveals how the automobile was – at least by implication – perceived among a group that was itself changing in status. The proliferation of articles on, and advertisements for, cars in *Elle* reflects the growing importance of the female driver; a trend that saw more attention paid to women as potential drivers and car owners. This new market, allied with the strong readership that the magazine was gaining, can shed light on the specifically feminine desire to buy a car. From 1945 to 1950, *Elle* sold an average of 110,000 copies weekly, more than tripling to 340,000 in the 1950s and levelling off at 500,000 in the 1960s, with some special issues selling more than 1 million copies.[11]

L'Express was conceived as a more obviously news-dominated magazine than *Paris Match*. Founded in 1953, its initial strength was its focus on decolonization, functioning as 'opinion journalism' (*journal d'opinion*) until its transformation into a more photograph-oriented news magazine along the lines of the American *Time* in September 1964. As previously noted, Françoise Giroud was editor of *Elle* from 1946 to 1953; she then joined forces with her lover, Jean-Jacques Servan-Schreiber, to create *L'Express*. Servan-Schreiber was as prominent a figure as Giroud and was particularly noted as a commentator on France's relationship with America, advocating 'a discriminating Americanization.'[12] He also commented incisively on French colonial issues; indeed, he was conscripted to serve in the Algerian War in 1956 and famously wrote a critical account of his experiences.[13] In its early years, *L'Express* adopted a progressive stance *vis-à-vis* the French colonies as it promoted their transformation into autonomous states and openly supported Pierre Mendès-France in his

10   '*Elle* devait participer pleinement à la reconstruction du pays, apporter sa pierre à cette œuvre exaltante en procurant aux femmes – qui, pour la première fois dans l'histoire de l'humanité, avaient autant souffert de la guerre que les hommes – le rayon de soleil tant attendu afin de redécouvrir les plaisirs de la consommation, de la séduction, de la frivolité.' Soulier, Vincent. 2008. *Presse féminine: la puissance frivole*. Paris: L'Archipel, p. 108.

11   Jamet, *La Presse périodique en France*, p. 61.

12   Ross, *Fast Cars, Clean Bodies*, p. 66.

13   Servan-Schreiber, Jean-Jacques. 1957. *Lieutenant en Algérie*. Paris: Julliard.

ultimately successful attempt to become prime minister.[14] In order to survive, the publication moved to a more centrist stance, adopting a news magazine style, divided into seven sections – 'France,' 'Monde,' 'Économie,' 'Vie Moderne,' 'Spectacles,' 'Livres,' 'Madame Express.' This change saw a growth in interest from companies looking for a more cost-effective way of advertising their products. The new version of *L'Express* combined increased readership with lower advertising charges than daily newspapers; as such, it became a very advertisement-oriented weekly. Weekly readership grew from 152,917 in 1964 to 261,823 in 1965 and 614,101 in 1972.[15]

These three magazines together exemplified a media form that was itself modernizing during the Trente Glorieuses. The development of colour photography on magazine covers and in inside articles added to their allure. With average weekly sales of 702,000 in 1952, which grew to 1.8 million copies in 1957, the expansion of news magazines at the time was due to a combination of technical and stylistic changes that made them both more attractive and more accessible.[16] The growth in news magazines was reflected in the increase in their share of the market for commercial advertising in comparison with the daily press. As weekly publications, magazines offered advertisements that were more cost-effective than those in daily newspapers; they were also of better quality in appearance. The fact that weekly periodicals were more nationally oriented than the Paris-based dailies also aided this increase.[17]

The distinctive nature and focus of the magazines meant that advertisements could also be better targeted than in the daily press. This progression appears to have reached its peak in 1968, when the fallout from the events of May–June of that year – perceived as a rejection of the consumer society by a segment of the French population – translated into a fall-off in weekly press advertisements, while daily advertisement rates remained steady.[18] The growth of news

14   Delporte, Christian. 2001. '*L'Express*, Mendès France et la modernité politique (1953–1955).' *Matériaux pour l'histoire de notre temps* 63 (1): 96–103 (p. 96).
15   Jamet, *La Presse périodique en France*, p. 72.
16   Feyel, Gilles. 2001. 'Naissance, constitution progressive et épanouissement d'un genre de presse aux limites floues: le magazine.' *Réseaux* 1: 19–51 (p. 40).
17   Feyel, 'Naissance, constitution progressive et épanouissement,' p. 44.
18   Charon, *La Presse magazine*, p. 12.

magazines up to 1968, together with the seeming slump in the political and literary press, as seen in the conversion of *L'Express* to a magazine format, appeared to mirror Trente Glorieuses society as it embraced an American style of consumerism in which commodities were assimilated into the fabric of everyday life. The malleability of news magazines allowed for changing trends and offered the possibility of covering all aspects of a rapidly shifting society that was also becoming more segmented.[19] Analysing the growing presence of the automobile in these three magazines from 1945 to 1973 provides a window on the evolution of perceptions of the car through articles dedicated to it and also advertisements selling it. The changing coverage of the Salon de l'Automobile provides a valuable site in which to gauge this evolution as the car gains importance in the general cultural consciousness.

Our examination of these three news magazines may conveniently be divided into three sections aligned with three key periods while acknowledging some chronological overlaps during what was a rapid process of modernization. As far as representations of the automobile are concerned, the immediate post-war period can be defined by its references to modernity and by the conception of the car in terms of grandeur and desirability. The second period, which covers the 1950s, is a transitional one during which the automobile and modernity in general are still fetishized as aspirational, yet there are also examples of the car becoming more accessible and more commonplace. This transitional period coincides with the extension of paid holidays and runs until near the end of the decade as the car becomes ubiquitous. The final period (1960–73) is one of acceptance and even rejection, in which the automobile has been converted from a commodity coveted for its social status to a Baudrillardian need. While the car was still not possessed by the majority of French households until a date between 1965 and 1970,[20] demand grew on average by 5 per cent every year until 1973.[21] However, by 1960, its image in contemporary magazines had already evolved substantially; this continuing shift was reflected in editorial coverage as well as in advertisements, together with cartoons, throughout the final decade of the Trente Glorieuses.

19   Feyel, 'Naissance, constitution progressive et épanouissement,' p. 46.
20   Chanaron, *L'industrie automobile*, p. 120.
21   Sauvy, Jean. 1984. *L'industrie automobile*. Paris: Presses universitaires de France, p. 93.

1945–50: An Object of Desire

As *Elle* began publication in the immediate aftermath of the Second World War, it was best positioned to examine French attitudes towards modernity as the country emerged from the conflict. With the suppression of *Marie-Claire* for collaboration after the Liberation (until its relaunch in 1954),[22] *Elle* was able to enter an established female market, its first issue appearing in November 1945.[23] Overtly aimed at a female readership, as its name suggests, *Elle* offered editorial content that combined the aspirational (skiing holidays, 5 December 1945) and the practical ('Tricotons' ('Let's knit'), 19 December 1945). The first reference to the automobile appeared on 28 January 1946, when a young woman modelling a knitted jumper embroidered with telephone numbers was depicted sitting at the steering wheel of a convertible. This fusion of two emblems of modernity, the telephone and the automobile, would become a familiar trope. In the very next edition, a 'scene from everyday life' ('scène de vie courante') depicts a woman and her need for a telephone: 'As the diver needs an air line to breathe underwater, the modern girl cannot live without a telephone. It is a truth of our time that is apparent all over the world: in Paris as in London and New York.'[24] Through its comparison to the diver's air line, albeit in an exotic setting, this commodity begins to be treated as a need. It is a comparison that is similarly afforded to the car in a later issue of *Elle*, as we see actress Josette Day announce: 'I drive like I breathe.'[25]

Elle portrayed itself as a liberating and progressive magazine intent on advancing the rights of women. With Françoise Giroud as editor, *Elle* 'was a powerful instrument of liberation in the service of women.'[26] Early issues combined allusions to modernity with advice on everything

---

22   It was relaunched in 1954. See Feyel, 'Naissance, constitution progressive et épanouissement,' p. 42.
23   Charon, *La Presse magazine*, p. 11.
24   'Comme le scaphandrier a besoin d'un tuyau d'air pur pour respirer sous l'eau, la jeune fille moderne ne peut vivre sans le téléphone. C'est une vérité de notre temps qui se vérifie sous toutes les latitudes: à Paris comme à Londres et à New York.' *Elle*, 30 January 1946, p. 8.
25   'Je conduis comme je respire.' *Elle*, 16 October 1950, p. 15.
26   'fut un puissant instrument de libération au service des femmes.' Soulier, *Presse féminine*, p. 111.

from fashion to fitness, all of which was explicitly targeted at *la femme moderne*. Such editorial content was often linked to depictions of the automobile, which was increasingly perceived as a desired commodity, and as such associated with female celebrities – and, indeed, with celebrities in general. Thus, much of the column space devoted to the car was accompanied by references to stars of the time, generally of stage or screen. This linkage between stars and the new brand of 'glossy' magazines has been highlighted by John Gaffney and Diana Holmes: 'At the simplest commercial level, star figures functioned to sell newspapers, magazines (such as the new postwar *Paris Match* and *Elle*), books, films and all kinds of other products that could play on the consumer's desire to acquire something of the star's aura.'[27] This was particularly true of the automobile. While the typical magazine story focused on the star, reference would also be made to the car the person drove, thus simultaneously increasing the desire-value of the vehicle and the prestige surrounding the star. This was a reciprocal exchange, one which was particularly prevalent in the late 1940s and early 1950s. For instance, in its edition of 7 May 1946, *Elle* highlighted the opulence of summer holidaymaking on the Côte d'Azur on the occasion of the 'The Grand Prix d'Élégance Automobile, in Nice, [which] was contested in front of a crowd which experts estimate at 50,000 people.'[28] The image of film star 'Martine Carroll, son chien et sa Packard' ('Martine Carroll, her dog and her Packard car') accompanies this article.[29] In such representations, the Côte d'Azur, while growing in popularity, remains the domain of the wealthy, as does the automobile. Through this triumvirate of privileged location, social distinction and sought-after possession, the magazine instilled in the French population a desire for pleasures that were still primarily restricted to the upper classes.

In these post-war magazines, representations of the automobile are generally accompanied by a star at the wheel; for instance, Tyrone

27   Gaffney, John, and Diana Holmes. 2007. 'Stardom in Theory and Context.' In *Stardom in France*, edited by John Gaffney and Diana Holmes. Oxford: Berghahn, pp. 7–25 (p. 8).

28   'Le grand prix d'élégance automobile, à Nice, a été disputé devant une foule que les compétences évaluent à cinquante mille personnes. Il faisait beau. Le ciel était bleu. La cohue joyeuse …' *Elle*, 7 May 1946, p. 4.

29   Martine Carroll was a prominent French cinema star during the late 1940s and early 1950s. Packard was an American luxury automobile marque which was merged with Studebaker in 1954.

Power is photographed giving an autograph to a fan while at the wheel of his white convertible.[30] Indeed, the close association of stars with particularly desirable cars, and especially convertibles, served further to fuel the attractiveness of both. Convertibles suggested holidaying in the sun; they also evoked an image of America and the American car, an association which Lazareff and Giroud at *Elle* were intent on promoting.[31] As the newest cars were launched at the Salon de l'Auto, this annual autumn event provided the perfect opportunity for rapidly expanding social engagement with the automobile. In late 1949, *Elle* highlighted the gender dimension of this evolving public interest while also suggesting the grandeur and opulence of the vehicles on display as post-war austerity came to an end:

> [F]or the first time since the war, anyone is free to buy any car presented [at the Salon], with the certainty of it being delivered within a reasonable time frame (it would seem). Women say, 'Have you seen the little fuchsia red Simca-6 with tartan lining like my coat? The Nile green Dyna-Panhard? The Cadillac make-up box?' Men say: 'Have you seen the telescopic steering wheel? The folding dashboard?' Everyone is mad for 'convertibles,' 'semi-convertibles' and 'sunroofs' (recommended for feathered hats).[32]

Clearly, the journalist's suggested distinction in approaches to car buying among men and women is both stereotypical and gendered, as women focus on colour and accessories, while men are attracted by mechanics. Convertibles are also recommended for women, as the author humorously suggests that they are ideal if you want to wear 'a feathered hat.' More broadly, the article highlights the most opulent and iconic of large American cars, the Cadillac, as an object of continuing fascination for

---

30   *Elle*, 3 October 1949, p. 7.
31   Ross, *Fast Cars, Clean Bodies*, p. 79.
32   'pour la première fois depuis la guerre, n'importe qui est libre d'acheter n'importe quelle voiture présentée, avec la certitude d'être livré dans des délais raisonnables (paraît-il). Les femmes disent: "Vous avez vu la petite Simca-6 rouge fuschia, doublée d'écossais comme mon manteau? La Dyna-Panhard vert nil? La boîte à maquillage de la Cadillac?" Les hommes disent: "Vous avez vu le volant télescopique? Le tableau de bord rabattable?" C'est la grande folie des "décapotables", des "découvrables" et des "toits ouvrants" (recommandées pour chapeaux à plumes).' *Elle*, 17 October 1949, p. 5.

the French public, not least because of its radical inaccessibility for the great majority of French people. The Cadillac will be further explored later when we examine the 1961 film *La Belle Américaine*, in which a working-class family's life is changed dramatically by its acquisition.

As the Salon came to be covered more regularly by *Elle*, the magazine took an increasing interest in the practicalities of driving for its female readership. In 1950, an article entitled '*Elle* et les voitures' studied the number of women who succeeded in obtaining a driver's licence, going on to examine the types of cars driven by women, and also to explain how, statistically, women were better drivers than men:

> 43,445 women did a driving test last year, only 38.9 per cent did not get it. Eighteen- to 30-year-old women have the best chances of passing: examiners have confirmed this adding that 'They are more careful than men.' They incur – proportionately – fewer fines than men: prefecture registers attest to this. They choose convertibles and small, series-produced cars.[33]

Here again, an allusion to convertibles reflects a preoccupation with the aesthetic aspects of car ownership; while attainability may be suggested by the numbers of women obtaining their driving licence, appearance and desirability are still explicit. Leading cultural critics have considered both aspects of this increasing feminine access to the automobile. Obtaining one's driving licence is a rite of passage, as Baudrillard notes in his *Le Système des objets*.[34] *Elle*'s treatment of the surface appearance of the automobile echoes Barthes's critique of images of food in the same magazine, which foregrounds 'the very finality of the coating, which belongs to a visual category, and cooking according to *Elle* is meant for the eye alone.'[35] According to Barthes, the recipes in *Elle* were fantasies

---

33   'Elles ont été 43 445 à passer leur 'permis' l'an passé, 38,9% seulement ne l'ont pas obtenu. Elles ont, entre 18 et 30 ans, le maximum de chances pour réussir: les examinateurs l'affirment; et ils ajoutent: 'Elles sont plus prudentes que les hommes'. Elles encourent – proportionnellement – moins de contraventions que les hommes: les registres de la préfecture en font foi. Elles choisissent les cabriolets décapotables et les petites voitures de série.' *Elle*, 16 October 1950, p. 14.
34   Baudrillard, *Le Système des objets*, p. 93.
35   'la finalité même du nappé, qui est d'ordre visuel, et la cuisine d'*Elle* est une pure cuisine de la vue.' In a 'Mythology' entitled 'Cuisine ornementale' Barthes questions the need for photos of food to be made to look attractive, exploring the tension between being modern yet remaining at home. See

for the magazine's working-class readership, an idealization that its readers were unable to attain. By speaking of convertibles, *Elle* was fuelling similar dreams at a time when car ownership was still relatively low, with less than 20 per cent of households actually possessing a vehicle.[36] This 1950 article concludes with a previously noted quotation from Josette Day,[37] which echoes a sentiment expressed about the telephone three years previously: 'I drive like I breathe.' Still an object of desire, the car was being commodified and had been designated a need by the rich and famous. That the automobile had still not entered the domain of the everyday is suggested by the assertion, in a review of the year, that 'In 1950, we drive, we wear, we read, we caress, we covet.'[38] While ownership statistics suggest that it was not entirely accurate to say that 'we drive,' the car was undoubtedly becoming more visible and thus increasingly desired. *Elle* continued to afford attention to the automobile primarily as a plaything of the stars; however, it was increasingly of interest as a commodity that might realistically be acquired by some, at least, of its female readers. In a 1952 article entitled 'No, Don't Dress Like This,' *Elle* highlights the fact that fashion does not always sit well with the automobile and that many dresses are not meant to be worn in a car.[39] It also offers a number of tips on how to dress appropriately to look good in a car, once again highlighting the continuing tension between freedom and social expectations.

Image was of central importance in glossy magazines. The close association of the automobile with style and, more specifically, with celebrities was also apparent in the other news magazines of the era. From its creation in 1949, *Paris Match* had included abundant images and devoted significant space to the automobile as an indicator of distinction, as part of a broader movement towards modernity.[40]

Barthes, 2003 [1957], *Mythologies*, p. 120; Barthes, Roland. 1972, *Mythologies*. Translated by Annette Lavers. London: Vintage, p. 78; Mathieu, Patrick, and Frédéric Monneyron. 2015. *L'imaginaire du luxe*. Paris: Éditions Imago, p. 78.
36   Chanaron, *L'industrie automobile*, p. 120.
37   Josette Day was a famous actress and lover of Marcel Pagnol. She appeared in a number of his films, but is best known for her role as la Belle in Jean Cocteau's *La Belle et la bête* co-starring Jean Marais.
38   'En 1950, on roule, on porte, on lit, on caresse, on convoite.' *Elle*, 13 November 1950, p. 19.
39   'Non, ne vous habillez pas comme ceci.' *Elle*, 6 October 1952, p. 22.
40   Gaffney and Holmes, 'Stardom in Theory and Context,' pp. 14–15.

References to the automobile in *Paris Match* typically highlight opulence and well-known drivers. Michèle Morgan[41] appears on the cover of the 4 June 1949 edition at the wheel of a convertible with a caption reading 'You can be young 20 years longer.'[42] The linking of youth – or, more accurately, the appearance of youth – with convertibles again reinforces the automobile's desirability and, indeed, its mythical potential. Susan Weiner's study of *Mythologies* (1957) and *Les Stars* (1957) notes that both the cultural critic Roland Barthes and the sociologist Edgar Morin had:

> observed the same odd principle at work in mass culture, odd in light of the apparent thrall of technology in the postwar period. That principle was myth: technology, paradoxically, had the power to renew the ancient imaginative function of mythic thinking in contemporary industrial society. Through the mass media, the mythic was rendered visible, palpable, legible and ubiquitous.[43]

Thus, Weiner argues that although it was becoming more ubiquitous, technology continued to play a fetishized role in society.

From the Russian foreign minister Andrey Vychinsky (4 June 1949) to Greta Garbo (6 August 1949), references to the car in *Paris Match* frequently depict the cars driven by politicians and celebrities as symbols of their success. In the same August 1949 edition, Henri Vidal[44] is photographed standing beside his Lancia, thus imbuing the *marque* with a fetishized quality as the car of predilection of this famous actor. In November 1949, there is a similar image of Rita Hayworth: 'This photograph was taken last week as Rita Hayworth was leaving for her daily outing. Rita driving (a convertible Cadillac marked M.A.K.) to a tearoom.'[45]

---

41   Michèle Morgan was an actress who appeared in a series of French films over three decades and was also moderately successful in Hollywood. Her most famous role was in *La Symphonie pastorale* (1946).

42   'Vous pouvez être jeune vingt ans de plus.' *Paris Match*, 4 June 1949, front cover.

43   Weiner, Susan. 2007. '1950s Popular Culture: Star-Gazing and Myth-Making with Roland Barthes and Edgar Morin.' In *Celebrity and Stardom in France*, edited by John Gaffney and Diana Holmes. Oxford: Berghahn, pp. 26–39 (p. 28).

44   Henri Vidal was a prominent actor in the 1940s and 1950s. Reputedly discovered by Édith Piaf, his most notable roles were in *Les Maudits* (1947) and *Une Parisienne* (1957), which co-starred Brigitte Bardot.

45   'Cette photographie a été prise la semaine dernière au moment où Rita Hayworth partait pour sa promenade quotidienne. Rita se rend en voiture

Once again, the importance of the brand is indicative of the star quality of its owner. Also in November 1949, *Paris Match* covered Charles Lindbergh's[46] visit to France, noting that 'Lindbergh explores Europe in a 4CV.'[47] In this instance, a modest car is driven by the famous aviator. Lindbergh had previously visited the Citroën factories on the Quai de Javel and saw himself as a man of the people.[48] His choice of this model may be seen to reflect his construction of this image for himself: 'In Paris, Charles Lindbergh bought a Renault 4CV. He got his long legs in with difficulty and, his wife by his side, he set off on the roads of Europe to make up his own mind on the situation in Europe.'[49] From these early post-war beginnings, and as the Trente Glorieuses progressed, stars would still be used to market cars; however, the association was less relevant as possession of the car became fetishized differently. In the late 1940s and early 1950s, articles engaged with the car as a more attainable commodity, thereby dismantling to some extent the image of opulence associated with it.

The 1949 Salon de l'Auto was given a front-cover spread on *Paris Match*. Significantly, the periodical highlighted a selection of models that included the Citroën 2CV, the Renault 4CV and the Simca 3CV, all smaller cars reflecting a growing public interest in these functionality. At this time, *Paris Match* also covered the altogether more down-to-earth Foire aux Autos or second-hand motor show:

> One million French people visited the Salon de l'Automobile. Some tens of thousands have ordered a new car there. The others, those who cannot raise 300,000 francs, the minimum price of a small car, those who only go to the Salon to nurture

(une Cadillac décapotable marquée M.A.K.) dans un salon de thé.' *Paris Match*, 12 November 1949, p. 7.
46   Charles Lindbergh's arrival in Paris in 1927 is important as it highlighted his symbolic role as an icon of modernity and mobility. See discussion on this in Chapter 3.
47   'Lindbergh explore l'Europe en 4CV.' *Paris Match*, 19 November 1949, p. 7.
48   Barthes commented on the fact that Lindbergh flew wearing a lounge suit; this, he suggests, underlines his humanity as opposed to distancing himself from it. See Barthes, 2003 [1957], *Mythologies*, p. 89.
49   'A Paris, Charles Lindbergh s'est procuré une 4CV Renault. Il y a péniblement casé ses longues jambes et, sa femme à son côté, il est parti sur les routes d'Europe pour se faire une idée personnelle de la situation en Europe.' *Paris Match*, 19 November 1949, p. 7.

their dreams, those who return home by *métro*, still have hope: the used car. We find them at the Car Fair, at the Porte de Versailles. The cars for sale are surprisingly clean and shiny.[50]

While the existence of this second-hand *foire* suggests that would-be owners could now envisage purchasing a car, magazine coverage continued to prioritize luxury vehicles, thereby maintaining the automobile's historic association with the social elite.

In advance of the 1951 Salon de l'Automobile, *Paris Match* showcased one of the cars due to star at the event:

> In front of the Grand Palais, a month early, our reporters photographed the new Grégoire which will be one of the highlights of the show from October 4. It is a 5-seater, 13 HP, 4-speed front-wheel drive that reaches 150 km/h. At the wheel, its potential owner, dressed by Christian Dior, is wearing a beige woollen and fur coat.[51]

The accompanying picture underlines the continuing close association between a desirable car and a fashionable woman, strengthening the impression that the automobile remains fetishized as an object of desire. By the same token, the Salon's opening was the occasion for front-page coverage in *Paris Match* with the picture of a spectacular car, Le Sabre. Inside, the edition is almost entirely dedicated to the Salon and specifically to the purchase of a car: 'Of the 38 new cars selected by *Paris Match*, which one will be yours?'[52] This imagined step in the generalization of motoring is the beginning of the magazine's

---

50   'Un million de Français ont visité le Salon de l'Automobile. Quelques dizaines de milliers y ont passé commande d'une voiture neuve. Les autres, ceux qui ne peuvent pas réunir trois cent mille francs, prix minimum d'une petite voiture, ceux qui ne vont au Salon que pour nourrir leur rêve, ceux qui rentrent chez eux en métro, ceux-là ont encore un espoir: la voiture d'occasion. On les retrouve à la Foire aux Autos, à la porte de Versailles. Les voitures à vendre y paraissent étonnamment propres et brillantes.' *Paris Match*, 22 October 1949, p. 17.
51   'Devant le Grand Palais, avec un mois d'avance, nos reporteurs ont photographié la nouvelle Grégoire qui sera, à partir du 4 octobre un des clous du salon. C'est une traction avant à 5 places, 13 CV, 4 vitesses qui atteint 150 km/h. Au volant son éventuelle propriétaire, habillée par Christian Dior, porte un manteau de lainage beige et longs poils.' *Paris Match*, 8 September 1951, p. 19.
52   'Des 38 nouvelles voitures sélectionnées par Paris Match, laquelle sera la vôtre?' *Paris Match*, 13 October 1951, p. 24.

portrayal of the car as an obtainable commodity while still maintaining its desirability as a luxury object.

In 1953, the year of its foundation, *L'Express* asked, 'À quoi pourrait servir le salon?' ('What use is the Salon?'):

> The Salon, an operation which consists of filling hotels and restaurants with customers for two weeks, theatres with spectators less demanding than saturated Parisians, the notebooks of parking agents and the portfolio of organizers with good incomes, the Salon thus conceived has only one flaw: it exhibits what you can easily see driving in the street at no cost.[53]

Thus, in its first reference to the Salon, this new magazine suggested that a growing familiarity with the automobile meant that its status as an object of desire was similarly evolving.

It will be apparent from the foregoing that post-war coverage of the Salon de l'Automobile was largely ceremonial in nature, introducing magazine readers to static exhibits rather than imparting practical knowledge of the car. Instead of offering vehicles for practical testing, the annual event placed automobiles on stands to be admired for their physical appearance. However, both the representation and the consumption of the car in France were about to undergo a radical transformation.

The 1950s: Learning about the Car

We turn now to the 1950s, during which the car goes through a gradual process of demystification. In this intermediate period, the automobile may still be associated with wealth and status; however, this representation is diluted as these magazines introduce the car to a broader public. Attempts are made to educate the reader about the workings of the car as well as about affordable ways of owning one.

---

53 'Le Salon, opération qui consiste à garnir pendant deux semaines les hôtels et les restaurants de clients, les théâtres de spectateurs moins exigeants que les Parisiens saturés, les carnets des agents de contraventions et le portefeuille des organisateurs d'honnêtes revenus, le Salon ainsi conçu n'a qu'un défaut: il expose ce qu'à moindres frais on peut en toute tranquillité voir rouler dans sa rue.' *L'Express*, 26 September 1953, p. 10.

We also see a growth of the Salon de l'Automobile, which begins to engage with a broader audience as the 2CV and the 4CV attract more coverage during this period. Rather than depict stars, magazine articles induce the reader to discover more about the car itself. During this second period, the democratization of the car is more accepted, as is its potential to give its owners great freedom. We see examples of the car being addressed through the life of its owner with articles entitled 'Votre voiture et vous' ('your car and you'), for example. Here, the automobile is no longer merely an aspiration; it is now a realistic goal for readers of these magazines.

To celebrate the opening of the 1955 Salon de l'Auto, *Elle* ran four images of a car on its cover. In two of these, a woman is at the wheel, in the third she is driving accompanied by a young boy and in the fourth a man is driving with a woman seated beside him. In all four images, the woman is wearing a fur coat, and the caption runs, 'She loves cars, furs ... and jams.'[54] The linkage with furs suggests a continued fetishizing of the car as a luxury item; however, the reference to jam in the same context suggests that the car is beginning to be perceived as more commonplace. Car possession was undoubtedly becoming more generalized, as highlighted by the use of the 'infomercial' to advertise cars. In an October 1952 edition of *Paris Match*, we see a full-page item, which under the guise of providing information to the reader is actually selling a product (in this case, the Renault Frégate), while depicting its driver, an elegantly dressed woman, leaving her car and going into a detached house with a beautifully maintained front garden.[55] This new form of advertising targeted prospective customers while at the same time serving to increase knowledge about the product. It was also indicative of a move towards a new market for automobile manufacturers. Articles discussing the affordability of the car, as well as increasing customer awareness of the makes and model available, became more prevalent as working-class spending power increased.[56]

These articles gave the automobile a new prominence within French society. Moreover, they invited a new category of potential

54   'Elle aime les voitures, les fourrures ... et les confitures'. *Elle*, 3 October 1955, front cover.
55   *Paris Match*, 4 October 1952, p. 10.
56   Jouin, Pierre. 1995. *Une liberté toute neuve: culture de masse et esthétique nouvelle dans la France des années 50*. Paris: Klincksieck, p. 26.

buyers to consider the acquisition of a car as a realistic possibility for the first time. This new narrative reflected the greater spending power of the French working classes and the widening opportunities for acquiring a car. An *Elle* article which appeared in October 1954 entitled 'Pouvons-nous acheter une voiture?' ('Can We Buy a Car?') presents a conversation between husband and wife Jean and Marceline as they try to calculate whether such a purchase is within their means.[57] What follows is a breakdown of the costs involved in the acquisition and running of a vehicle. However, the final paragraph of the article is of particular interest as all these factors no longer seem to matter; for, while it may not make financial sense to buy a car, the affective quality of car ownership is such that it is worthwhile:

> Unless you travel a lot and with a minimum of 2 people, you will not save money compared to the train and public transport. But you will make a dream come true. 'Admit it,' Marceline told me, 'that it's well worth 19,000 francs per month.' Well, she was right.[58]

The realization of a dream, rather than the utilitarian value of the car, is deemed to justify the expense. Nevertheless, affordability was a theme which became more prevalent during this second period. The cover of *Elle* in October 1957 portrays a well-dressed woman standing up in a car, while the caption runs 'A new little queen: the Vespa 2CV.'[59] Inside the magazine, this same car, while still depicted as beautiful, is also described as 'economically unbeatable.'[60] As advertising rhetoric evolves, we thus see the assimilation of the car into the household budget.

As early as 1952, an article entitled 'Why the French Have Reasons Not to Be Happy'[61] had lamented the fact that waiting lists for all makes of cars lagged behind increasing consumer demand. Confidently

---

57   *Elle*, 4 October 1954, p. 32.
58   'A moins de voyager ou de circuler beaucoup et à un minimum de 2 personnes, vous ne réaliserez pas une économie par rapport au train et aux transports en commun. Mais de toute façon, vous réaliserez un rêve. Avoue, m'a dit Marceline, que ça vaut bien 19 000 fr. par mois. Ma foi, elle avait raison.' *Elle*, 4 October 1954, p. 32.
59   'une nouvelle petite reine: la Vespa 2CV.' *Elle*, 7 October 1957, front cover.
60   'imbattable sur le plan économique.' *Elle*, 7 October 1957. p. 3.
61   'Pourquoi les Français ont des raisons de ne pas être contents.' *Paris Match*, 4 October 1952, p. 32.

declaring that 'Since the liberation, the French only dream of cars,' *Paris Match* argued that the French automotive industry was allowing itself to fall behind its international rivals.[62] In the same article, the journalist attempts to explain 'why France let the luxury automobile die'[63] and suggests that possession of a luxury car is an 'outward sign of wealth. It has become infinitely more compromising to have a Salmson or a Talbot than to wear diamonds or a mink coat.'[64] Thus, the image associated with the possession of a luxurious car is no longer necessarily a good one. This perceived fall in the popularity of luxury cars occurred at the same time as more modest cars were enjoying significant growth.[65] The Renault 4CV and Citroën 2CV in particular cost significantly less than larger cars. Moreover, their running costs could be as little as half that of their larger counterparts.[66] The car was coming to attract interest less for its image than for its functional capacity. Marx's commodity fetish is still present in this evolved perception of the car as something more than a vehicle. The luxury commodity was disappearing; however, the notion of the automobile as a purveyor of freedom, additionally offering the ability to emulate higher social classes, remains enshrined in the desire for a car in this period.

The next edition of *Paris Match* carried a story which reinforces the view that the automobile was no longer perceived as something mysterious. Paradoxically entitled 'The Mystery of the Salon: A Car That Hides Nothing,'[67] it describes a Simca with a shell made from transparent material in order to display its workings. It is significant that as the automobile was entering the everyday sphere, becoming a target purchase for the lower orders, Simca sensed the timeliness of this marketing approach. The motor car, hitherto shrouded in mystery with a variety of fetishized images hiding its true nature, was now

62   'Depuis la libération, les Français ne rêvent plus que d'automobiles.' *Paris Match*, 4 October 1952, p. 32.
63   'pourquoi la France a laissé mourir l'automobile de luxe.' *Paris Match*, 4 October 1952, p. 32.
64   'signe extérieur de richesse. Il est devenu infiniment plus compromettant d'avoir une Salmson ou une Talbot que de porter des diamants ou un manteau de vison.' *Paris Match*, 4 October 1952, p. 32.
65   Loubet, *Histoire de l'automobile française*, p. 284.
66   Loubet, *Histoire de l'automobile française*, p. 282.
67   'le mystère du Salon: une voiture qui ne cache rien.' *Paris Match*, 11 October 1952, p. 17.

Figure 14 Transparent Simca Aronde from Salon de l'Auto, Paris (1952). © Getty images/Walter Carone.

fully exposed with this nakedness forming the centrepiece of the Simca collection. Cordoned off from the public, the car was continuously surrounded as patrons examined this curiosity. The transparent Simca Aronde is indicative of the change in the perception of the automobile in the early 1950s. It shows that the car manufacturers themselves were eager to move on from the fetishized commodity that had been sold to date. Less an object of wonder, the car was becoming part of the everyday, and the 1952 Salon – labelled 'the Salon for buying' ('celui de l'achat') – was an ideal platform to project a new and overtly utilitarian image of the automobile.

Two years later, *Paris Match* launched its coverage of the Salon with a piece entitled 'Eleven Stars Introduce the French Cars of 1955.'[68] Unlike previous incarnations in which stars are depicted with cars as a symbol of wealth and success, this article states from the outset that 'The stage and screen artists who posed for *Paris Match* behind the wheel of the cars at the 41st Salon de l'Auto are not the owners, they

68 'Onze vedettes présentent les voitures françaises 55.' *Paris Match*, 2 October 1954, p. 29.

correspond to the types who will buy them.'⁶⁹ Here, *Paris Match* is creating an associative linkage. These cars are not owned by the stars, but if one identifies with the personality of a featured celebrity, the car they are paired with is perhaps one you should consider buying. This is a middle ground between a fetishized object and an obtainable commodity which is consumed in its use as well as through its image.

The mid-1950s was a period during which the automobile was portrayed as a commodity that could be purchased by the majority of the French population. In a series of editorials for *Elle*, prominent journalist and later a member of General de Gaulle's cabinet, Jean Duché, examines the positive and, more often, negative aspects of automobilization. This series of articles begins in 1955 with 'L'Automobile?,' which draws clichéd comparisons between a man's desire for a car and for a woman. Duché also suggests that it is the woman who applies common sense with regard to the car, while men expect a car to possess qualities that go beyond those of a vehicle:

> From a car, men expect incredible things. They want it to be robust, shiny, flexible, economical, soft, silent, nervous, manageable and elegant; they want it to be trustworthy, to have elegance, class ... Wouldn't you think they were dreaming of an ideal woman? You'd think that they require their car to have charm [...] in choosing a car, as in driving it, women clearly show the practicality of their minds when men view these issues in too romantic a way.⁷⁰

The subtitle of the article – 'for a man: captivating like a woman, for a woman: becoming like a dress' – portrays the different views of

69 'Les artistes de la scène et de l'écran qui ont posé pour "Paris Match" au volant des voitures du 41e Salon de l'Auto n'en sont pas les propriétaires, ils correspondent aux types de ceux qui les achèteront.' *Paris Match*, 2 October 1954, p. 29.
70 'D'une voiture, les hommes attendent des choses incroyables. Ils la veulent robuste, brillante, souple, économique, moelleuse, silencieuse, nerveuse, maniable et racée; ils veulent qu'elle soit digne de confiance, qu'elle ait de la tenue, de la classe ... Ne croirait-on pas qu'ils sont en train de rêver à quelque femme idéale? Pour un peu, ils exigent de leur auto qu'elle ait du charme [...] dans le choix d'une voiture, comme dans sa conduite, les femmes manifestent clairement le côté pratique de leur esprit quand les hommes considèrent ces problèmes d'une façon trop romanesque.' *Elle*, 3 October 1955, p. 30.

men and women about cars.[71] This suggests that the desire for, and desirability of, a car remains, while also suggesting enduring gender hierarchies. It must, however, be remembered that Duché is writing for a predominantly female readership and may here be indulging in a compensating tactic, suggesting that men remain enthralled by the car. It is noteworthy, moreover, that in both these articles, it is the person who is under the spell of the car who is ridiculed, while the one who has accepted its ordinariness is seen as a genuinely modern individual.

An article dedicated to the car the following October, in 1956, entitled 'Il faut créer la légion d'honneur de l'automobiliste' ('We Must Create a Motorist's Legion d'Honneur'), makes reference to the ubiquity of the car and to the fact that this very ubiquity has contributed to eliminating the freedom aspired to by the driver. Duché asks what pushes somebody to buy a car: 'It is, they say, convenience. Is there anything more practical, in fact, to get to work, than to sit in a box with wheels moving by its own means, provided that other similar boxes do not force you to stop when you want to ride, and to ride further when you want to stop?'[72] The car as a ubiquitous commodity can be seen to play a more prominent role in later 1950s France. That this is followed by a reference to rush hour in Paris on a workday morning, with fears of worse to come, illustrates that the car's popularity has grown and that it has become a commodity once aspired to and now universally attainable. In stating that a car is purchased for convenience, Duché refers to its utilitarian value, as he explains its use in transporting its owner to work. Its utilitarian value is not the reason for its popularity, however, according to Duché. It is rather the car's ability to provide its owner with a feeling of freedom, the freedom to go where he or she wants, when he or she wants. This is a rush hour impossibility, but at the weekend, the car is still capable of both symbolizing and providing autonomy:

> If it's not in the convenience, what is it that drives a motorist?
> Maybe a feeling of freedom, of independence? The motorist is an

71   'pour un homme: captivante comme une femme, pour une femme: seyante comme une robe.' *Elle*, 3 October 1955, p. 30.
72   'C'est, dit-on, la commodité. Est-il rien de plus pratique, en effet, pour se rendre à son travail, que de s'asseoir dans une boîte à roulette se déplaçant par ses propres moyens, sous réserve que d'autres boîtes similaires ne vous contraignent pas à vous arrêter quand vous voudriez rouler, et à rouler plus loin quand vous voudriez vous arrêter?' *Elle*, 1 October 1956, p. 7.

autonomous man. He goes where he wants, as he wants, when he wants, all alone. To the countryside, for example. This is clearly seen on Sunday evening at the gates of big cities.[73]

It is particularly interesting that Duché, while writing for *Elle*, refers to the car owner as a man. In doing so, he reinforces gender hierarchies; the car is capable of providing the freedom to its owner to go wherever *he* alone wants.

Duché's by now annual article on the car, coinciding with the Salon de l'Auto, is considerably more negative in 1957 than in previous years. One year after agreeing that the automobile was a symbol of freedom, Duché now asks: 'In the end, I wonder if it's a very good sign that we need so badly to travel just for the simple fact of travelling. Would we be so uneasy, [if we stayed] still, where we are?'[74] The weekend trip has now also become as overcrowded as the work-time rush hour of the previous year. Duché refers to the Salon de l'Auto as follows: 'I realize that when this column comes out, France will be celebrating in the hustle and bustle and the vapours of unburnt petrol its annual cult of modern times, the automobile. On which point, I wonder if we are not losing the plot.'[75] Thus, while Duché describes the Salon as a 'cult of modern times,' he questions the car, suggesting that it may be playing too central a role in our lives. He proceeds to refer to non-drivers in ironically pejorative terms as it seems incomprehensible that anyone could function without a car:

> I do not mean any harm to the auto industry or to motorists. Besides, everyone knows that a pedestrian is a loser, an outcast, a nobody, a Cro-Magnon half-wit, so I drive a car, like everyone

---

73   'S'il n'est pas dans la commodité, où donc est-il, ce moteur de l'automobiliste? Peut-être dans un sentiment de liberté, d'indépendance? L'automobiliste est un homme autonome. Il va où il veut, comme il veut, quand il veut, tout seul. A la campagne, par exemple. Cela se voit clairement le dimanche soir aux portes des grandes villes.' *Elle*, 1 October 1956, p. 7.

74   'Je me demande enfin s'il est très bon signe que nous ayons si grand besoin de bouger pour bouger. Serions-nous si mal à l'aise, immobiles, là où nous sommes?' *Elle*, 7 October 1957, p. 7.

75   'Je m'avise que lorsque cette chronique paraîtra, la France célébrera dans le tohu-bohu et les vapeurs de gaz imbrulées son culte annuel des temps modernes, l'automobile. Sur quoi je me demande si nous ne serions pas en train de perdre les pédales.' *Elle*, 7 October 1957, p. 7.

else, and I even enjoy it sometimes. But is it the melancholy of autumn? It seems to me that this instrument designed to serve us, every day enslaves us a little more.[76]

Duché explains this feeling as 'automobile snobbery' and associates it with a mystification of the car:

There is an automobile snobbery that may well be some sort of mysticism. If the average Frenchman says he doesn't have a car, we worry: what's wrong with him? We always talk about the housing crisis: it sounds like a bad joke, when we consider that we spend two or three times as much to drive on roads on Sundays than on accommodation for the week.[77]

References to the Salon, the automobilist, the non-automobilist and the general image of the car are hyperbolic in an attempt to poke fun at the position assumed by the automobile. Interestingly, Duché feels that the car is a commodity that has been so democratized that it seems now almost strange not to own one. The mystification of the car has changed, however, from one associated with its form to a fetishizing of the need for one. In comparing expenditure on personal transport with that on housing, which by 1957 was eventually beginning to meet public demand,[78] Duché questions why the automobile has come to be perceived as a need alongside the more obvious necessity of housing. The car has at this stage reached a tipping point in becoming a commodity which is increasingly perceived to be so 'needed' that it 'every day enslaves us a little more.'[79]

---

76 'Je ne veux aucun mal à l'industrie automobile ni aux automobilistes. D'ailleurs, chacun sait qu'un piéton est un pauvre type, un paria, un minus, un demeuré de Cro-Magnon, donc je roule en auto, comme tout le monde, et même il m'arrive d'y prendre bien du plaisir. Mais est-ce la mélancolie de l'automne? Il me semble que cet instrument conçu pour nous servir, nous réduit chaque jour un peu plus en esclavage.' *Elle*, 7 October 1957, p. 7.

77 'Il y a un snobisme de l'automobile qui pourrait bien être une espèce de mystique. Si un Français moyen déclare qu'il n'a pas d'auto on s'inquiète: qu'est-ce qui ne va pas chez lui? On parle toujours de la crise du logement: cela a tout l'air d'une mauvaise plaisanterie, quand on songe que nous dépensons deux ou trois fois plus pour rouler sur les routes le dimanche que pour nous loger dans la semaine.' *Elle*, 7 October 1957, p. 7.

78 Rioux and Sirinelli, *La France, d'un siècle à l'autre*, p. 307.

79 'nous réduit chaque jour un peu plus en esclavage.' *Elle*, 7 October 1957, p. 7.

By highlighting both the utilitarian and fetishized qualities of the car, it is apparent that Duché, and by extension late-fifties France, is struggling with this changing order as the car becomes more recognized for inconveniences caused by its ubiquity than by its previously heralded qualities. The further commodification of the car, reflected in the growth in automobile use,[80] inevitably led a number of writers to question the merits of this surge in traffic on French roads. Cartoonists, in particular, were among the first to question this development, and they began to parody the public infatuation with cars. While, initially, these cartoons lampooned the luxurious nature of the cars, the cartoons can also tell much about how the car has been accepted into society.

Possessing a motor car as a contributing factor to how one is viewed by society is parodied in a cartoon in which a woman says to her husband: 'Understand me, Edmond, it is not about denying your peasant origins ...'[81] as they step out of an elegant car to be met by a butler wielding an umbrella. As members of the *petite bourgeoisie* or *nouveaux riches*, this couple illustrates the effects of the rural exodus in which large numbers left to work in cities.[82] The car as an indicator of wealth is underlined here as this couple has acquired a car and a butler in order to demonstrate their newfound wealth. Desirability and the elegance associated with possession of a car are apparent at the end of the forties. In another cartoon, which appears in the 9 July 1949 edition of *Paris Match*, entitled 'L'élégance automobile' ('Automobile Elegance'), we see a man driving an expensive-looking car. Having crashed, he is transported away in an expensive-looking hearse.[83] Indeed, the automobile seems to become an object of derision for cartoonists, or rather, the image that ownership of a car conveys. In its first edition of 1951, a *Paris Match* cartoon shows a woman crashing into a car driven by a man. The caption reads, 'Bonne Année!' ('Happy New Year!').[84]

80　The percentage of homes that owned a car increased from 14 per cent in 1938 to 21 per cent in 1953, to 30 per cent in 1960 and 47.5 per cent in 1965. See Chanaron, *L'industrie automobile*, p. 120.

81　'Comprenez-moi bien, Edmond, il ne s'agit pas de renier vos origines paysannes.' *Paris Match*, 25 June 1949, p. 33.

82　Rioux and Sirinelli, *La France, d'un siècle à l'autre*, p. 271.

83　*Paris Match*, 9 July 1949, p. 7.

84　*Paris Match*, 6 January 1951, front cover.

A cartoon in August 1952 parodies the image of the car as the plaything of the rich while also constructing an image of opulence for whoever owns one. Here, a middle-aged couple dressed in fine clothes leave a shop called 'Snob'; a porter or doorman opens the door of the large modern car parked in front of the shop, the couple duly gets in, proceeds to get out the opposite door, and then gets into another – more modest – car which is parked adjacent to the first.[85] The second car is dilapidated and dates back to the 1920s. While possession of a car is once again associated with wealth, the simple fact of ownership no longer suffices as a marker of conspicuous consumption. Although this couple possesses a car, it would seem that, as we enter the 1950s, it is ownership of a modern, fashionable car that is fetishized. Car possession alone has taken a step towards being normalized as is seen as this couple is ridiculed for trying to portray an image of wealth by 'merely' possessing a car, one that is no longer desirable.

A cartoon that appeared the following month, in September 1951, also plays on the image of car ownership. It portrays a man standing on the driving seat of his car, as his wife seated beside him says: 'Come on! if you have to get on the seat every time to see what's going on in front of your bonnet ....'[86] In contrast to the previous cartoon, here, the couple is in a modern, fashionable car. Once again, however, the owner of the car is ridiculed. By poking fun at the car owner for buying a vehicle too large for his needs, we might infer that public opinion is moving towards a utilitarian viewpoint. However, the man standing on the seat of his car may be attempting to draw attention to himself and his recent purchase. The fetishizing of the car is ridiculed through questioning the 'need' to possess a large car in order to obtain autonomy and freedom. In choosing a large car, which is superfluous to his needs, the car owner is engaging in a fetishizing that was increasingly at odds with the perceptions of the French public. The shift from desiring an automobile to needing one is becoming apparent as cars previously coveted in image are increasingly questioned as the idea of a more utilitarian automobile begins to hold more importance. Thus, while mass ownership was not yet a *fait accompli*, *Paris Match* showed a public that was beginning to

---

85   *Paris Match*, 1 August 1952, p. 27.
86   'oh alors! si tu dois à chaque fois monter sur la banquette pour voir ce qui se passe devant ton capot.' *Paris Match*, 6 September 1952, p. 47.

take a new interest in the automobile in the early 1950s. As *Elle* had already suggested, with particular regard to its target readership, as women were now taking more of an interest, it was for its utilitarian possibilities as well as those related to image. The affective quality of the car, particularly its fetishized image, appeared to be changing as the automobile took a more central position in society.

A sketch by the cartoonist Chaval, which appears to coincide with the 1954 Salon, pokes fun at man's obsession with the automobile.[87] With an apparent nod at Simca's attempt at openness with its transparent car at the Salon of the previous year, Chaval depicts an X-ray of a car with someone at the wheel. The driver appears so fused with the vehicle that he and car are one, a cyborg creation resulting from man's dependency on the car. The cartoon calls to mind the Futurist man-machines, as posited by Marinetti.[88] Chaval is aware of the fact that Simca has made a conscious effort to win over the general public. He is suggesting the consequences of a possible over-reliance on the car with his dystopian vision in which a mutated being almost goes unnoticed due to its very mundanity. The fusion of car and driver pokes fun at this perceived over-reliance on the car as more and more time is spent at the wheel.

It will be apparent from the foregoing that women were still conspicuous by their absence from many of these representations. In the next section, we will explore this omission, which must be considered alongside the process whereby the car was increasingly perceived as a household appliance as France moved into the latter half of the 1950s. An advertisement for the Simca Aronde in October 1955 makes this linkage explicit by presenting an image of a woman climbing into an Aronde which has entered the family home and is parked beside the armchairs. The caption reads 'Just like in your living room.'[89] The commodification of the automobile as a 'needed' appliance is the transparent aim of this advertisement. The car is taking up its rightful place and no home should be without one; the industrial product and the cultural construct together enter the realm of the Baudrillardian commodification of need.[90]

87   *Paris Match*, 3 October 1954, p. 81.
88   See Marinetti, Filippo Tommaso. 1983. *Manifesto of Futurism*. New Haven, CT: Yale Library Associates.
89   'Comme dans votre salon.' *Paris Match*, 22 October 1955, p. 29.
90   Baudrillard, *Pour une critique de l'économie politique du signe*, p. 155.

In the same issue, we find an info ad for the Renault 4CV that again offers an illustration of the fetishizing of the automobile: 'At the Salon, Fernand Raynaud dresses his 4CV in 1956 fashion.'[91] An image shows this comic actor, who was renowned for playing recognizably ordinary French types, standing beside a 4CV with assorted car body parts at his feet.[92] He is wearing one of his trademark confused looks and we read that 'Fernand Raynaud presents the 70 accessories approved by the Régie Renault that can turn this 4CV Affaires into a luxury car.'[93] This is accompanied by a list and a process for all the parts. As Kristin Ross has observed, 'the 4CV was the first French car produced to be affordable on a mass level, the first "people's car" from what had been until then a successful luxury industry.'[94] However, while this vehicle may have remained the car of popular predilection due to its price and economical running costs, it is apparent from such *Paris Match* coverage that its low-cost image was perceived to be unappealing to many potential buyers. Thus, the illustrated 70-piece kit allows the owner to 'dress' the 4CV so that it is 'à la mode 1956' and 'une voiture de grand luxe' ('a luxury car'). We may conclude that, while the practical democratization of the car was taking place, particularly in lower-end vehicles, the continued opportunity for individual indulgence in collectively crafted desire was still provided to buyers. In short, the societal shift of car ownership from luxury to mundanity was not yet complete.

Further evidence for this view is offered by the front-page coverage given by *Paris Match* to the 1956 Salon, depicting Maurice Chevalier[95] at the wheel of a convertible: 'Two stars of Paris: the Salon and

91   'Au Salon Fernand Raynaud habille sa 4CV à la mode 1956.' *Paris Match*, 22 October 1955, p. 42.
92   Fernand Raynaud was one of the best-known French comic actors during the 1950s and 1960s. He appeared in a large number of films and also penned and performed many popular comic sketches. He was killed in a car accident in 1973.
93   'Fernand Raynaud vous présente les 70 accessoires homologués par la Régie Renault qui peuvent faire de cette 4CV Affaires une voiture de grand luxe.' *Paris Match*, 22 October 1955, p. 42.
94   Ross, *Fast Cars, Clean Bodies*, p. 24.
95   Maurice Chevalier was a world-renowned French actor and cabaret singer. In a career that spanned over 50 years he was twice nominated for an Oscar and appeared in a number of successful Hollywood musicals, including *Gigi* (1958) and *Can-Can* (1960).

Maurice Chevalier.'[96] As cars became more commonplace, there remained an obsession with those that were beyond the reach of less well-off buyers. It was these cars that gave the Salon a new relevance as distinct from that provided by what could be called more everyday models. The perception of the need for an affordable car in French households thus does not preclude a fetishizing of powerful, high-speed and image-based vehicles. By 1956, the Salon was still immensely popular but it no longer served the purpose of announcing to the French population what their first car could be. It functioned now as a platform to display newer, more unobtainable models. However, as car ownership had become more common, only the more spectacular cars would henceforth attract attention. Indeed, it is probable that those who now attended the Salon were no longer ordinary people but rather motoring enthusiasts, who remained hungry for novelty while the majority of previous visitors had had their thirst quenched by the incipient ubiquity of the car.

Late 1955 is perhaps the beginning of the transition period during which the car moved from being desired as a vehicle of distinction to one of mundanity. Yet Yonnet suggests that the car *still* has some value for class distinction when he examines the sales figures for that year:

> In 1955, 7 per cent of new car buyers in France were working-class, compared to 2 per cent in 1949. They made up 38 per cent of 4CV buyers. In 1951, four out of five households did not own a car (in 1981, seven out of ten households did). This was a time when analysis of car ownership still had the value of class opposition and can be generalized from similar observations on the restricted distribution of other durable goods (fridge, washing machine, television).[97]

---

96 'Deux vedettes de Paris: le Salon et Maurice Chevalier.' *Paris Match,* 6 October 1956, front cover.
97 'En 1955, 7% des acheteurs de voitures neuves en France sont des ouvriers, contre 2% en 1949. Ils constituent 38% des acheteurs de 4 CV. En 1951, 4 ménages sur 5 ne possèdent pas d'automobile (en 1981, 7 ménages sur 10 en possèdent une). C'est l'époque où l'analyse de la possession automobile a encore valeur d'opposition de classe et peut être généralisée à partir d'observations similaires sur la diffusion restreinte d'autres biens durables (frigo, machine à laver, télévision).' Yonnet, Paul. 1985. *Jeux, modes et masses 1945–1985.* Paris: Gallimard, p. 266.

A similarly slow transition is suggested in an article in *L'Express*. While its author acknowledges that the Salon is still popular, they question its relevance and suggest that it is no longer of use to the public as it continues to fetishize past images of power while the French public has moved on. This normalization of the car due to its proliferation was examined by *L'Express* at the Salon of 1955:

> In a few days, the prodigious growth of the most dynamic branch of French industry, the automobile, will receive its annual consecration: the 1955 Salon. This event, during which provincial France gravitates to Paris every year and which causes giant traffic jams in the capital, allows us to measure the place that the car now holds in the life of each of us – even those who do not have one.[98]

The five essential characteristics mentioned in the article are of interest as they encompass both forms of the fetishization of the car. The first two mentioned, mechanics and bodywork, can be associated with a fetishizing of desire, particularly the importance of form; engine size is central in the desirability of the automobile, as already seen through the fetishizing of motor racing. The last three characteristics, however, are associated with a more mundane commodity; safety, comfort and affordability are characteristics that suggest that the automobile is less perceived as a desired product but rather as a one that has entered the realm of the everyday. The car which comes out on top in the comparison in this article is the Citroën Traction Avant, a model that was first built in 1934. This might indicate a lingering nostalgia for larger cars that carry a certain amount of prestige. It also suggests that there was a dearth of quality new cars in spite of the huge demand which had seen production rise from 34,000 in 1945 to 285,000 in 1949, and to 600,000 in 1954. Purchase of a Citroën 2CV still entailed a two-year wait for delivery. The 2CV and the Renault 4CV made up 20 per cent of all car sales in 1955, while the four large manufacturers

---

98 'Dans quelques jours, l'essor prodigieux de la branche la plus dynamique de l'industrie française, l'automobile, va recevoir sa consécration annuelle: le Salon 1955. Cette manifestation, qui draine chaque année la province vers Paris et vaut à la capitale des embouteillages géants, permet de mesurer la place que tient désormais l'auto dans la vie de chacun de nous – même de ceux qui n'en possèdent pas.' *L'Express*, 24 September 1955, p. 10.

sold 93.5 per cent of all cars on French roads to an increasingly diversified market in which the most dynamic sector was that of the working class, increasing modestly from 9.4 per cent to 11.8 per cent.[99]

The second of our identified periods (1950–60) is marked by an opposition between the desire which the automobile continued to incarnate and its banalization. By the end of the 1950s, it was becoming clear that a desire for the automobile was making way for an acceptance of the car due to its ubiquity. This intermediate period is characterized by magazine articles which engaged with the car in different ways, some introducing it, others questioning its position in society. As we move into the 1960s, these contradictions become fewer as the car seems to have been accepted as we move towards a Baudrillardian commodification of need for a car.

1960–73: Fetishizing the Mundane

The third and final period of the Trente Glorieuses, as seen through these three news magazines, is one during which the transition of the car from a fetishized object of desire to fetishized need is more complete. The social necessity of the car is more apparent by the end of the 1960s. In July 1970, a new regular section appeared in *Paris Match* entitled 'Mieux vivre' ('Better Living'), and it is here that news on automobiles begins to appear rather, than in a specially dedicated section. Here again, the annual Salon de l'Automobile continues to offer a privileged site for our close reading of evolving representations of automobility. Thus, the 1970 Salon is covered briefly under this new rubric as the everyday car is presented as a way of improving quality of life. 'Mieux vivre' involves improving what one already has. The car is no longer a commodity desired for its aesthetics alone, its use–values are now part of its fetishized properties, and the resulting saturation of the roads has led to inevitable problems with traffic and accidents. Indeed, this third period is punctuated by growing public outrage over such unintended and unexpected consequences.

Jean Duché's editorials in *Elle* in the 1950s questioned the need for the car to play such a large part in French society. In the 1960s, his

99   *L'Express*, 24 September 1955, p. 10.

articles move towards a rejection of the car for all of the problems it caused. Traffic and road safety issues are at the forefront of his columns that coincide with the annual Salon de l'Automobile in Paris. In October 1960, Duché 'welcomes' the Salon with an ironic article about the automobile. He makes explicit reference to traffic issues and refers to the car as no longer a symbol of freedom:

> These beautiful machines that offer temptation at the Salon de l'Automobile seem to me a symbol of our absurdity: the more we buy, the less we can use them [...] For my part, I solved the problem by walking, taking the bus and taking a taxi; so the car in the garage – or parked in the street – costs me 1,000 francs a day (depreciation, insurance, etc.) to do nothing. Smart, isn't it?[100]

Even the practical freedom which the car can provide outside town is affected by traffic jams and offers merely a brief respite in comparison with city streets. The car has become part of everyday life, an example of mundanity which has its advantages and disadvantages much like any other commodity. The utilitarian value of the car, for which it is now consumed, has come to the foreground as its ostentation has been surpassed. This practical aspect of the car becomes apparent in *Elle*. In September 1961, the magazine published an article entitled 'Seat Belt: Pros and Cons.'[101] This is followed in the next edition by an article entitled 'Motorist Manners.'[102] We are here witnessing the genesis of a universal automobile culture, where rules of acceptability are being decided and where accession to the car has become a way of life. The car is once again discussed in a 1961 article as the behaviour of drivers towards other road users is examined. It asks why men, in particular, lose their manners once they get behind the wheel of a car. The establishment of a code of conduct whilst driving is indicative

---

100   'Ces belles machines qui proposent leurs tentations au Salon de l'Automobile me paraissent un symbole de notre absurdité: plus nous en achetons, moins nous pouvons nous en servir [...] Pour ma part, j'ai résolu le problème par la marche, l'autobus et le taxi; voilà donc une voiture au garage – ou le long du trottoir – qui me coûte mille francs par jour (amortissement, assurances, etc.) à ne rien faire. C'est intelligent, n'est-ce pas.' *Elle*, October 1960, p. 6.
101   'Ceinture de sécurité: les pour et les contre.' *Elle*, 29 September 1961, p. 31.
102   'Des manières d'automobiliste.' *Elle*, 6 October 1961, p. 4.

of the development in the cultural standing of the car amongst the population and, more specifically, within the family. However, this also has gender implications and Duché's explanation for any lack of manners resides mainly in the unlikelihood of a (male) driver being taken to task for his transgression.

The proliferation of cars also leads to questions being asked about their viability due to road casualties. The first reference to this in *Elle* is again by Jean Duché, in a 1962 article entitled 'Trees and Cars,'[103] in which he questions the need for the trees that traditionally border country roads to be cut down in order to reduce the number of fatal injuries from road accidents. The question of fatalities is addressed on a number of occasions in *Elle*, *L'Express* and *Paris Match*. Attitudes to automobile accidents in general change throughout the sixties. For instance, editorials in *Elle* note that holidaymakers die more frequently in car crashes than any other population segment, while the dangers of drink-driving are also raised. In 1969, *Elle*'s position was much stronger than earlier in the decade as one article posited that: 'to punish the killers of the road … we must change the penal code. They are more dangerous with a car than with a gun.'[104] The questioning of the causes of motor accidents continued, and the problem is again highlighted in October 1969 when *Elle* tries to discover the factors involved in the choice of a new car.[105] Price is identified as the number one factor, while safety figures last on the list.

By 1970, this media questioning extends to the motor industry's annual Parisian shop window. *L'Express* marks the opening of the Salon by ironically accepting that the car is part of modern life:

> Man is the noblest conquest of the automobile; you just have to be in a traffic jam at 6 o'clock in the evening to be convinced! However, a gigantic 'rally' of motorists – veterans and neophytes – is taking place in Paris from October 6: thousands of men from all over France and even from around the world will meet in the capital; they all have one goal, to visit the Salon de l'Automobile; one meeting point, the Grand Palais; and one dream, to acquire

103   'Arbres et autos.' *Elle*, 5 October 1962, p. 7.
104   'pour punir les assassins de la route … il faut changer le code pénal. Ils sont plus dangereux avec une voiture qu'avec un revolver.' *Elle*, 29 September 1969, p. 10.
105   *Elle*, 13 October 1969, p. 8.

the new model and – if possible – to enrich their motor stable with a few more horses.[106]

The article then goes on to question the function of the Salon. Given that the car is now an integral part of society, and recognized as such, the magazine wonders 'What use is the Salon?': 'Does the Salon de l'Automobile, where French manufacturers do not have any new models, still have a *raison d'être*?'[107] This piece effectively argues that the Salon continues to present the car as a fetishized commodity, and is consequently no longer in touch with modern life. It may thus actually have a negative effect on the status of the car:

> Of course, October's Salon gives constructors deep moral satisfaction: does it not give a brief image of the world of which they dream? For 11 days, all of Parisian life is organized around the goddess car. The 'season' of theatres, cinemas, etc. begins under its evocation. But this extraordinary animation is like a caricature of the current capitalist economy, focused on the automobile industry like that of the 19th century was on the cotton industry. The Salon presents this caricature dangerously to the public: by creating record congestion in Paris, it clearly shows all the drawbacks of an anarchic development of individual means of transport.[108]

---

106   'L'homme est la plus noble conquête de l'automobile; il suffit de se trouver à 6 heures du soir dans un embouteillage pour s'en persuader! Or, un gigantesque 'rallye' d'automobilistes – vétérans et néophytes – se déroule à Paris à partir du 6 octobre: des milliers d'hommes venus des quatre coins de France et même du monde entier vont se retrouver dans la capitale; ils ont tous un but: visiter le Salon de l'auto, un point de rencontre: le Grand Palais et un rêve: acquérir le nouveau modèle et – si possible – enrichir leur écurie-moteur de quelques chevaux supplémentaires.' *L'Express*, 6 October 1970, p. 28.
107   'Le Salon de l'Automobile où aucun constructeur français ne présente plus de nouveaux modèles, a-t-il encore une justification?' *L'Express*, 6 October 1970, p. 31.
108   'Certes, le Salon d'octobre procure aux constructeurs une profonde satisfaction morale: ne donne-t-il pas l'image en raccourci du monde auquel ils rêvent? Pendant onze jours, toute la vie de Paris est organisée autour de la déesse-voiture. La "saison" des théâtres, des cinémas, etc. commence sous son évocation. Mais cette extraordinaire animation est comme la caricature de l'économie capitaliste actuelle, axée sur l'industrie automobile comme celle du XIXe siècle l'était sur l'industrie cotonnière. Cette caricature, le Salon la présente dangereusement au public: en créant des encombrements records à Paris,

Echoing Barthes's celebrated characterization of the car as a *déesse*, Chavanne suggests that the Salon de l'Automobile transforms the city into an automobile-centric hub, reminding us in turn of Le Corbusier's 1924 dystopian vision of a world where 'with traffic fury increasing, leaving your home meant that once you crossed the threshold you became a possible prey to death, in the form of countless engines.'[109] While Salon attendance remained high, with 800,000 visitors in 1959, the perception of the car had changed.

Thus, the proliferation of cars on French roads had become the main cause of media concern and even consternation. The car was no longer a purveyor of freedom but a victim of its own popularity as, in an effort to escape cities, travellers were caught in traffic jams that roads could not handle: 'On the motorway on Sunday evening, you can easily reach 35 kilometres per hour.'[110] A cartoon in the same October 1960 issue of *Paris Match* makes fun of the seemingly eternal traffic jams which drivers are forced to face as we see two men sitting in a queue in their respective cars playing chess, while a woman in another car is catching up on her knitting. While these cartoons show the lighter side of a topical issue, Raymond Cartier wrote an article asking, 'Why is the *route des vacances* not a motorway?,' in which he highlights the significant safety issues that arise from such an abundance of cars:

> Several million cars have taken city dwellers on holidays over the past three weekends. Before the sun and the rest, there was the travel ordeal: congestion, lost time, accidents; 108 killed, 2,703 injured in the first three days of July. Why? Because France, which has the largest vehicle fleet in Europe (8 million cars) and the densest road network in the world, has virtually no motorways.[111]

il montre à l'évidence tous les inconvénients d'un développement anarchique des moyens de transport individuels.' *L'Express*, 6 October 1970, p. 31.

109 'la fureur de la circulation grandissant, quitter votre maison signifiait qu'une fois le seuil franchi, vous deveniez une proie possible de la mort, sous forme d'innombrables moteurs.' Le Corbusier, *Urbanisme*, p. 3.

110 'Sur l'autoroute le dimanche soir, vous roulez facilement à 35 kilomètres/ heure.' *Paris Match*, 8 October 1960, p. 149.

111 'Plusieurs millions de voitures ont emmené ces trois derniers week-ends les citadins vers les vacances. Avant le soleil et le repos ce fut pour eux l'épreuve du voyage: encombrements, temps perdu, accidents: 108 tués, 2.703

Thus, the Route Nationale 7, having been fetishized as a *lieu de mémoire*, was now perceived as an obstacle. The lack of a motorway network to enable automobility and to improve road safety was just one social issue which the campaigning Cartier explored, and can perhaps be seen as part of his anticolonial agenda as he promoted the advancement of the French *métropole* at the expense of its colonies.[112] Cartier followed up this article with another in the following issue of *Paris Match* entitled 'How to Give France the Motorways it Needs.'[113] This was an indictment of the state of the road network and also a message about the broader need for France to modernize.

The proliferation of the car, allied with the ensuing problems of road accidents and traffic jams, became the focus of numerous articles in the late 1950s and the early 1960s.[114] A 1963 advertisement for mineral water is revealing of the new position of the car in the French imaginary. The caption over the image of a large traffic jam reads: 'Are you tense? ... annoyed? ... Watch out for high cholesterol! Drink Hépar.'[115] In selecting this image, the advertiser highlighted an experience to which modern France had become accustomed. More broadly in such coverage, the automobile had taken on negative connotations. This theme was reinforced by the deaths of a number of high-profile celebrities nationally and internationally. While the death of iconic American actor James Dean in 1955 was remembered as the fusion of fast living and sheer speed,[116] the deaths of the celebrated writers Albert Camus in 1960 and Roger Nimier in 1962, coupled

blessés pour les trois premiers jours de juillet. Pourquoi? Parce que la France, qui possède le plus grand parc automobile d'Europe (8 millions de voitures) et le réseau routier le plus dense du monde, n'a pratiquement pas d'autoroutes.' 'Pourquoi la route des vacances n'est-elle pas une autoroute?', *Paris Match*, 21 July 1962, p. 42.

112   Batailler, Francine, Alain Schifres and Claude Tannery. 1963. *Analyses de presse*. Paris: Presses universitaires de France, p. 55.

113   'Comment donner à la France les autoroutes dont elle a besoin.' *Paris Match*, 28 July 1962, p. 66.

114   There were 8,000 road deaths in the 1950s and 16,000 road deaths in the 1970s. Assailly, *Homo automobilis ou l'humanité routière*, p. 151.

115   'Êtes-vous tendu? ... énervé? ... Attention à l'excès de Cholestérol! Buvez Hépar.' *Paris Match*, 19 October 1963, p. 22.

116   According to Ross, Dean 'provided a legend of angst-ridden mobility, a particularly appealing package of the American myth of speed and freedom.' Ross, *Fast Cars, Clean Bodies*, p. 46.

with the large-scale loss of more modest French lives, predominantly holidaymakers on overcrowded roads, meant that the allure once displayed by the car was now fading quickly.[117]

The continued growth of car numbers on roads incapable of accommodating them is a recurrent theme in Raymond Cartier's critical articles for *Paris Match*. In August 1966, high season for holiday-making, he published a piece entitled 'We are not ready for the leisure civilization,'[118] in which he refers to 'two huge issues in France: housing and the roads.'[119] While work is being done to improve the road network, it is not being done quickly enough, and this is particularly evident during the summer holidays:

> To drive on the *routes de vacances* is to live dangerously. It has been calculated with precision that 46 per cent of fatal accidents take place during the great summer car migrations and during the weekends from May to September [...] in 1970, it is expected that it [the road] will be almost entirely motorway to the Italian border. Unfortunately, in 1966, it still remains for 'vacationers' a motley assemblage of buckled surfaces and dangerous crossroads separated by too short passages on the existing sections of motorways.[120]

Cartier builds on this with a piece in the following edition entitled 'Warning! We Will Soon Have the Worst Roads in Europe,' in which he calls for the construction of 9,000 km of motorways by 1985.[121]

---

117 The link between luxury cars and death is explored in Mathieu and Monneyron, *L'imaginaire du luxe*, p. 11.
118 This echoes Joffre Dumazedier's thesis in *Vers une civilisation du loisir?*, which places leisure at the centre of modern society.
119 'Nous ne sommes pas prêts pour la civilisation des loisirs'; 'deux lacunes béantes en France: le logement et la route.' *Paris Match*, 20 August 1966, p. 36.
120 'Rouler sur les routes de vacances c'est vivre dangereusement. On l'a calculé avec précision, 46% des accidents mortels ont lieu durant les grandes migrations automobiles de l'été et durant les week-ends de mai à septembre [...] en 1970, il est prévu qu'elle sera presque entièrement autoroute jusqu'à la frontière italienne. Malheureusement, en 1966, elle demeure encore pour les "vacanciers" un assemblage hétéroclite de chaussées déformées et de carrefours pièges entrecoupés de trop courts passages sur les tronçons d'autoroutes existants.' *Paris Match*, 20 August 1966, p. 42.
121 'Attention! Nous serons bientôt le dernier pays routier d'Europe.' *Paris Match*, 27 August 1966, p. 35.

The president of the Union routière de France, George Gallienne, addressed many of Cartier's questions in an article in October of the same year, just as the Salon de l'Auto was about to open, in which he acknowledged that this issue was given more newspaper space than any other focusing on the car in the 1960s.[122]

In the graphic sphere, similar sentiments were regularly expressed by magazine contributors. Two cartoons appear on the same page of the 9 October 1965 edition of *Paris Match*, both of which ridicule the impotence of the automobile in the face of its growing ubiquity. In the first, we see a driver observe a snail overtaking him as he sits stationary in a traffic jam.[123] The second cartoon also pokes fun at the fight for the freedom supposedly provided by the car: a rather smart gentleman abandons his car in the middle of a traffic jam so that his chauffeur can carry him to his destination. While both cartoons depict a traffic jam, the socially differentiated protagonists are a reflection of the car's ubiquity. Traffic jams are not only an affliction of the common man; not even the upper-class automobile user, chauffeur-driven, can escape them.

In a work by the celebrated artist Sempé,[124] originally published in his collection *Rien n'est simple* (1962),[125] and later in *L'Express*, 'L'histoire de l'automobile … vue par Sempé,'[126] we see a series of five situations involving two individuals in the same setting. We start with a man walking past the gates of an opulent house, from which we see emerge a man pedalling an old-fashioned bicycle. The second image has the same passer-by walking past the same house, while the man emerging from the property is at the wheel of a turn-of-the-century automobile, much like the Renaults used in the first Grands Prix. The third image shows the same passer-by, this time on a bicycle, as he observes the owner of the opulent house leave in a large 1920s-style car. The fourth image shows the passer-by still on a bicycle and still observing the rich man, who once again leaves the grounds of his mansion ahead of him,

122   *Paris Match*, 1 October 1966, p. 17.
123   *Paris Match*, 9 October 1965, p. 132.
124   Sempé is a renowned French cartoonist who mainly contributed to *Paris Match*. He is best-known for his illustrations of *Le Petit Nicolas*. See Corten-Gualtieri, 'L'humour visuel de Sempé.'
125   Sempé, Jean-Jacques. 1962. *Rien n'est simple*. Paris: Folio.
126   *L'Express*, 8 October 1963, p. 21.

this time at the wheel of a large American-styled car. The final image shows the passer-by arriving at the gates of the opulent house, this time in a car that resembles a 2CV. He observes the rich man leaving his grounds on a bicycle just ahead of him; however, the passer-by is unable to overtake him as there is so much traffic that the bicycle can easily overtake everyone else. By comically inverting the desires of the rich and less well-off over time, Sempé shows how the modern car, while initially maintaining its prestige, was less fetishized as an object of desire as a result of it becoming democratized. Moreover, this same process would see the automobile itself become a barrier to the freedom that it had for so long embodied.

The 1968 Salon was 'greeted' in *L'Express* by an article highlighting the number of deaths caused by cars. The author, Françoise Giroud herself, dramatically compares the car to a weapon: 'If there were in Paris a Salon for firearms, inaugurated by the President of the Republic, where the most recent models of rifles, revolvers and machine guns were displayed, free of charge, we would be surprised, shocked, disapproving.'[127] It is significant that Giroud, who would later serve in the French government, questions the fact that the head of state continued overtly to promote the automobile. Having been part of the modernizing process in France with her editorial role at *Elle* and then *L'Express*, this hyperbolic critique from Giroud indicates the extent to which the automobile and, more specifically, road accidents had negatively impacted society. The dangers of the road constituted a theme which continued to be widely discussed in the print media.

In the later 1960s, the amount of space dedicated to the Salon de l'Automobile was drastically reduced as the negative impact of the car took up more column space. The annual event remained a site where the car was fetishized as a desire; however, disenchantment with the car as a result of its own success meant that the relevance of the Salon was questioned. Its evolution can thus be seen to mirror the way in which the car itself came to be viewed. While still desired, the automobile had come to form part of the new system of needs of a France that had been rapidly and radically modernized since the Liberation.

127   'S'il y avait à Paris, un Salon de l'Arme à feu, inauguré par le Président de la République, ou seraient exposés, en vente libre, les plus récents modèles de carabines, de revolvers et de fusils mitrailleurs, nous serions surpris, choqués, désapprobateurs.' *L'Express*, 14 October 1968, p. 89.

Conclusion

While aimed at distinct readerships and possessing their own formal and conceptual characteristics, the post-war glossy magazines *Elle*, *Paris Match* and *L'Express* were united in their shifting perception of the automobile over the course of the Trente Glorieuses. We have charted an evolution from a fetishizing of desire to a new need-based fetishization. Towards the end of this period of economic expansion, there was almost a rejection of the car as its ubiquity and an inadequate road network prone to traffic jams together negated the car's utility by bringing it to a stop. The number of deaths in car accidents also climbed, and negative reactions were reflected in the growing number of articles which, if not actually rejecting the car outright, at a minimum called for a road network that matched the needs of the modern automobile. This move from fetishizing the car as an object of desire to fetishizing it as a need fully inscribed in the modern French home, may be observed in the evolution in advertisements for cars as well as in the articles dedicated to them.

Focusing on three major publications and highlighting their combined coverage of the French motor industry's annual flagship event, the Salon de l'Automobile, this chapter has identified three stages in the evolving representation of the car over the course of the Trente Glorieuses. Pre-war conceptions were maintained in the early post-war period as the car continued to represent an object of desire which appeared to be unobtainable and, therefore, was associated with opulence and the wealthy celebrities of the time. A transitional period followed, which placed the expansion of paid holidays and emerging affluence alongside the launch and increasing availability of the Citroën 2CV and the Renault 4CV. This period may be best represented by the transparent Simca Aronde, as the car began to be perceived as attainable while remaining an object of desire. The third period identified in these magazines encompassed the adoption of the car as part of the household. As the car became more ubiquitous, these magazines portrayed a modernized France that had overwhelmingly accepted the car. They thus bore witness to a conceptual transformation of the automobile from a desired object of wonder to a socially created need, the object of a Baudrillardian desire for its practical acquisition. In the next chapter, representations of the car in other media will be explored, notably including two foundational works by

Roland Barthes on the evolving social significance of the automobile. We will also examine representations of the automobile in cinema, highlighting two of the most important directors of the era, Jean-Luc Godard and Jacques Tati.

Chapter 6

Evolving Critiques of the Car

In the print media in post-1945 France, the automobile gradually shifted from being perceived as a highly desired commodity to being considered a need. With this in mind, we now focus on cultural representations of the car, with the aim of charting the evolution of its fetishized status in French society. The selected depictions include one of the most famous pieces ever to be written on the subject, 'La Nouvelle Citroën,' by Roland Barthes, published in his 1957 collection *Mythologies*. The evolution in Barthes's perception of the car will be critically explored and placed in the context of the Trente Glorieuses through a close reading of a further essay written by him in 1963. In addition, the changing status of the automobile and its contribution to the modernization of France have been portrayed in the films of leading directors Jacques Tati and Jean-Luc Godard. Their works mirror a broader cultural evolution in which the car was central.

The Car According to Barthes

Barthes's initial analysis of the mythology of the automobile strongly echoes Marx's theory of the commodity fetish. More specifically, his deconstruction of the reification of the Citroën DS, including notably the attribution of godlike characteristics to the car, reveals that it is the 'spiritual' form of the post-war vehicle that is consumed rather than its use-value. In 1963, six years after the publication of his *Mythologies* in book form, he would associate a very different image with the car. In 'La Voiture, projection de l'égo,' published in *Réalités*, he appears to reject or at least update his more famous piece on the DS.[1] The automobile is no longer a luxury item; in the eight years since the launch of the DS, the automobile has become more neutral in social terms, more of a domestic appliance, like the fridge. Barthes maintains that while the car still holds a dominant position in French discourse, its mythical standing has changed. For Barthes, it now has an intermediate status; it is the next thing that will be bought for the household. The car has lost its dreamlike quality. The characteristics that were shrouded in obscurity have dissipated, and the car has become a somewhat more banal part of everyday existence. This shift in its status from an object of desire to an object of quotidian consumption would be examined in turn by Barthes and Jean Baudrillard. As noted in the Introduction, while there may be limitations to these theorists' approaches, as historically specific expressions of then prevailing Marxian intellectual orthodoxies, their joint conclusion that fetishizing does not disappear, but rather mutates, remains a valuable analytical tool. The specific social context within which this mutation occurs becomes evident in Barthes's and Baudrillard's respective writings, which we will examine in turn.

Barthes's critical mobilization of religious terminology in his 1957 essay echoes Marx's conception of organized religion to explain the way in which the 'real' values of an object are shrouded in mystery. His use of such imagery also draws attention to older forms of fetishizing, such as idolatry and animism, to identify the integral characteristics of the automobile as sacred:

> We must not forget that an object is the best messenger of a world above that of nature: one can easily see in an object at once a perfection and an absence of origin, a closure and a brilliance, a transformation of life into matter (matter is much more magical than life), and in a word a silence which belongs to the realm of fairy-tales.[2]

---

1   See Barthes, *Œuvres complètes*, pp. 1136–42. (First published as *La voiture, projection de l'égo*, in *Realités*, October 1963.)

2   'Il ne faut pas oublier que l'objet est le meilleur messager de la surnature: il y a facilement dans l'objet, à la fois une perfection et une absence d'origine, une clôture et une brillance, une transformation de la vie en matière (la matière est bien plus magique que la vie), et pour tout dire un silence qui appartient à l'ordre du merveilleux.' Barthes, 2003 [1957], *Mythologies*, pp. 140–41; 1972, *Mythologies*, p. 88.

Figure 15 President Charles De Gaulle leaving the presidential DS after assassination attempt (1962).
© Keystone Press/Alamy Stock Photo.

While the automobile in general, and the DS in particular, may embody such epistemological blurring, this is certainly not a new phenomenon, and it cannot be restricted to automobiles, as Kaika and Swyngedouw's discussion of early water towers shows.[3] Barthes, in his treatment of the DS, examines a vehicle that was fetishized in its form and through the desired image that it created. He refers to the quasi-religious experience involved in the consumption of the DS, which exemplifies the fetishizing of an object as its true character becomes obscured through the process of commodification.

While the Citroën DS did not appear until 1955, the concept of the car was proposed in the immediate aftermath of the war. An issue for manufacturers was that the process from the original concept to production could take from five to ten years; therefore, when they eventually left the production line, many vehicles no longer satisfied

3   Kaika and Swyngedouw, 'Fetishizing the Modern City,' p. 128.

the demands of the market.[4] As a revolutionary automobile, which improved on many aspects of top-of-the-line cars of its time, the DS was arguably not the vehicle that was desired by the majority of prospective car owners. Although a success in terms of sales, the DS had its greatest impact on a middle- and upper-class clientele; it thus had little effect on the democratization of the car or on its commodification as a utilitarian object.

In Barthes's celebrated analysis 'La Nouvelle Citroën,' he describes the appearance of the iconic DS at the Salon de l'Automobile in 1955, where it is accompanied by film star Gina Lollobrigida. In his introduction, he compares modern cars to a gothic cathedral which is 'consumed in image if not in usage,' as they are appropriated as 'a purely magical object.'[5] Éric Cobast argues that such terminology is designed to shock our sensibilities.[6] Barthes's consciously challenging representation of the DS begins by drawing critical attention to the vehicle's name. The DS can be read in French as *déesse* ('goddess'), which at once connotes the car in religious terms and simultaneously as an object of adoration. In 1965, a luxury upgrade to the DS emerged, the DS Pallas, named after Greek goddess Pallas Athena; this is, once again, an example of the reification or mythologizing of this car.[7] Barthes is explicit in his analysis of this fetishizing of the DS; this vehicle has all the trappings of an otherworldly being. His direct reference to an 'absence of origin'[8] echoes Marx, and this is expanded upon in the following paragraph as the author compares the car's shell to Christ's outer garment. This comparison serves to highlight the impression that the car appeared fully formed with as little trace of its construction as Christ's seamless robe, which, during his crucifixion at Calvary, was not destroyed, but for which lots were drawn to see who would get it in its entirety. Not only does the examination have recourse to the Marxian 'mists of religion' in a direct reference to the car as a goddess, it also underlines its fetishized nature by highlighting its apparent absence of origin:

4   *Paris Match*, 15 October 1955, p. 40.
5   'consommée dans son image, sinon dans son usage'; 'un objet parfaitement magique.' Barthes, 2003 [1957], *Mythologies*, p. 140; 1972, *Mythologies*, p. 88.
6   Cobast, Éric. 2002. *Mythologies de Roland Barthes: premières leçons*. Paris: Presses universitaires de France, p. 82.
7   Rémond, Rogé. 2000. *La DS*. Paris: Hermé, p. 46.
8   'absence d'origine.' Barthes, 2003 [1957], *Mythologies*, p. 141; 1972, *Mythologies*, p. 88.

There are in the D.S. the beginnings of a new phenomenology of assembling, as if one progressed from a world where elements are welded to a world where they are juxtaposed and hold together by sole virtue of their wondrous shape, which of course is meant to prepare one for the idea of a more benign Nature.[9]

More prosaically, Barthes also notes the tactile reaction of the public: 'one keenly fingers the edges of the windows, one feels along the wide rubber grooves which link the back window to its metal surround.'[10] This petting of the fetishized object imbues the vehicle with a further quality of desire, as it is viewed as animate as it is caressed. Gilles Néret refers to this section of the essay as 'a searing erotic homage' to the DS.[11] The earlier tradition of depicting the car as female adds credence to this erotization.

Barthes argues that the otherworldly quality of the DS even extends to its physical construction: 'As for the material itself, it is certain that it promotes a taste for lightness in its magical sense.'[12] For its part, the vehicle's streamlining suggests a more relaxed style of design; it does not express speed in the aggressive way that was employed up to this point. It is in the glasswork, however, that Barthes primarily locates 'spiritualization': 'The *Déesse* is obviously the exaltation of glass, and pressed metal is only a support for it.'[13] In Le Corbusier's conception of Paris, towering glass structures which house the population in an automobile-centred civilization form a striking aspect of the modern city.[14] Jacques Tati's 1967 film *Playtime*

---

9   'Il y a dans la DS l'amorce d'une nouvelle phénoménologie de l'ajustement, comme si l'on passait d'un monde d'éléments soudés à un monde d'éléments juxtaposés et qui tiennent par la seule vertu de leur forme merveilleuse, ce qui, bien entendu, est chargé d'introduire à l'idée d'une nature plus facile.' Barthes, 2003 [1957], *Mythologies*, p. 141; 1972, *Mythologies*, pp. 88–89.

10   'on tâte furieusement la jonction des vitres, on passe la main dans les larges rigoles de caoutchouc qui relient la fenêtre arrière à ses entours de nickel.' Barthes, 2003 [1957], *Mythologies*, p. 141; 1972, *Mythologies*, p. 88.

11   'un hommage […] d'un érotisme brûlant.' Néret and Poulain, *L'art, la femme et l'automobile*, p. 7.

12   'Quant à la matière elle-même, il est sûr qu'elle soutient un goût de la légèreté, au sens magique.' Barthes, 2003 [1957], *Mythologies*, p. 141; 1972, *Mythologies*, p. 89.

13   'la DS est une exaltation de la vitre, et la tôle n'y est qu'une base.' Barthes, 2003 [1957], *Mythologies*, p. 141; 1972, *Mythologies*, p. 89.

14   Le Corbusier, *Urbanisme*, p. 6.

echoes this Corbusian future, a critical construction of modern Paris that will be discussed later. For Tati, as we shall see, shiny glass-and-metal structures only serve to sanitize and dehumanize modern life. In contrast, for Barthes, glasswork can make an object more organic; indeed, he views the cutting-edge design of the DS as a considered attempt to give life to this particular vehicle.

Barthes's attention to these overlapping processes of sacralization and anthropomorphization does not preclude his appreciation of shifting attitudes towards the automobile in French society. Specifically, he suggests that the DS marks a change in the mythology of cars as it does not symbolize sheer power alone:

> Until now, the ultimate in cars belonged rather to the bestiary of power; here it becomes at once more spiritual and more objectlike, and despite some concessions to neomania (such as the empty steering wheel), it is now more homely, more attuned to this sublimation of the utensil which one also finds in the design of contemporary household equipment.[15]

Through this paradoxical focus on the domestic sphere, we can see that, even in terms of this luxurious vehicle, Barthes is beginning to see the car as commodified in a new way. In leaving the realm of the 'bestiary of power,' the DS is fetishized as a part of the household and, therefore, as a socially constructed need. He underlines this evolution in his reading of the vehicle's interior:

> The dashboard looks more like the working surface of a modern kitchen than the control-room of a factory: the slim panes of matt fluted metal, the small levers topped by a white ball, the very simple dials, the very discreteness of the nickel-work, all this signifies a kind of control exercised over motion, which is henceforth conceived as comfort rather than performance.[16]

---

15 'Jusqu'à présent, la voiture superlative tenait plutôt du bestiaire de la puissance; elle devient ici à la fois plus spirituelle et plus objective, et malgré certaines complaisances néomaniaques (comme le volant vide), la voici plus ménagère, mieux accordée à cette sublimation de l'ustensilité que l'on retrouve dans nos arts ménagers contemporains.' Barthes, 2003 [1957], *Mythologies*, p. 142; 1972, *Mythologies*, p. 89.

16 'Le tableau de bord ressemble davantage à l'établi d'une cuisine moderne qu'à la centrale d'une usine: les minces volets de tôle mate, ondulée, les petits

Here, we observe a desire for comfort rather than performance, thus moving away from a fetishized surplus capacity as the common denominator in the perception of the car. The alchemy of speed, which was most ostentatiously fetishized prior to any real democratization of the car, is gradually replaced by 'a relish in driving.'[17] As the car becomes more widespread, it is placed within what Urry calls the system of automobility, which is defined as:

> [T]he major item of *individual consumption* after housing which provides status to its owner/user through its sign-values (such as speed, security, safety, sexual desire, career success, freedom, family, masculinity); through being easily anthropomorphized by being given names, having rebellious features, seen to age and so on.[18]

It was the desire to be part of this system that, in the post-war period, became a need for the French public. Ross has argued that mass car ownership was preceded by engagement with it in the mass media and popular culture.[19] Barthes's treatise on the DS would seem to support this view. The final paragraph of his mythology suggests that the vehicle, and the automobile more generally, may have become less fetishized in terms of desire as a result of the practical familiarization offered by the Salon de l'Automobile:

> In the exhibition halls, the car on show is explored with an intense, amorous studiousness: it is the great tactile phase of discovery, the moment when visual wonder is about to receive the reasoned assault of touch (for touch is the most demystifying of all senses, unlike sight, which is the most magical).[20]

---

leviers à boule blanche, les voyants très simples, la discrétion même de la nickelerie, tout cela signifie une sorte de contrôle exercé sur le mouvement, conçu désormais comme confort plus que comme performance.' Barthes, 2003 [1957], *Mythologies*, p. 142; 1972, *Mythologies*, p. 89.

17   'une gourmandise de la conduite.' Barthes, 2003 [1957], *Mythologies*, p. 142; 1972, *Mythologies*, p. 89.

18   Urry, 'The "System" of Automobility,' p. 26.

19   Ross, *Fast Cars, Clean Bodies*, p. 27.

20   'Dans les halls d'exposition, la voiture témoin est visitée avec une application intense, amoureuse: c'est la grande phase tactile de la découverte, le moment où le merveilleux visuel va subir l'assaut raisonnant du toucher (car le toucher est

While a form of fetishization is implied in this petting of the desired object, Barthes posits that in the act of fetishizing, the fantastic object is paradoxically demystified. Through petting, this totem ceases to function as such; its materiality displaces its mystified image: 'The bodywork, the lines of union are touched, the upholstery palpated, the seats tried, the doors caressed, the cushions fondled; before the wheel, one pretends to drive with one's whole body.'[21] Through familiarity with the fetishized object, one can see beyond its fantastic qualities. Nevertheless, as a symbol of progress, and specifically social promotion, the DS continues to exert its powerful attraction as a desired marker of distinction: 'The object here is totally prostituted, appropriated: originating from the heaven of *Metropolis*, the Goddess is in a quarter of an hour mediatized, actualizing through this exorcism the very essence of petit-bourgeois advancement.'[22]

Barthes would return to these themes of automotive appropriation and familiarization in 'L'Automobile, projection de l'égo' (1963). Although a less celebrated analysis than his 1957 essay in *Mythologies*, it offers a window on how interaction with the car evolved over the intervening six years of sustained economic expansion in France. Barthes explains the rationale for and the modalities of his latest engagement with automobility in the following terms:

> Today, it is easy to imagine the complexity of the representations attached to the automobile: there is not a man, at first glance, in our societies, who does not talk about it (if he has one) or who dreams of it (if he doesn't have one). What are these dreams, these words? How are the mental images organized of this automobile that every man today carries 'in his head'? How do these images evolve, according to the development of society? A series of open interviews, conducted quite recently, will perhaps

le plus démystificateur de tous les sens, au contraire de la vue, qui est le plus magique).' Barthes, 2003 [1957], *Mythologies*, p. 142; 1972, *Mythologies*, p. 90.

21   'Les tôles, les joints sont touchés, les rembourrages palpés, les sièges essayés, les portes caressées, les coussins pelotés; devant le volant, on mime la conduite avec tout le corps.' Barthes, 2003 [1957], *Mythologies*, p. 142; 1972, *Mythologies*, p. 90.

22   'L'objet est ici totalement prostitué, approprié: partie du ciel de Metropolis, la Déesse est en un quart d'heure médiatisée, accomplissant dans cet exorcisme, le mouvement même de la promotion petite-bourgeoise.' Barthes, 2003 [1957], *Mythologies*, p. 142; 1972, *Mythologies*, p. 90.

allow us to approach this inner universe that the Frenchman of today builds around the car he owns, covets or refuses.[23]

While there is no indication of the percentage of men and women interviewed in this study, it is quite apparent that Barthes is examining this question from a male perspective. In referring to 'every man' and 'the Frenchman of today,' we can legitimately question if this step towards banalization of the car is available to all of society.

In this essay, while a Marxian conceptual frame remains with references to the 'automobile-object' ('l'objet-automobile'), Barthes's representation of the car as a differentially fetishized commodity effectively prefigures the work of Jean Baudrillard:

> The car has ceased to be a luxury, it has become a need; it is therefore no longer the object of a utopian discourse, we no longer dream of it in a fabulous way, its image is no longer 'photogenic,' it has definitively joined the class of domestic objects, where nothing, except its price, separates it from appliances such as the telephone or the shower.[24]

Barthes makes it clear that while the social status of the car has evolved significantly, this does not mean that it has become a ubiquitous object, as the majority of people still do not own one. Nevertheless, he underlines the continuing shift in the perception of the automobile from fetishized desire to mundanity:

> We see here that a banal object is not necessarily – today – a universal object; the automobile poses financial problems of

---

23   'On imagine sans peine, aujourd'hui, la complexité des représentations attachées à l'automobile: pas un homme, à première vue, dans nos sociétés, qui n'en parle (s'il l'a) ou qui n'en rêve (s'il ne l'a pas). Quels sont ces rêves, ces paroles? Comment s'organisent les images mentales de cette automobile que tout homme de maintenant porte "dans la tête"? Comment ces images évoluent-elles, au gré du développement de la société? Une série d'interviews libres, menées tout récemment, va peut-être nous permettre d'approcher cet univers intérieur que le Français d'aujourd'hui construit autour de la voiture qu'il possède, qu'il convoite ou qu'il refuse.' Barthes, *Œuvres complètes*, p. 1136.

24   'L'auto a cessé d'être un luxe, elle est devenue un besoin; elle n'est donc plus l'objet d'un discours utopique, on ne la rêve plus sur un mode fabuleux, son image n'est plus "photogénique", elle a définitivement rejoint la classe des objets domestiques, où rien, sinon son prix, ne la sépare de l'électroménager, du téléphone ou de la douche.' Barthes, *Œuvres complètes*, p. 1136.

purchase and maintenance for the vast majority of French people; six out of seven French people do not own a car; this does not prevent the car from being now a perfectly tamed object, entirely passed from fairyland to reality, even when you do not own it.[25]

An important part of this process of domestication would be the increasing availability of more mundane alternatives to the luxury durably epitomized by the DS. As Peter Wollen suggests, the Panhard Dyna Z, which was in production from 1954 to 1959, is a perfect example of such resolutely 'homely' models.[26] Increasingly disregarded as an object of desire, and no longer primarily craved for its mystified properties, the automobile had, by 1963, taken on an intermediary status: 'The car is not yet a universal accessory for the French, but it has ceased to be a fabulous object; neither incredible luxury nor absolute need, it has an intermediate status: it is what we are going to buy; it is no longer a dream, but a project.'[27]

The transition from an object of desire to an almost mundane object is one which Baudrillard has explored in his analysis of the Marxian commodity fetish.[28] Within this analytical framework, the automobile has become inscribed in everyday society as an object or appliance. Regarded as such, it has become a need for the 1960s French family and has thus become refetishized. This reworking of Marx's theory amounts to a critical acceptance of the concept of the commodity fetish, but it also implies its extension from the realm of exchange-value to the fetishizing of use-value. As Barthes had argued in 1957, the automobile as gothic cathedral was worshipped in image solely. It was not as a transport provider that it was desired but rather for the magical qualities with which it was imbued. Marx did not allow for

25   'On voit ici qu'un objet banal n'est pas forcément – aujourd'hui – un objet universel; l'automobile pose à la grande majorité des Français des problèmes financiers d'achat et d'entretien; six Français sur sept ne possèdent pas d'auto; cela n'empêche pas la voiture d'être désormais un objet parfaitement apprivoisé, entièrement passé de la féerie à la réalité, même quand on ne la possède pas.' Barthes, *Œuvres complètes*, p. 1136.

26   Wollen, *Autopia*, p. 351.

27   'L'auto n'est pas encore, pour les Français, un accessoire universel, mais elle a cessé d'être un objet fabuleux; ni luxe inouï, ni besoin fatal, elle dispose d'un statut intermédiaire: elle est ce qu'on va acheter: elle n'est plus rêve, mais projet.' Barthes, *Œuvres complètes*, pp. 1136–37.

28   Baudrillard, *Le Système des objets*, p. 70.

the use-value of an object to be fetishized, yet it is this Baudrillardian rereading of the Marxist commodity that Barthes was effectively invoking in this 1963 essay:

> For use-value – indeed, utility itself – is a fetishized social relation, just like the abstract equivalence of commodities. Use-value is an abstraction. It is an abstraction of the system of needs cloaked in the false evidence of a concrete destination and purpose, an intrinsic finality of goods and products. It is just like the abstraction of social labor, which is the basis for the logic of equivalence (exchange-value), hiding beneath the 'innate' value of commodities.[29]

Using the term 'infuse,' Baudrillard echoes Marx's original text on the concept. His argument that a use-value can also be fetishized is particularly applicable as the 'innate' value of the automobile has been placed within this system of needs. This is something that Barthes had recognized, if not directly formulated, in his own essay of a decade earlier.

There Barthes explores the utilitarian nature of the car as he explains how it has become a mundane object. He argues that the fact that it no longer functions as a symbol of social status ('standing social,' as he calls it) is an indication of its integration into everyday society, hence of its banality. He also posits that it is no longer 'un objet de classe ou de promotion' as 'man can no longer invest his vanity in an instrument whose purchase plan is almost universal; now a mass object, the car ceases to arouse, at least in itself, a psychology of distinction: the object itself has become socially neutral, it no longer displays.'[30]

---

29 'La valeur d'usage, l'utilité elle-même, tout comme l'équivalence abstraite des marchandises, est un *rapport social* fétichisé, – une abstraction, celle du *système des besoins*, qui prend l'évidence fausse d'une destination concrète, d'une finalité propre des biens et des produits – tout comme l'abstraction du travail social qui fonde la logique de l'équivalence (valeur d'échange) se cache sous l'illusion de la valeur "infuse" des marchandises.' Baudrillard, *Pour une critique de l'économie politique du signe*, p. 155; Baudrillard, *For a Critique of the Political Economy of the Sign*, p. 131.

30 'l'homme ne peut plus investir sa vanité dans un instrument dont le projet d'achat est à peu près universel; devenue objet de masse, l'auto cesse d'exciter, du moins en soi, une psychologie de la distinction: l'objet lui-même est devenu socialement neutre, il n'affiche plus.' Barthes, *Œuvres complètes*, p. 1137.

Here, Barthes posits that the automobile has become so pervasive that it no longer has the ability to represent social 'distinction'; a term which, in this case, anticipates the work of Pierre Bourdieu, effectively excluding the automobile from the mechanisms of class distinction famously explored by the sociologist in his own foundational work.[31] Barthes, rather hyperbolically, suggests that this goes further than simple possession of a car; it extends to the various car brands that exist on the market. The *marques* and models of car no longer carry any form of fetishized value as they have all come to be seen as homogenous: 'of course, the types do not appear absolutely uniform, we continue to distinguish, affectively, a 403 from a DS; but from a mythological point of view – which we retain here alone – the automobile consciousness seems to really recognize only one personalized car (semanticians would say: marked).'[32]

The only exception to this semiotic blurring is that of the Citroën 2CV, as this is the only car capable of capturing the imagination. According to Barthes, 'The entire French fleet thus seems to be reduced to a significant opposition between the 2 CV and "the rest" in which the subjects do not feel any need, despite the price differences, to introduce differences in signs, that is to say, standing.'[33] The way the 2CV still captures the imagination seems unclear: is it because it is the only car that the lower classes can afford and is a reminder of their growing automobilization? Even if this is the case, it is not because of the aesthetic qualities of the car. However, Barthes suggests that there are still some remnants of a fantastic image of the automobile, as this needs to exist in order to form a counterpoint to the homogenous nature of the French car market. This fetishizing is now to be found in the representation of imported foreign cars, as 'the Jaguar and the Mercedes are still dreamlike, probably because of their comfortable

31   Bourdieu, *La Distinction*, p. 164.

32   'certes, les types n'apparaissent pas absolument uniformes, on continue de distinguer, affectivement, une 403 d'une DS; mais du point de vue mythologique – que l'on retient seul ici – la conscience automobile ne semble reconnaître vraiment qu'une seule voiture personnalisée (les sémanticiens diraient: *marquée*).' Barthes, *Œuvres complètes*, p. 1137.

33   'tout le parc français semble ainsi se réduire à une opposition signifiante entre la 2 CV et «le reste» dans lequel les sujets n'éprouvent nul besoin, en dépit des différences de prix, d'introduire des différences de signes, c'est-à-dire de standing.' Barthes, *Œuvres complètes*, p. 1137.

sportiness.'[34] Thus, while everyday cars have become normalized, larger sports cars have remained fetishized as they retain a certain cachet of unavailability and thus otherworldliness.

As Barthes suggests, there exists a paradox in this transition, since while the automobile may have been banalized through ubiquity, it remains a 'place of extremely rich psychological investment.'[35] The linkage between the car and the post-war nuclear family is the key to its affective power. Typically, the type of car owned by an individual is reflective of his/her family situation, with a succession of updated vehicles reflecting its evolution. While Barthes suggests that there is no tension between husband and wife with regard to the car – 'the interviews here deliver no problem: in front of their car, the spouses really seem to be one'[36] – his examination of the family car contains strong gender assumptions as neither wife nor daughter is mentioned in this relationship. On the male side, what was once an object of desire for the father has become mystified differently, and is now both desired and rejected by the son in a paradox which is explained thus:

> when the son does not yet have a car, the father's car is both a coveted object and a rejected model (*I will never buy the same brand as my father*), so that borrowing the father's car is always, for the son, an ambiguous act which testifies to both an obligation and a subjection (most memories of the car begin with this relationship between a father who has and a son who does not).[37]

Barthes elucidates this filial dilemma of desire and rejection as he explores how the car has become crucial in the son's passage from childhood to adulthood. The son's first car, which generally will have

34 'la Jaguar et la Mercedes font encore rêver, sans doute en raison de leur sportivité confortable.' Barthes, *Œuvres complètes*, p. 1137.
35 'lieu d'investissements psychiques extrêmement riches.' Barthes, *Œuvres complètes*, p. 1137.
36 'les interviews ne livrent ici aucun problème: devant leur auto, les époux ne semblent vraiment faire qu'un.' Barthes, *Œuvres complètes*, p. 1137.
37 'lorsque le fils n'a pas encore d'auto, celle du père est à la fois objet convoité et modèle rejeté (*je n'achèterai jamais la même marque que mon père*), en sorte qu'emprunter l'auto du père est toujours pour le fils un acte ambigu qui témoigne à la fois d'une obligation et d'une sujétion (la plupart des souvenirs d'auto commencent par ce rapport entre un père qui a et un fils qui n'a pas).' Barthes, *Œuvres complètes*, pp. 1137–38.

previously been the father's car, constitutes the first tangible example of ownership in the younger man's life. Barthes characterizes it as a new form of fetish, marking an important step in the male life course: 'the son's first car functions essentially as his first property, more substantial than the first communion watch, more accessible than the future house; it is therefore here a rite-object, an object of initiation, the acquisition of which marks the full accession to adulthood.'[38] This is echoed by Baudrillard in his *Le Système des objets*, where he refers to the driver's licence as a symbol of freedom and thus adulthood:

> Travel is a necessity, and speed is a pleasure. Possession of a car implies more: the driving licence is a sort of passport, a letter of credit from an aristocracy whose domain is the very latest in engine compression and speed. Disqualification from driving is surely tantamount to an excommunication, to a kind of social castration.[39]

In both Barthes's and Baudrillard's works, and with echoes of Freud here, perhaps, the automobile continues to be fetishized; its centrality in the accession to adulthood of French youth underlines how much more democratized the automobile has become as we move towards the end of the Trente Glorieuses. The gender assumptions of both texts, such as Baudrillard's image of social castration, would support the impression that banalization was largely restricted to male drivers. Baudrillard admits to this later in the same discussion:

> Very often the car remains a male preserve. 'Daddy has His Peugeot,' runs one advertising slogan, 'and Mummy has HER Peugeots': the father gets the Peugeot car and the mother gets the Peugeot egg-beater, the Peugeot coffee mill and the Peugeot

38   'la première auto du fils fonctionne essentiellement comme sa première propriété, plus conséquente que la montre de première communion, plus accessible que la maison future; elle est donc ici un objet-rite, un objet d'initiation, dont le contact marque le plein avènement de l'adulte.' Barthes, *Œuvres complètes*, p. 1138.
39   'Le déplacement est une nécessité et la voiture est un plaisir. La possession d'une automobile est plus encore: une espèce de brevet de citoyenneté, le permis de conduire est la lettre de créance de la compression et la vitesse de pointe. Le retrait de ce permis de conduire n'est-il pas aujourd'hui une espèce d'excommunication, de castration sociale?' Baudrillard, *Le Système des objets*, p. 93; *The System of Objects*, p. 66.

electric mixer. The family universe is a universe of foods and multifunctional appliances; as for the man, he rules over the world outside, the effective sign of which is the automobile: he himself does not appear in the picture.[40]

This juxtaposition of male automobility and the female domestic sphere should be nuanced by a brief mention of Barthes's analogy between the mundanity of the car and bread, 'fundamental in the lives of the French.'[41] Bread maintained a powerful, real and symbolic quality during the century before the writing of this essay and has a strong emblematic link with the French Revolution. By 1963, Barthes suggests, the automobile had achieved much the same status as bread; it had become a banalized object but had not yet reached the stage of triviality. Its mythical status was thus evolving and would likely disappear in the near future:

> The automobile, it seems, has arrived at the last moment of this trip; we fight for it, to buy it, to maintain it (hence the acuteness of the consciousness it provokes), but already commonplace, it would take little for it to become insignificant (there is no refrigerator mythology in America). As this is not yet the case, some mythical traces remain in the French automobile, but these traces are weak, probably temporary.[42]

The mythical remnants still apparent in the automobile are the only obstacle to it becoming as everyday as bread. It may be argued that the

---

40   'La voiture reste en effet souvent l'apanage de l'homme. "Papa a SA Peugeot, Maman a SES Peugeot," dit une réclame. A l'homme la voiture, à la femme le batteur, le moulin à café, le robot électro-culinaire, etc. L'univers familial est celui des aliments et des appareils multifonctionnels. L'homme, lui, règne à l'extérieur, sur un monde dont le signe efficace est la voiture: on ne le voit pas sur l'image.' Baudrillard, *Le Système des objets*, pp. 96–97; *The System of Objects*, p. 68.
41   'fondamental dans la vie des Français.' Barthes, *Œuvres complètes*, p. 1138.
42   'L'automobile, semble-t-il, est arrivée au dernier moment de cet itinéraire; on lutte pour elle, pour l'acheter, pour l'entretenir (d'où l'acuité de la conscience qu'elle provoque), mais déjà banale, il suffirait de peu pour qu'elle devienne insignifiante (il n'y a aucune mythologie du réfrigérateur en Amérique). Comme ce n'est pas encore le cas, il reste dans l'automobile française des traces mythiques, mais ces traces sont faibles, probablement provisoires.' Barthes, *Œuvres complètes*, p. 1138.

analogy with a fridge might be taking the comparison too far as the fridge may symbolize a new, clean France *à la* Ross, but it nonetheless did not and could not enthral potential customers to the same extent as the automobile.

In this context, new ways of standing out from the increasingly motorized crowd become essential. The pure speed technically made possibly by the automobile's surplus capacity, and historically the object of fetishization (see Chapter 1), is no longer a possibility in the regulated modern world. So, Barthes argues, what is left is the opportunity to differentiate oneself in the pursuit of 'the exercise of a certain individualism,'[43] an insight that would be developed by Bourdieu through his concepts of cultural capital and distinction. Sport, as the ludic expression of individuality, may offer one such sphere for self-expression within a Urryan system of automobility[44] exemplified by conformity to the rules of the traffic jam:

> The 'sporting' is therefore shifted towards behaviours: travelling at unusual times (that is to say when the others are not travelling), aimlessly driving along a motorway (to let off steam), this is the 'sporting' nature of the automobile, above all an ethical virtue which consists in diverting the automobile from its mass uses in order to find through it a certain solitude.[45]

Thus, the deceleration of the car in the traffic jams caused by its ubiquity means that 'the sporting nature of the automobile' is now the mechanism by which the modern driver may stand out from others 'either by possessing, if one can, an object more complicated than the others, or by bending this object to singular behaviours.'[46] Such imaginative reinvention is also required because, in the new space

---

43 'l'exercice d'un certain individualisme.' Barthes, *Œuvres complètes*, p. 1138.
44 Urry, 'The "System" of Automobility,' pp. 25–39.
45 'Le "sportif" est donc déplacé vers des comportements: voyager à des heures inhabituelles (c'est-à-dire quand les autres ne voyagent pas), parcourir sans but une autostrade (pour se défouler), c'est là le "sportif" automobile, vertu surtout éthique qui consiste à détourner l'auto de ses usages de masse pour retrouver à travers elle une certaine solitude.' Barthes, *Œuvres complètes*, p. 1139.
46 'soit en disposant, si l'on peut, d'un objet plus compliqué que les autres, soit en pliant cet objet à des conduites singulières.' Barthes, *Œuvres complètes*, p. 1139.

age inaugurated by the 1957 launch of Sputnik 1, the mass-market automobile's transition to immobility is complete:

> But it is normal that the car loses all heroic fabulousness, because the adventure is today entirely absorbed by the exploration of sidereal space: in the face of cosmic machines, the automobile can no longer fulfil any dream of unknown movement: it is now a stationary object.[47]

The shift in social fascination from the automobile – via the aeroplane, historically – to the space rocket is also investigated by Jacques Tati in his 1971 film *Trafic*, as we shall see later in this chapter.

The representation of the car as a house, which is similarly explored and parodied in *Trafic*, forms an important part of Barthes's thesis. The acquisitions of both a house and a car are socially constructed needs. One does not choose one or the other, although Henri Lefebvre suggests a widespread predilection for a car, which he refers to as 'l'Objet-Roi,' when he says: 'it is true that, for a lot of people, their car is part of their "living," maybe even an essential part.'[48] Both are necessities that must be satisfied in order for the owner to be socially successful: 'The acquisition of a car, then of a home, is in no way seen as an alternative between two different needs, but as successive moments on a single journey.'[49] In this context, Barthes notes that car interiors are now being personalized as an exercise in individualism. The automobile has become 'a space to furnish, the equivalent of a household ornament.'[50] What is more, the automobile has become what Barthes describes as 'an extension to a house,'[51] as

47 'Mais il est normal que l'auto perde tout fabuleux héroïque, car l'aventure est aujourd'hui entièrement absorbée par l'exploration de l'espace sidéral: face aux engins cosmiques, l'automobile ne peut plus accomplir aucun rêve de mouvement inconnu: c'est un objet désormais immobile.' Barthes, *Œuvres complètes*, p. 1139.
48 'Il est vrai que, pour beaucoup de gens, leur voiture est un morceau de leur "habiter", voire le fragment essentiel.' Lefebvre, Henri. 1968. *La Vie quotidienne dans le monde moderne*. Paris: Gallimard, p. 100.
49 'L'acquisition d'une auto, puis d'un logement n'est nullement sentie comme une alternative posée entre deux besoins différents, mais comme les moments successifs d'un itinéraire unique.' Barthes, *Œuvres complètes*, p. 1139.
50 'un espace à meubler, l'équivalent du bibelot domestique.' Barthes, *Œuvres complètes*, p. 1139.
51 'une maison appendice.' Barthes, *Œuvres complètes*, p. 1140.

it serves as a sanctuary of familiarity while at work. This concept of the automobile is echoed in Eric Laurier's discussion of the car as a personal workspace,[52] and, to a certain extent, is the opposite of Augé's 'non-lieux' of hypermodernity.[53] Baudrillard also links home and the car as he sees both as capable of reinforcing the everyday: 'Indeed, relative to the social sphere, household and motorcar partake of the same *private* abstractness, and the binomial they thus constitute, when it is articulated with another, that of work and leisure, frames the entirety of everyday experience.'[54]

In the conclusion to his 1963 essay, Barthes states that the car itself can no longer be straightforwardly fetishized; instead, it is driving that has now become the mythology: 'the fantastic seems to move from the automobile object itself to the way of using it, that is to say of driving it.'[55] The very ubiquity of the automobile is posited as the reason for this change: 'The high number of cars on the road makes "sporty" driving more and more difficult, and moreover, the uniformity of models seems to condemn the very idea of technical performance; "normal" driving then becomes the narrow field, but the only possible field in which to invest fantasies of power and invention.'[56] The uniformity of the automobile market, where the numbers produced are beginning to meet demand, but at the same time are saturating road networks, means that opportunities to fetishize the everyday automobile are fast disappearing. The automobile has become a 'very ordinary thing.'[57] Thus, Barthes can anticipate the demise of the fetishized vehicle: 'It is no longer its forms or functions that will solicit the human dream, it

---

52   See Laurier, Eric. 2004. 'Doing Office Work on the Motorway.' *Theory, Culture & Society* 21 (4–5): 261–77.

53   See Augé, *Non-lieux*.

54   'En fait, par rapport à la sphère sociale, foyer et voiture participent de la même abstraction privée, – leur binôme venant s'articuler sur le binôme travail, loisir pour constituer l'ensemble de la quotidienneté.' Baudrillard, *Le Système des objets*, p. 96; *The System of Objects*, pp. 67–68.

55   'la fabulation semble se déplacer de l'objet automobile lui-même à la façon d'en user, c'est-à-dire de la conduire.' Barthes, *Œuvres complètes*, p. 1142.

56   'Le nombre élevé des voitures en circulation rendent de plus en plus difficile la conduite "sport", et d'autre part, l'uniformité des modèles semble condamner l'idée même de performance technique; la conduite "normale" devient alors le champ étroit, mais le seul champ possible où investir des phantasmes de puissance et d'invention.' Barthes, *Œuvres complètes*, p. 1142.

57   'truc très ordinaire.' Barthes, *Œuvres complètes*, p. 1142.

is its handling; and soon, perhaps, it will no longer be an automobile mythology that needs to be written, but a mythology of driving.'[58]

The shift seen in Barthes's perception of the car also occurs in French cinema. Two directors in particular engaged with technological modernity and, more specifically, its imbrication with the automobile during the Trente Glorieuses. Jean-Luc Godard was the Nouvelle Vague director *par excellence*, as he rejected literary influences to experiment with Hollywoodian and other cinematic techniques. Jacques Tati cannot be described as a Nouvelle Vague director, although his highly idiosyncratic work is from this same period. In the works of both these film-makers, we see a gradual rejection of the modernization of French society and of the automobile as a result.

Godard: From Americanization to *Week-end*

Two of Jean-Luc Godard's films, *À bout de souffle* from 1959 and *Week-end* from 1967, are important as they indicate Godard's own journey from a desire for American society to its rejection, as well as that of capitalism. Godard's interest in all things American at the time of the shooting of *À bout de souffle* is noted by Ross in terms that echo Barthes's nomenclature: 'things American have a mythical element which creates their own existence.'[59] Michel Poiccard (played by Jean-Paul Belmondo), the hero of *À bout de souffle*, is very taken with American popular culture; he steals and drives American cars and mimics the mannerisms of Humphrey Bogart, his cinematic idol. Godard's shift in attitude towards the Americanization of society and more specifically the role of the car echoes that which we have already seen in the analysis of Trente Glorieuses magazines. Having been initially embraced, desired and, indeed, fetishized in Godard's works, in *Week-end* the automobile is rejected for the way in which it has entered French society and obliterated the traditional way of life. In calling his film *Week-end*, still a relatively recent borrowing both

---

58   'Ce ne sont plus ses formes ou ses fonctions qui vont solliciter le rêve humain, c'est son maniement; et ce n'est plus bientôt, peut-être, une mythologie de l'automobile qu'il faudra écrire: c'est une mythologie de la conduite.' Barthes, *Œuvres complètes*, p. 1142.
59   Godard, qtd. in Ross, *Fast Cars, Clean Bodies*, p. 44.

linguistically and culturally, Godard highlights the car's creation or facilitation of notionally free time that must be consumed in the active pursuit of leisure. The automobile has, in effect, forced us to engage in leisure activity while at the same time becoming a barrier to it, as in the now-famous rolling shot early in *Week-end*.

In Godard's earlier work, *À bout de souffle*, we see Jean-Paul Belmondo at the wheel of the American car he has stolen, talking to himself insouciantly as he passes people and cars: 'If he thinks he's going to overtaking me, that asshole … Now I'm going for it … Why isn't she overtaking? Women are cowardice personified … You should never brake. Like old Bugatti said, cars are made to drive, not to stop.'[60] Poiccard as an anti-hero displays deeply anti-social characteristics while at the wheel of the car. However, this suggests that the automobile has become more mundane as it incarnates 'natural,' although negative, emotions. It is an everyday object in which both bad and good traits are possible. A pedestrian is killed by a car in Paris, yet it is still fetishized as an object of desire as Belmondo's character only steals powerful American cars. The car is reaching the intermediary stage that Barthes describes, where it is coming to be perceived as a constituent part of modern society.[61] Godard hints at the potential dangers of the car while at the same time giving it prominent space on screen.

Released in the same year as *Bonnie and Clyde*,[62] *Week-end* differs from this celebrated road movie as Godard refuses to valorize road travel as a means of escape from, or a form of rebellion against, society. In late Trente Glorieuses France, this 'need' for escape has become symbolic of a materialistic, Americanized society. Godard presents a middle-class couple as they encounter a series of bloody car accidents on their weekend trip away from the city. The clichéd image of an idyllic countryside to which one may escape is attacked as Godard rejects the notions of freedom and leisure associated with the car. Neil Archer has succinctly described this critique of the automobile world:

60   'S'il pense qu'il va me doubler, ce con … Maintenant, je fonce, Alphonse … Pourquoi elle dépasse pas? Les femmes, c'est la lâcheté personnifiée … Il ne faut jamais freiner. Comme disait le vieux père Bugatti, les voitures sont faites pour rouler, pas pour s'arrêter.' Boissel, Anne. 2004. 'L'accident ou la chair dévoilée.' *Champ psychosomatique* 4: 101–17 (p. 106).
61   Barthes, *Œuvres complètes*, p. 1136.
62   Penn, Arthur, dir. 1967. *Bonnie and Clyde*. United States, Warner Home Video.

Figure 16 Jean-Paul Belmondo at the wheel in Nouvelle Vague classic. © *À bout de souffle*, Jean-Luc Godard (1960).

'*Week End* does indeed make a mockery of automotive aspiration, and our received iconography of the road genre, through its reduction of car culture to mechanized manslaughter or the literal impasse of traffic jams.'[63] Godard replaces it with an almost post–apocalyptic landscape which has been destroyed by an overabundance of automobiles and associated consumerism. Gerald Silk has aptly characterized the striking depiction of this commodified world on screen:

> This sensation of numbness and ennui recurs in Jean-Luc Godard's film *Week-end*, in which car wrecks become symbolic of the paradox of progress. Through repetition and stylization of violent acts, Godard created a humorous situation that becomes a horrible one. After scores of crashes, the idea of another crash becomes ludicrous, but the viewer, catching himself laughing at these grisly events, feels shameful and confused about his

63   Archer, *The French Road Movie*, p. 19.

Figure 17 Infamous traffic jam scene with blood–soaked victims strewn along the road.
© *Week-end*, Jean–Luc Godard (1967).

> response. Both Warhol and Godard have pointed up the savage assault of mass culture on the mind and the body, and the reduction of 'advanced' civilization into a mental and physical wasteland.[64]

Annie Goldmann posits that the use of everyday scenes and their exaggeration are Rabelaisian in nature; however, they are used by Godard not in a comic way, but rather to ensure that the viewer is entirely focused on his message.[65] Jean Douin also makes reference to Rabelais in the context of *Week-end* as he refers to all travellers as 'hordes de Panurge.'[66] This carnivalesque hysteria, while severed from comedy, creates an atmosphere which serves to ridicule modern France, or at least Godard's impression of it; yet this is done in a very serious tone.

First and foremost, *Week-end* offers a negative image of the middle classes by inspiring dislike of the bourgeois couple who leave on their

64   Silk, *Automobile and Culture*, p. 135.
65   Goldmann, Annie. 1971. *Cinéma et société moderne*. Paris: Anthropos, p. 177.
66   'Un mouton de Panurge' is an expression referring to a person who is easily led. Douin, Jean-Luc. 2010. *Jean-Luc Godard, dictionnaire des passions*. Paris: Stock, p. 432.

weekend trip. They are portrayed as greedy, unfaithful and, once in their car, constantly angry. An early scene during which the couple, in a conversation, wish a fatal accident upon the father of the wife, cuts to a scene of road rage in the car park below, seen from the vantage point of the couple's apartment. David Laderman offers an illuminating reading of this episode:

> A long, high-angle shot exaggerates the cars as 'characters' more than the people (since the latter are so tiny in the frame), as two cars back into each other. The occupants then get out and fistfight. As demonstrated here, Corinne and Roland's relationship – full of hate, distrust, and selfishness – is contextualized by cars as vehicles of violence, extensions of human domination and abuse.[67]

Taking place in a leafy suburb, the surroundings contrast with the brutish characteristics of the cars' occupants as their overreaction to a minor incident conveys the message that acquisition of all these new symbols of modernity has not made people happier. The consumerist nature of competition amongst the characters, as they vie for superiority, first in their cars, and then physically, underlines the new world where possessions dominate, and thus the automobile assumes the characteristics of its owners. The spectacle of two couples fighting as they prepare to leave for the weekend, as the main characters are also doing, is framed by the title of the film, *Week-end*, which appears onscreen as their fight is in full flight.

The iconic travelling shot of the traffic jam early in the film conveys hyperbolically the overabundance of the automobile. The camera moves along in a tracking shot that lasts for over eight minutes as we see every type of person imprisoned in the vehicle that was designed to procure the liberty for which they have all departed on this particular weekend. People are playing cards while waiting, an image that had already been parodied in cartoons that appeared in magazines of the time. There are overturned cars, while others try to overtake in a vain attempt to make a minimum of progress. We also witness the barbaric behaviour of the occupants, which contradicts the clichéd image of the middle classes typically associated with the automobile and with

---

67   Laderman, David. 2002. *Driving Visions: Exploring the Road Movie*. Austin, TX: University of Texas Press, p. 256.

leaving for the weekend. Finally, the camera reaches the cause of the traffic jam, an accident where bodies are strewn in a bloody mess across the road. This famous scene is not constructed so as to be realistic; rather, it is apparent that the artificial world constructed by Godard is one which critiques modern-day society: 'This suggests that "good" middle-class people out on their weekend are false, prone despite the veneer of civility to cruelty and barbarism.'[68] More particularly, the extent of the traffic jam, allied with the clichéd image of interactions between drivers, presents a society destroyed by consumerism. It is Godard's rejection of the American road movie and of American automobile-centric society, as well as that of those Europeans who seek to emulate it. The burlesque nature of the scene is additionally reminiscent of France's Second World War *exode*, during which Paris was abandoned in the face of the German invasion of the city.

The variously symbolic clash of cultures is explored in a further accident. We see a sports car trying to overtake a tractor, and then hear a crash off-screen before cutting to a scene where the male driver of the sports car is dead. Almost unaware of her dead partner, the blood-spattered young woman who was accompanying the driver is arguing hysterically with the tractor driver over who had the right of way. This screaming match, which arguably signifies the collision of social classes, again underlines a rejection of modernity. By moving ahead too quickly, the nation has forgotten its roots, and it is not only the forgotten classes that suffer as a result. In its ever-increasing attempt to accelerate and attain its consumerist goals, France needs to be careful that it does not become a victim of its own modernizing aspirations. The similarity in the reaction of both parties to the crash counterpoints this collision between the classes. By reacting hysterically to each other, the only distinction between them can be seen in terms of their possessions. Thus, any Bordelian distinction is portrayed in this scene solely through the ownership of a vehicle. Laderman posits that this accident occurs off-screen in a rejection by Godard of the American cinema of the spectacular. It is the social consequences of Americanization that interest Godard rather than its cinematic conventions.[69]

Week-end is a film in which Godard demystifies social modernity, in particular by rejecting French devotion to American consumer culture.

68   Laderman, *Driving Visions*, p. 257.
69   Laderman, *Driving Visions*, p. 257.

The early car park scene in which members of the middle class attack one another is paralleled in a later episode where two hippie groups face off. Society in Godard's film is malfunctioning at all levels. The consumerist nature of modern life has led to society devouring itself – we see cannibalism later in the film as a trope for how life is literally consumed. Society seems to have become indifferent to this as the central couple initially drives and later walks past overturned cars and bodies strewn across the road with complete indifference. The deaths in *Week-end* occur amongst the middle classes and remind us of the leading writers Camus, Nimier and Sagan, amongst others, who were all involved in car accidents at this time.[70] Kristen Ross explores how incidents involving such well-known personalities were extensively covered in the press of the day:

> The violent automobile death of Nimier himself and novelist Sunsiaré de Larcone in 1962, along with those of Albert Camus and Michel Gallimard in 1960, Jean-René Huguenin in 1962, the two sons of André Malraux, the Ali Khan, and the near-fatal accident of Johnny Hallyday in the surrounding months, each produced a torrent of horrified, lurid articles.[71]

While initially seen as reflecting the desire for high-performance vehicles, in particular in the representation of James Dean, who died in 1955 in a Porsche 550 Spyder nicknamed 'Little Bastard,'[72] the adulation of speed, and specifically death at speed, was gradually supplanted by a growing discourse on the dangers of the car, reinforced, as Ross states, by the coverage these deaths received. It is in this context of the mediatized car accident that *Week-end* is set.

Week-end proved to be a commercial success in France, particularly amongst the middle classes, who apparently, ironically, identified with this rejection of modern society.[73] Godard's film uses the automobile to portray the rapid modernization of society and, more specifically, to signify one of the ways by which society may destroy itself:

---

70   See also Vidal, Ricarda. 2013. *Death and Desire in Car Crash Culture: A Century of Romantic Futurism*: Peter Lang.
71   Ross, *Fast Cars, Clean Bodies*, p. 27.
72   Raskin, Lee, and Tom Morgan. 2005. *James Dean: At Speed*. Phoenix, AR: David Bull, p. 101.
73   Kavanagh, Thomas M. 1973. 'Godard's Revolution: The Politics of Meta-Cinema.' *Diacritics* 3 (2): 49–56 (p. 52).

Godard, like many other postwar European filmmakers, forges a cinema that de-glamorizes the car and debunks Hollywood's myth of American automobility. But he does so in a newly Fordist society where the car, along with Hollywood films and other American consumer products, are quickly encroaching on everyday life.[74]

This rejection of 'American automobility' contrasts strongly with the valorization of the car in earlier productions such as *À bout de souffle* and can be seen to reflect the evolution of society as rapid modernization was being increasingly questioned. Jacques Tati's films through this period provide us with further evidence of this rejection. While Tati was not a Nouvelle Vague director and much more obviously comedy-oriented, his later films have been likened by a number of scholars to those of Godard.[75] However, his work did not undergo quite the same kind of evolution. A strong believer in tradition and community, Tati consistently shows us a changing France over a period of 20 years; a France which slowly abandons its roots, as the modernization of the nation removes any vestiges of a more humane society.

Tati: Critical Chronicler of Modernization

Jacques Tati's standing as a social observer and a critical chronicler of the post-1945 modernization and, more especially, the technicization of France has been widely examined.[76] The gradual evolution of his films from *Jour de Fête* (1949) up to *Trafic* (1971) may be seen as a reflection of – and an increasingly critical reflection on – that same modernization.[77] In *Jour de fête*, a postman who is enthralled

74   Green-Simms, Lindsey. 2009. *Postcolonial Automobility: West Africa and the Road to Globalization.* Minnesota, MN: University of Minnesota, p. 136.
75   See Darke, Chris. 2005. *Alphaville: Jean-Luc Godard, 1965.* Chicago, IL: University of Illinois Press, p. 29; Laufer, Laura. 2002. *Jacques Tati ou le temps des loisirs.* Paris: L'If, p. 20; François, Corinne. 2002. *Roland Barthes, Mythologies.* Paris: Bréal, p. 12.
76   See Laufer, *Jacques Tati ou le temps des loisirs,* p. 20; Ross, *Fast Cars, Clean Bodies,* p. 5; Goudet, Stéphane. 2002. *Jacques Tati: de 'François le facteur' à 'Monsieur Hulot.'* Paris: Cahiers du cinéma; Makeieff, Macha, and Stéphane Goudet. 2009. *Jacques Tati: deux temps trois mouvements.* Paris: Naïve.
77   Tati, Jacques, dir. 1949. *Jour de fête.* France, Voyager; Tati, Jacques, dir. 1971.

by mechanized American production methods decides to adapt these techniques to his own work, only to reject them to return to traditional ideals. Tati's last feature film, *Trafic*, as the title would suggest, uses the car as a means of critiquing modernism. In between these two films, there is an automotive shift from *Les Vacances de monsieur Hulot* (1953), in which the car is a rickety old banger, to a gleaming modern car in *Mon oncle* (1958).[78] In the latter film, we see two very different societies, divided by a crumbling wall.[79] There is the marginalized traditional community within which Hulot lives and in which his characteristic insouciance is given free rein. This is contrasted with the sterile house in which Hulot's brother-in-law lives on the other side of the collapsing wall. *Playtime* (1968), a further step in Tati's interpretation of a rapidly modernizing society, portrays a futuristic, Corbusian city,[80] in which traditional Paris has been replaced by glass-and-metal high-rise buildings.[81] Tati's acute sense of the visual creates a striking impression of Trente Glorieuses France. While he remains optimistic, particularly through the happy-go-lucky personality of Monsieur Hulot, played by Tati himself, the director condemns the constant and furious attempts to modernize the nation. Ross sees Tati's work as a reflection of how objects had become more dominant since the Second World War:

> If I return [...] to the films of Jacques Tati, it is because they make palpable a daily life that increasingly appeared to unfold in a space where objects tended to dictate to people their gestures and movements, gestures that had not yet congealed into any degree of rote familiarity, and that for the most part had to be learned from watching American films.[82]

Ross refers to Tati as 'the greatest analyst of postwar French modernization'[83] and, therefore, a vehicle-focused reading of the evolution of

Trafic. France, Ciné vidéo film.
78   Tati, Jacques, dir. 1953. *Les Vacances de monsieur Hulot*. France, Criterion Collection.
79   Tati, Jacques, dir. 1958. *Mon oncle*. France, Voyager.
80   Le Corbusier designed and built a series of modernist buildings throughout Europe, the first in Marseille and named 'Cité radieuse,' but which is locally called 'la maison du fada'. *Fada* means 'crazy/nutter' in Provençal.
81   Tati, Jacques, dir. 1967. *Playtime*. France, Les films de mon oncle.
82   Ross, *Fast Cars, Clean Bodies*, p. 5.
83   Ross, *Fast Cars, Clean Bodies*, p. 30.

his work is particularly worthwhile. The earlier films will set the scene for the change. *Mon oncle* will be considered as a reflection of a rapidly evolving society, while *Playtime* and *Trafic* may be read as explorations of the mechanics of the resulting change. These last two works merit special attention. Tati's outstanding ability to convey a serious critique of society within a popular medium makes his work particularly rich for this analysis.

Tati's work explored the technological advances within France in the 1950s and 1960s. The rapid urbanization and modernization, which included the expansion of the automobile sector, are examined as they are experienced in everyday society.[84] While *Jour de fête* and *Les Vacances de monsieur Hulot* do not prioritize these themes, the emergence of a France beginning to be impacted by Americanized culture can be seen. In *Jour de fête*, François, the rural postman, becomes so entranced with a promotional video short on the modern-ization of the postal service that he decides to do things 'the American way.'[85] In *Les Vacances de monsieur Hulot*, leisure time and, to a lesser extent, the automobile are examined as the importance of traditional community is highlighted. The trope of community is one which stands out in Tati's work. Similarly, the importance of family in the face of a more modern, business-oriented society is explored briefly in *Les Vacances de monsieur Hulot*, as the eponymous protagonist forms a stronger bond with a young boy than the latter is able to make with his own father, who is constantly on the phone engaged in business conversations while he is supposed to be on holiday. This theme forms the main thrust of *Mon oncle*, as Hulot remains part of the old France, while his brother-in-law and family become symbols of its modern counterpart. This tension is underscored in all of Tati's later films; as modernization takes hold, Tati's work reflects how society has dealt with this evolution.

Mon oncle was released in 1958 and saw Jacques Tati receive the Academy Award for best foreign-language film. It deals directly with the conflict between the old and the new France. These two worlds are separated physically and metaphorically by a crumbling brick wall, which Hulot, on one occasion, takes care not to destroy any further by carefully replacing a brick which he has inadvertently displaced. Hulot

84   See Bardou, Chanaron, Fridenson and Laux, *La révolution automobile.*
85   Ross, *Fast Cars, Clean Bodies*, p. 42.

manifestly belongs to old France, and his effort to physically maintain this rapidly crumbling wall is indicative of his desire to preserve the past. While happy to enter new France with all its technology and gadgets, Hulot prefers to reside in the people-centred community to which he is accustomed and which, through its refusal to move with the times, appears to have been marginalized from modern society. That Gérard, Hulot's nephew, and Monsieur Arpel's dog both choose to leave modern France to have fun is indicative of Tati's negative impression of the modernizing effect. Gérard appears delighted to be told that he can spend the afternoon with his uncle, much to the disapprobation of his own father. This conflict between the old and the new appears on a number of occasions in *Mon oncle*. More often than not, it is caused by Hulot's inability, voluntary or otherwise, to integrate into a cleaner, but also more sterile France.

Released in the year that the Fourth Republic gave way to the Fifth, *Mon oncle* can be seen as representing a pivotal point during the Trente Glorieuses as regards the modernization of France, and in particular the democratization of the automobile. In the opening sequence of the film, Monsieur Arpel takes his son, Gérard, to school. He pulls out of his house in his car to join three lanes of constant traffic moving in unison in a mid-1950s rush hour. While there are large numbers of cars, it is important to note that they are still moving; it is possible to make progress even though there are increased volumes of traffic. This is not the case in later Tati movies, such as *Playtime* and *Trafic*; both make use of the traffic jam to demonstrate how the ubiquity of the car has halted mobility. In another traffic jam in *Mon oncle*, we are introduced to some of the drivers making their way home from work when a children's trick leads them to believe that they have been crashed into, and they consequently engage in arguments with the drivers of the car behind. We meet a young businessman, referred to by Ross as the 'high priest of Fordism,'[86] as well as a young businesswoman and an elderly gentleman. In this scene, as in the early morning traffic jam, the vehicles are all large and American-looking, as the car appears to be reserved for the middle and upper classes. The drivers' reactions to the imagined accident are quite understated as a specific type of behaviour is expected of them. Here the automobile

86 Ross, *Fast Cars, Clean Bodies*, p. 7.

Figure 18 Traffic jam scene.
© *Playtime*, Jacques Tati (1967).

is clearly class-specific, and its possession alone is symbolic of social status, reflecting the broader reality of class distinction explored by Bourdieu.[87]

The couple's wedding anniversary provides an opportunity to examine their devotion to all things modern. Monsieur Arpel purchases a pink-and-green Chevrolet as a present for his wife while she surprises him with an automatic electric garage door. Both purchases are demonstrations of the couple's need to indulge in ostentatious acquisition and conspicuous consumption.[88] The Chevrolet, a 'belle Américaine' as in Robert Dhéry's film of the same name,[89] is displayed to Monsieur Arpel with the modern catchphrase 'Tout est automatique' ('Everything is automatic'). The couple's joy at their respective presents is short-lived, however, as they get trapped in the new Chevrolet when the automatic garage door is inadvertently closed, triggered by the couple's dog. This episode underlines Tati's message that life is not necessarily made any easier by all these new gadgets; in fact, the opposite may actually be true. The hysterical reaction of the maid when

87   Bourdieu, *La Distinction*, p. 164.
88   See Veblen, Thorstein. 2005. *The Theory of the Leisure Class: An Economic Study of Institutions*. Delhi: Aakar Books.
89   Dhéry, Robert, dir. 1961. *La Belle Américaine*. France, Matinee Classics.

asked to pass through the motion sensor in order to open the garage underlines the social differentiation that is reinforced by this rapid modernization. The maid's overpowering fear of being electrocuted almost prevents her from releasing her employers from their garage; an ironic image of enforced immobility in a location conceived as a domestic shrine to automobility.

Mon oncle was the first film by Tati in which he addressed the modernization of French society, juxtaposing the lifestyle of the eponymous lead character with that of his sister-in-law's family. The broader French predilection for shiny, metallic surfaces is further explored in *Playtime*, a futuristic work in which it seems that the entire population has become part of a mechanized and sanitized society. By the time *Playtime* came out in 1967, a number of social critics had engaged at length with the rapid modernization of France. In 1961, sociologist Henri Lefebvre brought out the second part of his study of everyday life, the first having been published in 1947. The third part of his *Critique de la vie quotidienne* appeared in 1981 in order to address how the category of the everyday had once again evolved. The 1961 volume has the subtitle *Fondements d'une sociologie de la quotidienneté*,[90] and in 1968 *La Vie quotidienne dans le monde moderne* was also published as Lefebvre updated his analysis of a still modernizing France. As a social analyst, he argued that the country was in a state of transition between a traditional country and one that was becoming modern too quickly. Building on this analysis, Jean Baudrillard also commented on this evolution and mentioned *Playtime* as an excellent illustration and critique of this rapid transformation, highlighting these competing national identities:

> We are still, in our service-consuming society, at the crossroads of these two orders. This was very well illustrated by Jacques Tati's film *Playtime*, which moved from traditional, cynical sabotage, the wicked parodying of services (the whole episode in the fancy restaurant, with the cold fish passing from one table to another, the malfunctioning systems, all the perversion of 'reception structures', and the breakdown of a world that is simply too new) to the useless instrumental functionality of reception

90   Lefebvre, Henri. 1961. *Critique de la vie quotidienne II: fondements d'une sociologie de la quotidienneté*. Paris: L'Arche.

rooms, armchairs and pot-plants, glass façades and 'impeccable' communication, all in the icy solicitude of the countless gadgets and a perfect ambience.[91]

Baudrillard thus explores the transition highlighted by Lefebvre and suggests that France was still at a 'crossroads of these two orders' in the late 1960s. As illustrated by Tati, a tension between personal relationships and a new, more sterilized world order is apparent as there seems to be no room for traditional warmth, as incarnated by Monsieur Hulot, in modern France.

Playtime, released in 1967, and the film which bankrupted Tati, is almost certainly his finest work. The film is set in a futuristic Paris in which, as Daney puts it, Tati 'built la Défense before la Défense existed.'[92] Tati replaces the city centre with Corbusian shiny glass-and-metal skyscrapers. These glass shells house enterprises within which workers are themselves placed in glass booths. The Arpels' modern house in *Mon oncle* is here condensed into an apartment with a large glass wall on its side, through which one can panoptically observe the uniformity of the occupants. These Foucauldian structures are explored by Martouzet and Laffont, who suggest that social practice in tandem with technology has created a homogenized country with no room for individuality or tradition.[93] The old Paris, which was evoked by its eccentric and interesting inhabitants in *Mon oncle*, is no longer visible. Indeed, the only glimpses we get of any recognizable Parisian structures are when we see the Eiffel Tower and the Arc de Triomphe

---

91   'Nous sommes encore, dans notre société de consommation de services, au carrefour de ces deux ordres. C'est ce qu'illustrait très bien le film de Jacques Tati: Playtime, où l'on passait du sabotage traditionnel et cynique, de la parodie méchante des services (tout l'épisode du cabaret de prestige, le poisson refroidi qui va d'une table à l'autre, l'installation qui se détraque, toute la perversion des «structures d'accueil» et la désagrégation d'un univers trop neuf) à la fonctionnalité instrumentale et inutile des salons de réception, fauteuils et plantes vertes, des façades de verre et de la communication sans rivages, dans la sollicitude glaciale des innombrables gadgets et d'une ambiance impeccable.' Baudrillard, *La Société de consommation*, p. 261; *The Consumer Society*, p. 164. See also Flonneau, Mathieu. 2016. *L'automobile au temps des Trente Glorieuses*. Paris: Loubatières, p. 164.
92   'construit la Défense avant que la Défense n'existe.' Serge Daney, qtd. in Hilliker, Lee. 2002. 'In the Modernist Mirror: Jacques Tati and the Parisian Landscape.' *The French Review* 76 (2): 318–29 (p. 320).
93   Martouzet, Denis, and Georges-Henry Laffont. 2010. 'Tati, théoricien de l'urbain et Hulot, habitant.' *L'Espace géographique* 39 (2): 159–71 (p. 164).

Figure 19 Reflections of Paris.
© *Playtime*, Jacques Tati (1967).

as reflections in the glass facades of these modern structures. The only link with the past is personified by the flower seller, as the rich colours of the flowers, and the reminders of nature, are in stark contrast to the grey and transparent structures that surround her.

In this dehumanized, sterile world, Monsieur Hulot appears to be homeless as he does not belong to modern Paris, yet we do not see where he goes. Hulot arrives from where he left in *Mon oncle*, the *non-lieu* of the airport: 'Finally, as a link between the two films, the viewer finds Mr. Hulot, ten years later, back in Paris through the same door from which he left: the airport.'[94] Hulot is as out of place in this new Paris as he was in the world inhabited by his sister and brother-in-law. However, in *Playtime*, Hulot's screen time is significantly diminished since Tati chooses to focus on the way in which, in this modernized setting, people all behave uniformly and become depersonalized due to the sterile nature of their surroundings. Much of the film is a sequence of sounds; automobile engines and horns provide the soundtrack for much of the film as human life and social interaction

94 'Enfin, en guise de trait d'union entre les deux films, le spectateur retrouve M. Hulot, une dizaine d'années plus tard, de retour à Paris par la même porte d'où il l'avait quitté: l'aéroport.' Martouzet and Laffont, 'Tati, théoricien de l'urbain et Hulot, habitant,' p. 165.

have been suppressed. The homogenous nature of modern life is underscored in one scene by four similarly dressed young businessmen simultaneously getting into four identical cars which are parked beside one another. The rush hour traffic, which moved at a relatively brisk pace in *Mon oncle*, has now been reduced to a crawl. In the film's final scene, there is a further demonstration of the homogenized nature of modern France: cars and buses alike crawl along in unison and circle roundabout after roundabout to the sound of carnival merry-go-round music. The Tatian carnival chimes strongly with Bakhtin's analysis of the same; but here, the carnivalesque serves to subvert modern rather than traditional social hierarchies.[95] The sheer ubiquity of the car means that all classes are able to converge on the streets of Paris and yet not necessarily interact. This mingling is noted by Lefebvre, who posits that real interaction is impossible: 'In automobile traffic, people and things accumulate, mingle without meeting.'[96] Thus, once again, Tati demonstrates how objects which were associated with modernity – with the car to the fore – through their proliferation merely serve to deprive people of their individuality. They are inserted into a system that functions (or ceases to function) over and above that for which these objects were conceived. As Martouzet and Laffont argue, Tati does not identify the car or any other commodity as the cause of this dystopian malfunction; rather, he accuses society of having allowed itself to become dependent on technical progress.[97]

Mon oncle and *Playtime* both reflect how modernization has impacted on Trente Glorieuses France. Tati himself was quick to highlight the fact that it is not the objects themselves that he ridicules in his films, but the impact they have had, or have been allowed to have, as they are consumed: 'The satire of the film is not about where we live but how we practice it.'[98] The urbanization of France as a result of the

95   Bakhtin, Mikhail. 1984 [1965]. *Rabelais and His World*. Bloomington, IN: Indiana University Press, p. 10.
96   'Dans la circulation automobile, les gens et les choses s'accumulent, se mêlent sans se rencontrer.' Lefebvre, *La Vie quotidienne dans le monde moderne*, p. 100.
97   Martouzet and Laffont, 'Tati, théoricien de l'urbain et Hulot, habitant,' p. 169.
98   'La satire du film ne porte pas sur le lieu où nous vivons mais comment nous le pratiquons.' Jacques Tati, qtd. in Martouzet and Laffont, 'Tati, théoricien de l'urbain et Hulot, habitant,' p. 167.

growth of the car provided Tati with fertile ground for much of his comedy. Both *Mon oncle* and *Playtime* explore a country increasingly controlled by technological modernity. In his final feature film, *Trafic*, Tati focuses his attention on the automobile as he moves away from housing and the workplace.

Trafic was released in 1971, just two years before the oil crisis of 1973. Much like Tati's more famous work, *Trafic* is a comedy that parodies society's devotion to the car as the epitome of modernity and also as a commodity that has made its way ubiquitously into everyday life. It has been said that *Trafic* was a step backwards for Tati after *Playtime*.[99] *Trafic* is set in a recognizable world, and it restores Monsieur Hulot as the primary source of comedy.[100] The film moves away from the futuristic society created in *Playtime*; Hulot is now employed, for the first time, as an automobile designer for a small car-making firm in Paris called Altra. Hulot's boss asks him to take their latest design, a small camper van or *camping-car*, to be displayed at the International Motor Show in Amsterdam. What follows is a series of misadventures on the road as Hulot and companions struggle with unforeseen obstacles only to arrive at the Salon just as it is closing. Hulot is promptly fired and left to make his own way in the world, walking off into the crowd as he has previously done in both *Mon oncle* and *Playtime*.

With Hulot's journey outside France, we are moving away from the modernizing post-war world into one characterized by globalization. Indeed, while place was important in Tati's earlier works, here it falls into the background. Film critic Michel Chion echoes Augé's theory of the *non-lieu* when he says that the road trip in *Trafic* is 'a journey between two places, neither of which has its own existence,' adding that Paris 'is a motorway exit and a glimpse of a square; Amsterdam an exhibition hall. Nothing exists but the journey.'[101] The car trip thus takes centre stage as *Trafic* becomes a commentary on the system of automobility that has taken over, not just in France, but right across continental Europe. We see motorways and various intersections; we

99   Chion, Michel. 1987. *Jacques Tati*. Paris: Seuil, p. 81.
100   The financial failure of *Playtime* was attributed to the absence of Hulot's character for large parts of the film.
101   'un trajet entre deux lieux dont aucun n'a d'existence propre … est une sortie d'autoroute et un coin de place entr'aperçu; Amsterdam un palais d'exposition. Plus rien n'existe que le trajet.' Chion, *Jacques Tati*, p. 82.

also see an overabundance of cars as numerous traffic jams display how the automobile is suffering from its own success. Interestingly, Hulot goes on this journey while Apollo 11 is making its way to the moon. At different points on Hulot's itinerary, we catch glimpses of the explorers in outer space as they are observed with awe by terrestrial society. In one scene, mechanics in a garage abandon their work to sit in front of a television and watch this new conquest of space. Tati pokes fun at this manifestation of modernization. While two men land on the moon, Hulot and his comrades are incapable of making it to Amsterdam in the same time; mankind's inability to adapt properly to technology in the everyday is counterpointed by the first steps on the lunar surface, with ironic echoes of Barthes's 1963 comments on the space rocket.

In fact, it is the overabundance of gadgets in Hulot's car that makes him late for the motor show. When investigated by the police, Hulot must demonstrate all of the appliances that have been integrated into his creation. As previously mentioned, Tati for the first time moves away from the theme of place in terms of buildings, housing and community. However, as Barthes and Baudrillard both suggested in their studies of the car, the automobile has become a substitute for the house in that it provides many of the comforts originally associated with a home, functioning as 'a house by proxy,' as Barthes puts it.[102] In *Trafic*, Tati parodies this development as the *camping-car* automatically extends in order to accommodate two people sleeping in the back. The various gadgets demonstrated to the police remind us of the gleaming appliances that are the pride and joy of Madame Arpel in *Mon oncle*. Hulot's creation has incorporated many of the modern appliances without which French homes were felt to be incomplete. There is a table and chairs which extend from the back, and which are surrounded by a canopy for privacy. Also at the back is a shower. On the front of the car, the grill can be converted into a barbecue. Inside, there is a stove, a sink, a coffee maker, a soap dispenser and an electric razor that extends from the steering wheel. The *camping-car* even has a television that comes out from the wall to be viewed by the inhabitants while in bed in their extended vehicle. Modernity has thus moved forward from the incorporation of such appliances into the modern house. The automobile has now become a substitute for the house and, in a world

102   'une maison par procuration.' Barthes, *Œuvres complètes*, p. 1139. See also Baudrillard, *Le Système des objets*, p. 65.

where one spends more and more time in the car, its conversion into a living space, where one can function 'normally,' is almost expected.

There are two further scenes in *Trafic* that are noteworthy: the pile-up on the motorway and the traffic jam at the end of the film. These scenes have become the most iconic images of a film that was not a box office success. The motorway collision occurs when a traffic warden losing his bearings, and two flows of traffic start running into one another. The iconic image of a DS going up on its two front wheels marks the beginning of this mass pile-up, which is very different from those seen in Godard's *Week-end*. In this scene, Tati turns things on their head by attributing unexpected sounds to various objects. As the DS comes back down onto four wheels, we hear the sound of an aeroplane landing. Throughout the entire scene, there is an absence of any human sounds; there are thus no exclamations or cries as we witness the crash as a kind of a mechanical ballet. In a scene that recalls the animism prevalent in Futurism, the vehicles almost seem to come to life as a Beetle chases a runaway wheel with its bonnet opening and closing like a predatory animal.[103] The humans, as they remove themselves from their crashed cars, appear to take on the characteristics of their machines as they silently stretch in exceptionally mechanized movements. Tati's transposition of mechanical characteristics onto humans, and vice versa, suggests that, by continually submitting to mechanization, it becomes difficult to differentiate subjects from objects. An image of a priest standing in front of his damaged Beetle is particularly symbolic as he addresses his vehicle as he would a church altar. The priest then kneels at the engine of his car and proceeds to hold a circular part of the engine aloft as if it were the host during the mass. In this striking scene, Tati shows us a vehicle that has become ubiquitous to the point of immobility, but which is nevertheless still fetishized and worshipped. As such, it is the object which best represents the position assumed by technology in modern France.

In the last scene in *Trafic*, Tati develops the link between the exponential growth of the car and the effect it has had on people and on life. In this second iconic sequence, the motion of the windscreen wipers of each car resembles the corporeal and behavioural characteristics of its driver. The wipers of an old man's car move with the greatest

---

103 Campbell, 'Vital Matters,' p. 161.

Figure 20 A priest worshipping at the altar of the car.
© *Trafic*, Jacques Tati (1971).

effort, while those of a fat driver move more slowly and deliberately. As David Bellos notes: 'The technology is humanized by Tati in order to emphasize that, after purchase, cars become indigenized, reworked and recast to some degree to suit the personalities of their users.'[104] This echoes Barthes's allusion to the car, which is 'bichonnée' or modified in order to make it resemble the personality of its owner, while at the same time differentiating it from that of its neighbour. This final scene, which was shot in a car park, depicts hundreds of cars stuck in a logjam that shows no signs of moving. We have moved from the limited ability to travel in space in *Mon oncle*, via the carnivalesque regularity with which vehicles make progress in *Playtime*, to a standstill in *Trafic*. In order to emphasize that we have gone full circle, Tati shows groups of people emerging from a *métro* station and opening their umbrellas as they make their way freely between the cars. This final scene suggests that the automobile itself has become the greatest

104   Bellos, David. 1999. *Jacques Tati: His Life and Art*. London: Harvill, p. 212.

obstacle to freedom, as Tati shows that returning to a simpler way of life is a means of moving forward. Thus, while Godard's work showed a considerable modification of his position with regard to modernity and the Americanization of France, Tati's work is more consistent in its goals. François the postman's attempts to modernize his work practice are gently lampooned in *Jour de fête*, while the automobile comes to symbolize modernity in *Les Vacances de monsieur Hulot* and, more overtly, in *Mon oncle. Playtime*, which Tati considered to be his best film, utilizes the car to highlight the homogenized world which has emerged from the Trente Glorieuses, a world in which traditional France has faded into the background. In his final role as Monsieur Hulot in *Trafic*, Tati depicts the harmful impact of the ubiquity of the automobile and society's inability adequately to deal with it. As a chronicle of modernization, Tati's work provides uniquely revealing insights into French society in the post-war period.

Conclusion

Roland Barthes's famous mythology of the DS presents a vehicle which is fetishized for its image quality, and desired for its ability to confer higher social status upon its owner. His reworking of this analysis in an essay published some six years later is reflective of the democratization of the automobile in Trente Glorieuses France. This rapid expansion of the car and of a commodity-oriented society is critiqued quite violently by Godard and more gently in Tati's comedies, which present us with an intriguing record of how France has desired and consumed these new symbols of modernity. From the modernity of the automatic appliances in Madame Arpel's kitchen to their integration into Hulot's *camping-car* in *Trafic*, we see representations of a French society which has accepted the modern and, indeed, has embraced it. The perception of the automobile evolved in the eyes of writers and film-makers, from an object broadly desired as a symbol of class distinction to one whose ubiquity in modern society meant that much of its capacity to differentiate between individuals and classes began to disappear.

Conclusion

Only recently has car culture entered the academic mainstream as a focus for the study of culture as broadly conceived. However, as an object that has been so systematically consumed as to become part of the fabric of society, the car's impact and perception make it 'a curiously precise tool for calibrating cultural values.'[1] As it grew in popularity, the automobile conditioned the texture of modern life. Hall posits that 'the automobile is just as much an expression of the culture as is the language and, therefore, has its characteristic niche in the cultural biotype.'[2] The particularly car-centred society of modern and contemporary France is thus apt for such an examination. Precisely because the automobile has become so ubiquitous, people from all classes have interacted with it, making it part of the national cultural fabric. The automobile consequently provides us with an accurate prism through which to examine the evolution of French society in the modern and postmodern eras.

As a vehicle which was democratized gradually, the automobile was consumed in image before it was actually purchased by large numbers of people. Thus, the way the public engaged with it, whether it be as an owner/driver or as a spectator, reflects closely both its own commodification and the growth of society's affluence. This study's relatively long timescale – from 1895 to 1973 – has allowed us to trace a durable progression in France's engagement with the automobile. The range of representations analysed, as well as the parallels established across

---

1   Bayley, *Sex, Drink and Fast Cars*, p. 62.
2   Hall, Edward T. 1990. *The Hidden Dimension*. New York: Anchor, p. 145.

these forms, indicate that the evolving role of the car reflects a broader societal transformation. This development can be explained using Marx's concept of the commodity fetish as a theoretical framework, supplemented and refined by the work of later thinkers.

Perhaps the clearest example of Marxian fetishizing of an object is that predicated on desire; indeed, a commodity can be so invested with imagined properties that it comes to be highly desired. These properties may vary widely depending on the specific good so invested. In particular, Marx made frequent reference to the use of religious imagery in the fetishizing process, in that the conferring of supernatural properties upon a product leads it to become a talisman. This phenomenon was explored with regard to the automobile in our opening chapters, where we observed that the car and speed have historically been linked to a range of mythological figures, as evoked by motor racing trophies. Such associations would also be noted by later cultural commentators on the car. Indeed, in what is arguably Roland Barthes's most famous mythology, he makes explicit use of the wordplay evident in the name of the Citroën DS (or Déesse), as he critiques the way in which the automobile has become venerated in modern society.[3]

We have seen that prominent intellectuals of the time explored cars in terms of fetishization, as this became the dominant intellectual response to consumer society, reflecting prevailing Marxist and early post-Marxist thought patterns. Such Marxian attempts to engage with a rapidly evolving economy and social structure, to which a new techno-logical dimension was added, led to the rejection of structuralism and would in time lead Baudrillard and others to formulate new theoretical approaches now characterized collectively as postmodernism. More fundamentally, Marx's analysis remains very useful in diagnostic terms; however, as has often been observed in other contexts, his prognosis has limits and blind spots, as do those of Barthes and Baudrillard. What has transpired is that the sign systems of the automobile have proven remarkably durable. The specific modes of fetishization of the automobile – as both an object and a sign – have consequently evolved, while Barthes's and Baudrillard's respective engagements with the legacy of Marx continue to shed light on one of the most iconic products of the 20th century.

3   Barthes, 2003 [1957], *Mythologies*, pp. 140–42.

In this study, we examined how the surplus capacity of the automobile was fetishized as cars were raced over increasing distances and at higher and higher speeds at a time when motor sport and, indeed, the industry itself were still both in their infancy. The Gordon Bennett races brought an international dimension to the sporting sphere, and French patriotism was underlined with victory in the first Grand Prix in 1905. The surplus capacity of the car was similarly promoted by the Citroën expeditions in Africa. With state backing, these militarized treks endorsed the automobile as a vehicle capable of crossing vast expanses of land. Moreover, as the latest incarnation of western technology, the expeditions were also notable for their geo-symbolic significance. By greatly facilitating the exploration and domestication of 'darkest' Africa, they contributed to France's self-appointed civilizing mission and, specifically, the promotion of modernizing championed by Albert Sarraut as Minister for the Colonies and culminating in the Exposition Coloniale Internationale of 1931. By highlighting the possibilities of the automobile to inhabitants of the colonies and, just as importantly, by widely publicizing this 'civilizing' effort back in France, the *raids Citroën* served to reinforce the notion that a confidently imperial 'Greater France' was entering a new technological age in which old beliefs were being displaced by scientific precision. The French colonies could now be crossed without difficulty thanks to this new technology, with the result that the Michelin company's promotion of tourism also became instrumental in this process of taming the extended national space. At home, the creation of the Michelin guide, which initially consisted of technical advice for the early driver, and subsequently the establishment of the tourist office and Michelin maps, were indications of a France reinventing itself thanks to these new and accurate tourist tools. People could now consider visiting a tourist destination which, according to the guidebooks, 'was worth a detour' as the country was beginning to be accessed and enjoyed by its increasingly motorized citizens.

This study has also explored how the automobile was ideologically and affectively invested during the Trente Glorieuses, in ways distinct from before the Second World War. The conceptual framework adopted was a Baudrillardian rereading of Marx, which stressed the possibility that a commodity may be fetishized not only for its exchange-value but also for its use-value. Thus, a product fits into a system of socially created needs in which, by representing membership of a class or a system, a commodified object may be designated as a need in order to fulfil the life of an individual. Baudrillard used the television, the fridge and, crucially, the automobile as examples of such fetishizing. While initially perceived as luxury items, the rapidly modernizing society of Trente Glorieuses France came to consider these commodities as a constituent part of this new world. The way in which the automobile came to be considered a collective need during this period casts light on how French society evolved at a time of intense social change.

The impact of the car on the growth of tourism was examined as the automobile continued to be fetishized as an object of desire and specifically as a Bordelian manifestation of class distinction. However, with the generalization of paid holidays on the basis of industrial expansion in the post-war years, the 'need' to depart on vacation grew as the use-value inherent in the car – the ability to transport people – now became fetishized. This was a gradual process, however, and one which was closely linked to a desire to emulate stars and the upper classes in frequenting heretofore exclusive resorts. The linking of certain stars to certain cars was a further indication of this association. Brigitte Bardot, the iconic Tropézienne *par excellence*, was a fitting candidate to sell Renault's latest convertible, the Floride. The strong connection between stars and cars was notably present in popular magazines in the late 1940s and early 1950s, as the automobile was still regarded as an exclusive commodity and was fetishized as such. However, a subtle evolution in this perception became apparent in the late 1950s. Vehicles were less often portrayed with stars at their wheel, and new magazines began to publish articles in which the automobile was portrayed as attainable and even necessary in modern France. Towards the end of the 1960s, road deaths and congestion became recurring themes as questions were asked about the car's ability to provide the use-values for which it had hitherto been fetishized.

The evolution of perceptions of the automobile can perhaps best be seen in the two critical essays that Barthes devoted to it in 1955/57 and 1963. We have scrutinized Barthes's celebrated analysis of the fetishization of the Citroën DS as an object which had seemingly descended from the heavens. This was juxtaposed with his treatment of the Citroën 2CV in 'La Voiture, projection de l'égo,' where he likens the altogether more commonplace vehicle to bread in terms of its now strictly limited desire-value. Barthes's critique suggests that while the automobile was initially desired for its seeming otherworldliness, the advent of the more affordable car to a large extent transformed it into an increasingly mundane need. In this way, the automobile 'joins the class of household objects, where nothing, if not its price, separates it from the household appliance, the telephone or the shower.'[4] Barthes, however, did not fundamentally question the continued social centrality of the car, as was to happen at the hands of both editorial writers and cartoonists in popular magazines of the late Trente Glorieuses. In fact, this cultural *mise en question* was to become most apparent in the cinema.

A clearly apparent evolution, if not actually a revolution, occurred in the work of Jean-Luc Godard, beginning with his epoch-making *À bout de souffle* in 1959, in which the protagonist, an anti-hero of sorts, loves everything American, and in particular large American cars. In contrast, the anarchic *Week-end* (1967) overtly rejects the Americanization of French society; however, it is the impact of the automobile that receives the most virulent criticism. The title of the film refers to the popular practice of getting away in one's car for the weekend; Godard transforms this perceived leisure time into a modern-day hell as epitomized by the now iconic traffic jam scene. The ubiquity of the car had by the late 1960s become the principal barrier to mobility. While Jacques Tati's films display throughout the closely associated themes of anti-Americanization and anti-modernization, an apparent evolution also takes place in his work. The portrayal of François the postman, in *Jour de fête* (1949), offers a gentle warning that more modern is not necessarily better. In *Mon oncle* (1958), *Playtime* (1968) and *Trafic* (1971), this questioning of the rapid transformation of society becomes more explicit. In the accident scene in *Trafic*, in which the priest holds part of his car aloft in an obvious allusion to the mass, we see a fetishizing of the car in terms of religious imagery once again. The car has become an integral part of society; indeed, it is now so needed that its presence is both reified and deified.

In these and related artistic productions, major cultural figures held up a mirror to a France which had, since the later 19th century,

---

4 'rejoint la classe des objets domestiques, où rien, sinon son prix, ne la sépare de l'électroménager, du téléphone ou de la douche.' Barthes, *Œuvres complètes*, p. 1156.

come to embrace the internal combustion engine and all its works. It first did so hesitantly, then enthusiastically in the interwar period, and finally, after 1945, almost obsessively. Of course, the automobile is highly important as an artefact not only in France but also in global culture. However, in France, the automobile industry developed quickly and distinctively, going on to play an essential role in the First World War. Having established its commercial and geo-symbolic credentials in the interwar period, it would become the foundation of the post-war economic miracle of the Trente Glorieuses, all of which underlines the continuing relevance of this automotive revolution for students of France and the French. For while this work is inherently interdisciplinary, touching on history, geography and sociology, as well as the arts, it remains primarily located within French studies. In consequence, its most basic argument is that, in much the same way as we might look to the country's acclaimed literature to provide insights into social and cultural change, by focusing on its myriad representations of the car, we may profitably expand our understanding of modern and contemporary France.

The automobile, particularly in its early years, became emblematic of new ways of doing things, and this led to new ways of seeing and thinking. The emergence of key figures such as André Citroën and the Michelin brothers had a significant impact as they marketed a society within which the car was democratized. Michelin's promotion of signposting, maps and tourist guides established a strong link between cartography and the mental mapping of this new France, together with its colonies, as new constructions of the national space were fostered. Thus, the automobile was instrumental in the creation of a country that became ever more accessible and which, with the affluence accrued during the Trente Glorieuses, was increasingly enjoyed by the mass of its citizens.

From an historical perspective, the rise of the car was synonymous with the giants of the French automobile industry, such as Louis Renault, André Citroën and the Michelin brothers, all of whom had a considerable influence on the automobile trade. Moreover, this impact stretched well beyond the factory walls, as the emergence of these entrepreneurs' businesses resulted in the automobile being represented in a variety of qualitatively new forms. Key moments in this automotive narrative range from Renault's *taxis de la Marne* through Citroën's African expeditions to the hydraulic system on the

DS that played a key role in saving President Charles de Gaulle's life in the assassination attempt at Petit-Clamart in the bloody endgame of French decolonization. Since the Second World War, with the car playing an ever-larger role in society, many aspects of the country's broader history were profoundly influenced by the automobile, the development of mass tourism being the most obvious example. Against this backdrop, the present study has sought to explore significant areas of structural change in France, thereby revealing, it is hoped, the profound cultural impact of mass automobility.

Bibliography

Allain, François. 2002. *Citroën 2 CV.* Boulogne-Billancourt: ETAI.

Althusser, Louis. 1970. 'Idéologie et appareils idéologiques d'Etat.' *La Pensée* 151 (May–June): 3–38.

Ambroise-Rendu, Anne-Claude. 2007. 'Dangers et tourments du sport.' *Le Temps des médias* 9 (2): 267–72.

Anderson, Susan C., and Bruce Tabb. 2002. *Water, Leisure and Culture: European Historical Perspectives.* Oxford: Berg.

Andrieu, Bernard. 2007. 'Du teint hâlé honni au bronzage de rigueur.' *Cerveau et psycho* 22: 54–65.

Aquin, Hubert, dir. 2012 [1961]. *Le Sport et les hommes.* Montreal, Office national du film du Canada.

Archambeau, Olivier, and Romain J. Garcier. 2001. *Une géographie de l'automobile.* Paris: Presses universitaires de France.

Archer, Neil. 2012. *The French Road Movie: Space, Mobility, Identity.* New York: Berghahn.

Arnaud, G. 1927. 'La Conquête automobile du Sahara.' *Annales de Géographie* 37: 173–76.

Ashmead, H. DeWayne. 'History and Articles: The History and Development of the Renault Caravelle.' *Renault Caravelle.* http://renaultcaravelle.com/the-history-and-development-of-the-renault-caravelle/.

Assailly, Jean-Pascal. 2018. *Homo automobilis ou l'humanité routière.* Paris: Imago.

Aubenas, Sylvie, and Xavier Demange. 2007. *Elegance: The Séeberger Brothers and the Birth of Fashion Photography, 1909–1939.* San Francisco, CA: Chronicle.

Augé, Marc. 1992. *Non-lieux: introduction à une anthropologie de la surmodernité.* Paris: Seuil.

Bakhtin, Mikhail. 1984 [1965]. *Rabelais and His World.* Bloomington, IN: Indiana University Press.

Bardou, Jean-Pierre, Jean-Jacques Chanaron, Patrick Fridenson and James M. Laux. 1977. *La révolution automobile.* Paris: Albin Michel.

Barjot, Dominique. 1999. 'Introduction.' In 'La Reconstruction économique de l'Europe (1945–1953).' Special issue of *Histoire, économie et société* 18 (2): 227–43.

Barthes, Roland. 1972. *Mythologies*. Trans. Annette Lavers. London: Vintage.

Barthes, Roland. 2002. *Œuvres complètes*. Paris: Seuil.

Barthes, Roland. 2003 [1957]. *Mythologies*. Paris: Seuil.

Barthes, Roland. 2004. *Le sport et les hommes*. Montréal: Les Presses de l'Université de Montréal.

Barthes, Roland. 2007. *What is Sport?* Trans. Richard Howard. New Haven, CT: Yale University Press.

Batailler, Francine, Alain Schifres and Claude Tannery. 1963. *Analyses de presse*. Paris: Presses universitaires de France.

Baudrillard, Jean. 1968. *Le Système des objets: la consommation des signes*. Paris: Gallimard.

Baudrillard, Jean. 1972. *Pour une critique de l'économie politique du signe*. Paris: Gallimard.

Baudrillard, Jean. 1981. *For a Critique of the Political Economy of the Sign*. Trans. Charles Levin. St. Louis, MO: Telos Press.

Baudrillard, Jean. 1986 [1970]. *La Société de consommation: ses mythes, ses structures*. Paris: Gallimard.

Baudrillard, Jean. 1986 [1983]. *Stratégies fatales*. Paris: Librairie générale française.

Baudrillard, Jean. 1996. *The System of Objects*. Trans. James Benedict. London: Verso.

Baudrillard, Jean. 1998. *The Consumer Society: Myths and Structures*. Trans. C.T. London: Sage.

Bayley, Stephen. 1986. *Sex, Drink and Fast Cars*. New York: Pantheon.

Bellos, David. 1999. *Jacques Tati: His Life and Art*. London: Harvill.

Bellu, Serge. 1978. *Le Sang bleu: 70 ans d'histoire des voitures françaises de grands prix*. Paris: EPA.

Bellu, Serge. 1984. *100 ans d'automobile française*. Neuilly-sur-Seine: L'Automobile Magazine.

Benjamin, Walter. 1999. *The Arcades Project*. Cambridge, MA: Harvard University Press.

Benton, Tim. 1990. 'Dreams of Machines: Futurism and l'Esprit Nouveau.' *Journal of Design History* 3 (1): 19–34.

Bertho-Lavenir, Catherine. 1999. *La Roue et le stylo: comment nous sommes devenus touristes*. Paris: Odile Jacob.

Bertho-Lavenir, Catherine. 2004. *La Visite du monument*. Clermont-Ferrand: Presses universitaires Blaise Pascal.

Besquent, Patrice. 1985. *La coupe Gordon-Bennett 1905*. Clermont-Ferrand: La Montagne.

Beyer, Antoine. 2004. 'La numérotation des routes françaises. Le sens de la nomenclature dans une perspective géographique.' *Flux* 55: 17–29.

Bliss, Brian. 1954. 'Nationalisation in France and Great Britain of the Electricity Supply Industry.' *The International and Comparative Law Quarterly* 3 (2): 277–90. doi: 10.2307/755537.

Bloom, Peter J. 2008. *French Colonial Documentary: Mythologies of Humanitarianism*. Minneapolis, MN: University of Minnesota Press.

Boissel, Anne. 2004. 'L'accident ou la chair dévoilée.' *Champ psychosomatique* 4: 101–17.

Boltanski, Luc. 1975. 'Les Usages sociaux de l'automobile: concurrence pour l'espace et accidents.' *Actes de la recherche en sciences sociales* 1 (2): 25–49.

Bonnet, Olivier, and Philippe Gazagnes. 2002. *Sur les traces de Michelin, à Clermont.* Clermont-Ferrand: Le Miroir.

Bonté, Michel, François Hurel, Jean-Luc Ribémon and François Bruère. 2006. *Le Mans: un siècle de passion.* Le Mans: Automobile club de l'Ouest.

Borden, Iain. 2013. *Drive: Journeys through Film, Cities and Landscapes.* London: Reaktion.

Bordes, François, ed. 1988. *L'automobile à la conquête de l'Afrique (1898–1932).* Aix-en-Provence: Centre des Archives d'Outre-Mer.

Bourdieu, Pierre. 1979. *La Distinction: critique sociale du jugement.* Paris: Minuit.

Boyer, Marc. 2007. *Le Tourisme de masse.* Paris: L'Harmattan.

Breyer, Victor. 1984. *La Belle époque à 30 à l'heure.* Paris: France-Empire.

Brosses, Charles de. 1988 [1760]. *Du culte des dieux fétiches.* Paris: Fayard.

Bruno [Augustine Fouillée], G. 1877. *Le Tour de la France par deux enfants: devoir et patrie.* Paris: Belin.

Buck-Morss, Susan. 1989. *The Dialectics of Seeing: Walter Benjamin and the Arcades Project.* Cambridge, MA: MIT Press.

Buffetaut, Yves. 1997. *La Citroën Traction de mon père.* Boulogne-Billancourt: ETAI.

Cadène, Jean. 2005. *L'automobile: de sa naissance à son futur.* Perpignan: Cap Béar.

Campbell, Timothy. 2009. 'Vital Matters: Sovereignty, Milieu, and the Animal in Futurism's Founding Manifesto.' *Annali d'Italianistica* 27: 157–73.

Carsalade, Yves. 1998. *Les Grandes Etapes de l'histoire économique.* Paris: Ellipses.

Ce que Michelin a fait pour le tourisme: guides Michelin, bureaux de tourisme, plaques indicatrices, cartes Michelin. [no place: no publisher], 1912.

Champeaux, Antoine. 2003. 'Bibendum et les débuts de l'aviation (1908–1914).' *Guerres mondiales et conflits contemporains* 209: 25–43.

Champeaux, Antoine. 2006. *Michelin et l'aviation, 1896–1945: patriotisme industriel et innovation.* Panazol: Lavauzelle.

Chanaron, Jean-Jacques. 1983. *L'industrie automobile.* Paris: La Découverte.

Charon, Jean-Marie. 1999. *La Presse magazine.* Paris: La Découverte.

Chion, Michel. 1987. *Jacques Tati.* Paris: Seuil.

Cobast, Éric. 2002. *Mythologies de Roland Barthes: premières leçons.* Paris: Presses universitaires de France.

Cohen, Yves. 1991. 'The Modernization of Production in the French Automobile Industry between the Wars: A Photographic Essay.' *The Business History Review* 65 (4): 754–80.

Corbin, Alain. 1995. *L'avènement des loisirs: 1850–1960.* Paris: Aubier.

Corten-Gualtieri, Pascale. 2006. 'L'humour visuel de Sempé: une pratique de la sagesse populaire.' *Communication et langages* 149 (1): 29–44.

Crossick, Geoffrey. 1994. 'Metaphors of the Middle: The Discovery of the Petite Bourgeoisie 1880–1914.' *Transactions of the Royal Historical Society* 4: 251–79. doi: 10.2307/3679223.

Culler, Jonathan. 2002. *Barthes: A Very Short Introduction*. Oxford: Oxford University Press.

Danius, Sara. 2001. 'The Aesthetics of the Windshield: Proust and the Modernist Rhetoric of Speed.' *Modernism/modernity* 8 (1): 99–126.

Danius, Sara. 2002. *The Senses of Modernism: Technology, Perception, and Aesthetics*. New York: Cornell University Press.

Dant, Tim. 1996. 'Fetishism and the Social Value of Objects.' *The Sociological Review* 44 (3): 495–516.

Darke, Chris. 2005. *Alphaville: Jean-Luc Godard, 1965*. Chicago, IL: University of Illinois Press.

Darmon, Olivier. 1997. *Le Grand Siècle de Bibendum*. Paris: Hoëbeke.

Darmon, Olivier. 2004. *La route autrefois*. Paris: Hoëbeke.

Dauncey, Hugh. 2008. 'Entre presse et spectacle sportif, l'itinéraire pionnier de Pierre Giffard (1853–1922).' *Le Temps des médias* 2: 35–46.

Dauncey, Hugh, and Geoff Hare. 2003. *The Tour de France, 1903–2003: A Century of Sporting Structures, Meanings, and Values*. London: Frank Cass.

Dauncey, Hugh, and Geoff Hare. 2014. 'Cosmopolitanism United by Electricity and Sport: James Gordon Bennett Jnr and the Paris *Herald* as Sites of Internationalism and Cultural Mediation in Belle Époque France.' *French Cultural Studies* 25 (1): 38–53.

de Beauvoir, Simone. 1979 'Brigitte Bardot et le syndrome de Lolita.' In *Les Écrits de Simone de Beauvoir*, edited by Claude Francis and Fernande Gontier. Paris: Gallimard, pp. 363–76 [originally published in *Esquire*, August 1959, pp. 32–38].

Delaperrelle, Jean-Pierre. 1986. *L'invention de l'automobile. Bollée: de la vapeur au turbo*. Le Mans: Cénomane.

Delporte, Christian. 2001. '*L'Express*, Mendès France et la modernité politique (1953–1955).' *Matériaux pour l'histoire de notre temps* 63 (1): 96–103.

de Penfentenyo, Jehan-Charles. 2016. *2, 3, 4 roues, le grand prix de Picardie de 1913*. Paris: Michel de Maule.

Deschamps, Eric. 1999. *Croisières Citroën: carnets de route africains*. Boulogne-Billancourt: ETAI.

Dettelbach, Cynthia Golomb. 1976. *In the Driver's Seat: The Automobile in American Literature and Popular Culture*. Westport, CT: Greenwood.

De Villiers, Marc. 1921. 'Comte Le Marois.' *Journal de la Société des Américanistes* 13 (1): 129–30.

Dhéry, Robert, dir. 1961. *La Belle Américaine*. France, Matinee Classics.

Dine, Philip. 2010. 'Dresser la carte sportive de l'Algérie «française»: vitesse technologique et appropriation de l'espace.' In *L'empire des sports*, edited by Pierre Singaravélou and Julien Sorez. Paris: Belin, pp. 105–16.

Dine, Philip. 2012. *Sport and Identity in France: Practices, Locations, Representations*. Oxford: Peter Lang.

Direction Générale des Entreprises. 2006. *Mémento du tourisme*. Ivry-sur-Seine: Observatoire National du Tourisme.

Dockès, Pierre. 1993. 'Les Recettes fordistes et les marmites de l'histoire (1907–1993).' *Revue économique* 44 (3): 485–528.

Douin, Jean-Luc. 2010. *Jean-Luc Godard, dictionnaire des passions*. Paris: Stock.

Dubois, Thierry. 2012. *L'automobile populaire*. Issy-les-Moulineaux: Le fil conducteur.

Dumazedier, Joffre. 1972 [1962]. *Vers une civilisation du loisir?* Paris: Seuil.

Dumond, Lionel. 2002. *L'épopée Bibendum: une entreprise à l'épreuve de l'histoire*. Toulouse: Privat.

Dumont, Pierre. 1973. *Quai de Javel, quai André Citroën*. Paris: Éditions pratiques automobiles.

Eagleton, Terry. 1991. *Ideology: An Introduction*. London: Verso.

Farrell, James J. 1987. 'The Crossroads of Bikini.' *Journal of American Culture* 10 (2): 55–66.

Featherstone, Mike, Nigel Thrift and John Urry, eds. 2005. *Automobilities*. London: Sage.

Feyel, Gilles. 2001. 'Naissance, constitution progressive et épanouissement d'un genre de presse aux limites floues: le magazine.' *Réseaux* 1: 19–51.

Fignon, Laurent. 2009. *Nous étions jeunes et insouciants*. Paris: Librairie générale française.

Flonneau, Mathieu. 1999. 'Georges Pompidou président conducteur et la première crise urbaine de l'automobile.' *Vingtieme siecle. Revue d'histoire* 61: 30–43.

Flonneau, Mathieu. 2008. *Les Cultures du volant: essai sur les mondes de l'automobilisme, XXe–XXIe siècles*. Paris: Autrement.

Flonneau, Mathieu. 2016. *L'automobile au temps des Trente Glorieuses*. Paris: Loubatières.

Forsdick, Charles. 2005. *Travel in Twentieth-Century French and Francophone Cultures: The Persistence of Diversity*. Oxford: Oxford University Press.

Fourastié, Jean. 1979. *Les Trente Glorieuses: ou la Révolution invisible de 1946 à 1975*. Paris: Fayard.

François, Corinne. 2002. *Roland Barthes, Mythologies*. Paris: Bréal.

Francon, Marc. 2001. *Le Guide vert Michelin: l'invention du tourisme culturel populaire*. Paris: Economica.

Frerejean, Alain. 1998. *André Citroën, Louis Renault: un duel sans merci*. Paris: Albin Michel.

Fridenson, Patrick. 1989. 'La Question de la voiture populaire en France de 1930 à 1950.' *Culture technique* 19: 205–10.

Frodon, Jean-Michel. 2010. *Le Cinéma français: de la nouvelle vague à nos jours*. Paris: Cahiers du cinéma.

Furlough, Ellen. 1998. 'Making Mass Vacations: Tourism and Consumer Culture in France, 1930s to 1970s.' *Comparative Studies in Society and History* 40 (2): 247–86.

Furlough, Ellen. 2002. '*Une leçon des choses*: Tourism, Empire, and the Nation in Interwar France.' *French Historical Studies* 25 (3): 441–73.

Gaffney, John, and Diana Holmes. 2007. 'Stardom in Theory and Context.' In *Stardom in France*. Oxford: Berghahn, pp. 7–25.

Gartman, David. 1994. *Auto Opium: A Social History of American Automobile Design*. New York: Routledge.

Gartman, David. 2004. 'Three Ages of the Automobile: The Cultural Logics of the Car.' *Theory, Culture & Society* 21 (4–5): 169–95.

Gartman, David. 2012. *Culture, Class, and Critical Theory: Between Bourdieu and the Frankfurt School.* New York: Routledge.

Godard, Jean-Luc, dir. 1967. *Week-end.* France, Athos Films.

Goldmann, Annie. 1971. *Cinéma et société moderne.* Paris: Anthropos.

Gonzalez, Pierre-Gabriel. 1995. *Bibendum: publicité et objets Michelin.* Paris: Le Collectionneur.

Goudet, Stéphane. 2002. *Jacques Tati: de 'François le facteur' à 'Monsieur Hulot'.* Paris: Cahiers du cinéma.

Gradis, Gaston. 1924. *À la recherche du grand-axe: contribution aux études transsahariennes.* Paris: Plon.

Green-Simms, Lindsey. 2009. *Postcolonial Automobility: West Africa and the Road to Globalization.* Minneapolis, MN: University of Minnesota.

Gunthert, André. 1987. 'La Voiture du peuple des seigneurs: naissance de la volkswagen.' *Vingtieme siecle. Revue d'histoire* 15: 29–42.

Haardt, Georges-Marie, and Louis Audouin-Dubreuil. 1923. *La première traversée du Sahara en automobile: de Touggourt à Tombouctou par l'Atlantide.* Paris: Plon.

Hadlock, Philip G. 2006. 'Men, Machines, and the Modernity of Knowledge in Alfred Jarry's *Le Surmâle*.' *SubStance* 35 (3): 131–48.

Hall, Edward T. 1990. *The Hidden Dimension.* New York: Anchor.

Hargreaves, Alec G. 2005. *Memory, Empire, and Postcolonialism: Legacies of French Colonialism.* Lanham, MD: Lexington Books.

Harp, Stephen L. 2001. *Marketing Michelin: Advertising and Cultural Identity in Twentieth-Century France.* Baltimore, MD: Johns Hopkins University Press.

Hébert, Didier. 2012. 'Deauville: création et développement urbain.' *In Situ. Revue des patrimoines* 6: 1–13.

Hilliker, Lee. 2002. 'In the Modernist Mirror: Jacques Tati and the Parisian Landscape.' *The French Review* 76 (2): 318–29.

Huchet, Isabelle. 1995. *50 ans à toute vitesse: l'automobile, les français et la société.* Paris: Hintzy Heymann.

Huggins, Mike. 1994. 'Culture, Class and Respectability: Racing and the English Middle Classes in the Nineteenth Century.' *The International Journal of the History of Sport* 11 (1): 19–41.

Inglis, David. 2004. 'Auto Couture: Thinking the Car in Post-War France.' *Theory, Culture & Society* 21 (4–5): 197–219.

Jacob, Jean-François. 1973. *Monte-Carlo: 60 ans de rallye.* Paris: Laffont.

Jacobs, Peter, Erwin De Decker and Isabelle Vanmaldeghem. 2009. *Nationale 7: la route des vacances. Le guide pour flâner de Paris à Menton.* Paris: Hachette.

Jamet, Michel. 1983. *La Presse périodique en France.* Paris: Colin.

Jemain, Alain, and Bernard Hanon. 1982. *Michelin: un siècle de secrets.* Paris: Calmann-Lévy.

Jouin, Pierre. 1995. *Une liberté toute neuve: culture de masse et esthétique nouvelle dans la France des années 50.* Paris: Klincksieck.

Joyce, James. 1926. *Dubliners.* New York: Modern Library.

Kaika, Maria, and Erik Swyngedouw. 2002. 'Fetishizing the Modern City: The Phantasmagoria of Urban Technological Networks.' *International Journal of Urban and Regional Research* 24 (1): 120–38.

Karlin, Daniel. 2007. *Proust's English*. Oxford: Oxford University Press.

Karpik, Lucien. 2000. 'Le Guide rouge Michelin.' *Sociologie du travail* 42 (3): 369–89.

Kavanagh, Thomas M. 1973. 'Godard's Revolution: The Politics of Meta-Cinema.' *Diacritics* 3 (2): 49–56.

Kellner, Douglas. 2020. 'Jean Baudrillard.' *Stanford Encyclopedia of Philosophy Archive* (winter edition), edited by Edward N. Zalta, https://plato.stanford. edu/archives/win2020/entries/baudrillard/.

Kelly, Michael. 2001. 'Holidays.' In *French Culture and Society: The Essentials*, edited by Michael Kelly. London: Arnold, p. 125.

Kerillis, Henri de. 1925. *De l'Algérie au Dahomey en automobile: voyage effectué par la seconde mission Gradis*. Paris: Plon.

Kuisel, Richard F. 1983. *Capitalism and the State in Modern France: Renovation and Economic Management in the Twentieth Century*. Cambridge: Cambridge University Press.

Laderman, David. 2002. *Driving Visions: Exploring the Road Movie*. Austin, TX: University of Texas Press.

Lanzoni, Rémi Fournier. 2004. *French Cinema: From its Beginnings to the Present*. New York: Bloomsbury Academic.

Laufer, Laura. 2002. *Jacques Tati ou le temps des loisirs*. Paris: L'If.

Laurier, Eric. 2004. 'Doing Office Work on the Motorway.' *Theory, Culture & Society* 21 (4–5): 261–77.

Laux, James Michael. 1976. *In First Gear: The French Automobile Industry to 1914*. Montreal: McGill-Queen's University Press.

Laux, James Michael. 1992. *The European Automobile Industry*. New York: Maxwell Macmillan.

Le Corbusier [Charles-Édouard Jeanneret-Gris]. 1994 [1924]. *Urbanisme*. Paris: Flammarion.

Lefebvre, Henri. 1947. *Critique de la vie quotidienne*. Paris: L'Arche.

Lefebvre, Henri. 1961. *Critique de la vie quotidienne II: Fondements d'une sociologie de la quotidienneté*. Paris: L'Arche.

Lefebvre, Henri. 1965. *La Proclamation de la Commune, 26 mars 1871*. Paris: Gallimard.

Lefebvre, Henri. 1968. *La Vie quotidienne dans le monde moderne*. Paris: Gallimard.

Lefebvre, Henri. 2000 [1974]. *La Production de l'espace*. Paris: Anthropos.

Lefebvre, Véronique. 2001. *Paris–Rhin–Rhône: histoires d'autoroutes*. Paris: Le Cherche Midi.

Leiss, William. 1976. *The Limits to Satisfaction: An Essay on the Problem of Needs and Commodities*. Toronto: University of Toronto Press.

Lelouch, Claude, dir. 1966. *Un homme et une femme*. France, Les Films 13.

Lelouch, Claude, dir. 2003 [1976]. *C'était un rendez-vous*. Paris, Spirit Level Film.

Lerivray, Bernard. 1975. *Guides bleus, guides verts et lunettes roses*. Paris: Le Cerf.

Levin, Miriam R. 2010. *Urban Modernity: Cultural Innovation in the Second Industrial Revolution.* Cambridge, MA: MIT Press.

Loste, Jacques. 1949. *L'Automobile, notre amie.* Paris: L'Argus de l'automobile.

Lottman, Herbert. 2003. *The Michelin Men: Driving an Empire.* New York: I.B. Tauris.

Loubet, Jean-Louis. 1990. 'Les Grands Constructeurs privés et la reconstruction. Citroën et Peugeot 1944–1951.' *Histoire, économie et société* 9 (3): 441–69.

Loubet, Jean-Louis. 1998. 'Citroën et l'innovation (1915–1996).' *Vingtième siècle. Revue d'histoire* 57: 45–56.

Loubet, Jean-Louis. 1999. 'L'industrie automobile française: un cas original?' *Histoire, économie et société* 18 (2): 419–33.

Loubet, Jean-Louis. 2001. *Histoire de l'automobile française.* Paris: Seuil.

MacKenzie, Scott. 1997. 'The Missing Mythology: Barthes in Québec.' *Canadian Journal of Film Studies* 6 (2): 65–74.

McLuhan, Herbert Marshall. 1967. *The Mechanical Bride.* London: Routledge.

Madsen, Axel. 2009. *Coco Chanel: A Biography.* London: Bloomsbury.

Makeieff, Macha, and Stéphane Goudet. 2009. *Jacques Tati: deux temps trois mouvements.* Paris: Naïve.

Marinetti, Filippo Tommaso. 1983. *Manifesto of Futurism.* New Haven, CT: Yale Library Associates.

Martouzet, Denis, and Georges-Henry Laffont. 2010. 'Tati, théoricien de l'urbain et Hulot, habitant.' *L'Espace géographique* 39 (2): 159–71.

Marx, Karl. 1990 [1867]. *Capital: A Critique of Political Economy.* London: Penguin.

Marx, Karl, and Friedrich Engels. 1988. *Economic and Philosophic Manuscripts of 1844.* Amherst, NY: Prometheus.

Mathieu, Patrick, and Frédéric Monneyron. 2015. *L'imaginaire du luxe.* Paris: Éditions Imago.

Mesrine, Jacques. 1977. *L'instinct de mort.* Paris: Lattès.

Michelin. 1900. *Guide Michelin, offert gracieusement aux chauffeurs.* Paris: Albouy.

Michelin. 1908. *Recueil. Documents techniques et publicitaires.* Clermont-Ferrand: Michelin et Cie.

Michelin. 1909. *Guide Michelin.* Clermont-Ferrand: Michelin-Guide.

Michelin. 2004. *La Saga du Guide Michelin: de 1900 à aujourd'hui, un formidable voyage à travers le temps.* Clermont-Ferrand: Michelin.

Miquel, René. 1962. *Dynastie Michelin.* Paris: La Table Ronde.

Mitchell, W.J. Thomas. 1986. *Iconology: Image, Text, Ideology.* Chicago, IL: University of Chicago Press.

Mom, Gijs. 2014. *Atlantic Automobilism: Emergence and Persistence of the Car, 1895–1940.* New York: Berghahn.

Monneyron, Frédéric. 2005. *Automobile et littérature.* Perpignan: Presses universitaires de Perpignan.

Moulin-Bourret, Annie. 1997. *Guerre et industrie. Clermont-Ferrand: la victoire du pneu.* Clermont-Ferrand: Institut d'études du Massif Central.

Mumford, Lewis. 1952. *Art and Technics.* New York: Columbia University Press.

Murray, Alison. 2000. 'Le Tourisme Citroën au Sahara (1924–1925).' *Vingtième siècle. Revue d'histoire* 68: 95–107.

Néret, Gilles, and Hervé Poulain. 1989. *L'art, la femme et l'automobile*. Paris: EPA.

Neupert, Richard John. 2002. *A History of the French New Wave Cinema*. Madison, WI: University of Wisconsin Press.

Nora, Pierre. 1997. *Les Lieux de mémoire*. Paris: Gallimard.

Pacey, Arnold. 1983. *The Culture of Technology*. Cambridge, MA: MIT Press.

Panhard, Jean. 1989. 'Petite histoire de l'automobile en France.' *Culture technique* 19: 29–42.

Parissien, Steven. 2013. *The Life of the Automobile: A New History of the Motor Car*. London: Atlantic Books.

Pawin, Rémy. 2013. 'Retour sur les «Trente Glorieuses» et la périodisation du second XXe siècle.' *Revue dhistoire moderne contemporaine* 1: 155–75.

Penn, Arthur, dir. 1967. *Bonnie and Clyde*. United States: Warner Home Video.

Perkins, Kenneth J. 2007. 'The Compagnie Générale Transatlantique and the Development of Saharan Tourism in North Africa.' In *The Business of Tourism: Place, Faith, and History*, edited by Philip Scranton and Janet F. Davidson. Philadelphia, PA: University of Pennsylvania Press, pp. 34–55.

Pietz, William. 1985. 'The Problem of the Fetish, I.' *RES: Anthropology and Aesthetics* 9: 5–17.

Pietz, William. 1993. 'Fetishism and Materialism: The Limits of Theory in Marx.' In *Fetishism as Cultural Discourse*, edited by E. Apter and W. Pietz. Ithaca, NY: Cornell University Press, 119–51.

Pinçon, Michel, and Monique Pinçon-Charlot. 1994. 'L'aristocratie et la bourgeoisie au bord de la mer: la dynamique urbaine de Deauville.' *Genèses* 16 (1): 69–93.

Pinkney, David H. 1958. *Napoleon III and the Rebuilding of Paris*. Princeton, NJ: Princeton University Press.

Plessix, René. 1992. 'Au berceau des sports mécaniques: Le Mans.' In *Jeux et Sports dans l'histoire. Tome II: pratiques sportives*. Aubervilliers: Éditions du CTHS, pp. 205–28.

Pociello, Christian, and Daniel Denis. 2000. *A l'école de l'aventure: pratiques sportives de plein air et idéologie de la conquête du monde, 1890–1940*. Voiron: Presses universitaires du sport.

Poirier, Léon, dir. 1926. *La Croisière noire. Film de l'expédition Citroën Centre-Afrique*. France, Gaumont.

Pompl, Wilhelm, and Patrick Lavery. 1993. *Tourism in Europe: Structures and Developments*. Wallingford: Cab International.

Poster, Mark. 1979. 'Semiology and Critical Theory: From Marx to Baudrillard.' *Boundary* 2: 275–88.

Proust, Marcel. 1907. 'Impressions de route en automobile,' *Le Figaro*, 19 November, p. 1.

Rachline, Michel. 1992. *La Genèse d'une automobile*. Paris: Albin Michel.

Rainis, Michel. 2000. 'French Beach Sports Culture in the Twentieth Century.' *The International Journal of the History of Sport* 17 (1): 144–58.

Raskin, Lee, and Tom Morgan. 2005. *James Dean: At Speed*. Phoenix, AR: David Bull.

Rauch, André. 1996. *Vacances en France: de 1830 à nos jours*. Paris: Hachette.

Rauch, André. 2002. 'Vacationing on France's Côte d'Azur, 1950–2000.' In *Water, Leisure and Culture: European Historical Perspectives*, edited by Susan C. Anderson and Bruce Tabb. Oxford: Berg, pp. 223–38.

Reiner, Silvain. 1958. *Des moteurs et des hommes*. Paris: Fayard.

Rémond, Rogé. 2000. *La DS*. Paris: Hermé.

Renou, Michel G. 1994. *Facel-Véga*. Paris: EPA.

Reynolds, John. 1996. *André Citroën: The Henry Ford of France*. New York: St. Martin's Press.

Ribeill, Georges. 1991a. 'From Pneumatics to Highway Logistics: André Michelin, Instigator of the Automobile Revolution, Part I.' *Flux* 3: 9–19.

Ribeill, Georges. 1991b. 'From Pneumatics to Highway Logistics: André Michelin, Instigator of the Automobile Revolution, Part II.' *Flux* 5: 5–19.

Ribémon, Jean-Luc, and Ray Toombs. 2010. *Deauville 1936: un grand prix près des planches*. Mulsanne: ITF.

Rioux, Jean-Pierre, and Jean-François Sirinelli. 1999. *La France, d'un siècle à l'autre, 1914–2000*. Paris: Hachette.

Rizet, Dominique. 1998. *100 ans de passion automobile: le salon de l'automobile, 1898–1998*. Paris: Mazarine.

Robin, Régine. 1991. *Masses et culture de masse dans les années trente*. Paris: Ouvrières.

Rojek, Chris. 2005. *Leisure Theory: Principles and Practice*. London: Palgrave Macmillan.

Rojek, Chris, Susan M. Shaw and Anthony J. Veal. 2006. *A Handbook of Leisure Studies*. London: Palgrave Macmillan.

Ross, Kristin. 1998. *Fast Cars, Clean Bodies: Decolonization and the Reordering of French Culture*. Cambridge, MA: MIT Press.

Rousseau, Jacques. 1985. *La Commémoration de la course Paris-Madrid: 24 mai 1903*. Bordeaux: Automobile-Club du Sud-Ouest.

Rouxel, Marie-Christine. 2003. *Renault en Afrique: croisières automobiles et raids aériens, 1901–1939*. Boulogne-Billancourt: ETAI.

Rowland, Michael. 1987. 'Michelin's *Guide vert touristique*: A Guide to the French Inner Landscape.' *The French Review* 60 (5): 653–64.

Rutsky, Robert L. 1999. 'Surfing the Other: Ideology on the Beach.' *Film Quarterly* 52 (4): 12–23.

Sabatès, Fabien. 1980a. *100 ans d'automobile: les coulisses du salon*. Neuilly-sur-Seine: L'Automobile.

Sabateş, Fabien. 1980b. *La Croisière noire Citroën*. Paris: E. Baschet.

Sagan, Françoise. 1954. *Bonjour tristesse*. Paris: Julliard.

Sahlins, Marshall David. 1976. *Culture and Practical Reason*. Chicago, IL: University of Chicago Press.

Sauvy, Jean. 1984. *L'industrie automobile*. Paris: Presses universitaires de France.

Schweitzer, Sylvie. 1994. 'Rationalization of the Factory, Center of Industrial Society: The Ideas of André Citroën.' *International Journal of Political Economy* 24 (4): 11–34.

Séguéla, Jacques. 1999. *80 ans de publicité Citroën et toujours 20 ans.* Paris: Hoëbeke.

Sempé, Jean-Jacques. 1962. *Rien n'est simple.* Paris: Folio.

Sempé, Jean-Jacques. 1964. *Sauve qui peut.* Paris: Denoël.

Serres, Olivier de. 2005. *Citroën DS: au panthéon de l'automobile.* Arcueil: Anthèse.

Servan-Schreiber, Jean-Jacques. 1957. *Lieutenant en Algérie.* Paris: Julliard.

Setright, Leonard. 2003. *Drive On! A Social History of the Motor Car.* London: Granta.

Sheringham, Michael. 1996. *Parisian Fields.* London: Reaktion.

Sheringham, Michael. 2010. *Everyday Life: Theories and Practices from Surrealism to the Present.* Oxford: Oxford University Press.

Silk, Gerald. 1984. *Automobile and Culture.* New York: Abrams.

Smith, Michael Stephen. 2006. *The Emergence of Modern Business Enterprise in France, 1800–1930.* Vol. 49. Cambridge, MA: Harvard University Press.

Smith, Paul. 2004. 'La Place de l'automobile dans le développement des stations.' *In Situ. Revue des patrimoines* 4: 2–20.

Soulier, Vincent. 2008. *Presse féminine: la puissance frivole.* Paris: L'Archipel.

Souvestre, Pierre. 1907. *Histoire de l'automobile.* Paris: H. Dunod.

Stein, Ralph. 1964. *Automobile.* Paris: Flammarion.

Studeny, Christophe. 1995. *L'invention de la vitesse.* Paris: Gallimard.

Sweeney, Carole. 2004. *From Fetish to Subject: Race, Modernism, and Primitivism, 1919–1935.* London: Praeger.

Tati, Jacques, dir. 1949. *Jour de fête.* France, Voyager.

Tati, Jacques, dir. 1953. *Les Vacances de monsieur Hulot.* France, Criterion Collection.

Tati, Jacques, dir. 1958. *Mon oncle.* France, Voyager.

Tati, Jacques, dir. 1967. *Playtime.* France, Les films de mon oncle.

Tati, Jacques, dir. 1971. *Trafic.* France, Ciné vidéo film.

Tylor, Edward B. 1970. *Religion in Primitive Culture.* Gloucester, MA: P. Smith.

Urry, John. 2002 [1990]. *The Tourist Gaze.* London: Sage.

Urry, John. 2004. 'The "System" of Automobility.' *Theory, Culture & Society* 21 (4–5): 25–39.

Urry, John. 2006. *Consuming Places.* London: Routledge.

Vadim, Roger, dir. 1956. *Et Dieu … créa la femme.* France, Cocinor.

Vantal, Anne. 1998. *Les Grands Moments du salon de l'auto.* Paris: EPA.

Varey, Mike. 2003. *1000 Historic Automobile Sites.* Oakland, CA: Elderberry.

Veblen, Thorstein. 2005. *The Theory of the Leisure Class: An Economic Study of Institutions.* Delhi: Aakar Books.

Viard, Jean. 2007. *Penser les vacances.* La Tour-d'Aigues: L'Aube.

Vidal, Ricarda. 2013. *Death and Desire in Car Crash Culture: A Century of Romantic Futurism.* Bern: Peter Lang.

Vincendeau, Ginette. 2000. *Stars and Stardom in French Cinema.* London: Continuum.

Volti, Rudi. 2004. *Cars and Culture: The Life Story of a Technology.* Westport, CT: Greenwood.

Weber, Eugen. 1976. *Peasants into Frenchmen: The Modernization of Rural France, 1870–1914.* Stanford, CA: Stanford University Press.

Weiner, Susan. 2007. '1950s Popular Culture: Star-Gazing and Myth-Making with Roland Barthes and Edgar Morin.' In *Celebrity and Stardom in France,* edited by John Gaffney and Diana Holmes. Oxford: Berghahn, pp. 26–39.

Wolgensinger, Jacques. 1974. *Raid Afrique.* Paris: Flammarion.

Wolgensinger, Jacques. 1991. *André Citroën.* Paris: Flammarion.

Wolgensinger, Jacques. 1995. *La 2 CV: nous nous sommes tant aimés.* Paris: Gallimard.

Wolgensinger, Jacques. 1996. *Citroën: une vie à quitte ou double.* Paris: Arthaud.

Wollen, Peter. 2002. *Autopia: Cars and Culture.* London: Reaktion.

Wood, Jonathan. 1993. *The Citroën.* Princes Risborough: Shire.

Yonnet, Paul. 1985. *Jeux, modes et masses 1945–1985.* Paris: Gallimard.

Index

Page numbers in *italics* refer to pages where topics appear in illustrations only.

Printed and bound by CPI Group (UK) Ltd, Croydon, CR0 4YY

16/04/2025

14658573-0005